A GANDHIAN THEOLOGY
OF LIBERATION

A GANDHIAN THEOLOGY
OF LIBERATION

IGNATIUS JESUDASAN, S.J.

ORBIS BOOKS

Maryknoll, New York 10545

The Catholic Foreign Mission Society of America (Maryknoll) recruits and trains people for overseas missionary service. Through Orbis Books Maryknoll aims to foster the international dialogue that is essential to mission. The books published, however, reflect the opinions of their authors and are not meant to represent the official position of the society.

Library of Congress Cataloging in Publication Data

Jesudasan, Ignatius.
   A Gandhian theology of liberation.

   Revision of thesis (Ph.D.)—Marquette University.
   Bibliography: p.
   Includes index.
   1. Gandhi, Mahatma, 1869–1948—Religion.   2. Gandhi,
Mahatma, 1869–1948—Political and social views.
3. Liberation theology.   4. Statesmen—India—Biog-
raphy.
DS481.G3J47   1984   294.5'178   83-19486
ISBN 0-88344-154-3 (pbk.)

To the memory of my father,
who taught his children by his example
a Gandhi-like love of truth as the highest value

Contents

Preface

This work is an exposition of Gandhi's theology of liberation. Although Gandhi did not produce a formal, systematic theology of liberation, he worked for the cause of liberation and laid down his life in that process, and he wrote and spoke about liberation, as about everything else, from a religious and theological perspective. The evolution of Gandhi's thought was coincidental with the events of his life, and the events of his life were closely interwoven with the history of India. This study, then, is an attempt at a systematic presentation of Gandhi's theology of liberation in the context of its development within the historical experience of India's liberation.

While that which is formally known as the theology of liberation is recent and Latin American in origin, the experience from which the impulse for such theologies arises is, as François Houtart points out, universal and hence pertinent to such social situations as are marked by alienation, enslavement, oppression, dependency, and underdevelopment, on the one hand, and a religio-political faith in and commitment to liberation, on the other. In this respect liberation theologies conform to the paradigm of the Passover or the exodus experience of the biblical Jews.

The problem of a Christian theology of liberation is one of conformity to the paradigm of the paschal experience of Jesus Christ. Whereas Latin American theologians of liberation have had to come to terms, both theoretically and practically, with a privatized, sacramental christology before they could actualize their beliefs in political terms, Mahatma Gandhi, a Hindu, was free to formulate his own christology, drawing inspiration from the life of Christ for political as well as spiritual liberation.

Gandhi's lifelong search for truth and the integration of that truth into his thought and action are explored in chapter 1. His life cannot be separated from India's struggle for freedom; thus history as narrative seems to be the appropriate introduction to a Gandhian theology of liberation.

Gandhi's concept of liberation, as uniquely suited to India, is exposed in chapter 2 in the discussion of his formulation of *swaraj*. This chapter conveys the dynamic character of Gandhi's conceptualization of *swaraj* and enumerates the types of reform that he advocated in order to bring it about.

Being rooted in his theological faith and his theo-political theory of action (*satyagraha*), Gandhi's theology of *swaraj* was effectively a political theology. Chapter 3 is an exposition of the theological roots of Gandhi's

ix

concept of *swaraj*, examining the ideas of God and humankind that underlie Gandhi's faith.

The Christological dimension in Gandhi's theology of liberation, both in conceptualization and in actualization, is explored in chapter 4 in terms of self-suffering brought to bear on the resolution of political, social, and religious conflicts.

Chapter 5 presents Gandhi's vision of a liberated society. This vision was global. God was the source and center of Gandhi's universalistic vision. Gandhi presented it as a critical alternative to both nominal democracy and totalitarian class-war. The book concludes with a discussion of the Christian significance of Gandhi and his challenge to Christianity in the light of his theology of religions.

This work is not a criticism of other theologies of liberation. No comparison or contrast with any of them is attempted here. Rather, I acknowledge my indebtedness to them for the inspiration to explore the concept of liberation in the life of Gandhi.

Gandhi's image of Christ was an inclusive one, which both confirmed and challenged Gandhi's Hindu paradigms, and therefore which, in Christianizing him on Gandhi's own terms, did so not by alienating him from his Hinduism but by making him a better Hindu. Though Christ was not for Gandhi the only begotten Son of God, he was a singular source of inspiration. In this sense, Gandhi's own life is a more likely witness to the uniqueness of Christ than that of many a conventional Christian.

This is a study, then, not only of a great religious figure in history, but of one whose faith led him to politics. Gandhi, like no one else before him, showed on the stage of world history that the process of liberation can be so Christian in style and inspiration as to demand the values symbolized by the cross. His example and his teaching might well be a factor in all political action and in all political and liberation theologies. Toward that goal, this study is a contribution.

At this point I must acknowledge my debt of gratitude to many who have helped me in the preparation and writing of this work. It was written initially as a dissertation for the degree of Doctor of Philosophy in Religious Studies at Marquette University, Milwaukee, Wisconsin. First I must thank my dissertation director, Father Matthew Lamb, whose conscientious guidance and judicious encouragement never failed through the months of my arduous labor. Professors Daniel Maguire and Donald Metz enthused me with their appreciative comments and suggestions. Fathers Joseph Bracken and William Kurz, S.J., shared with me their constructive comments and criticisms, many of which I have incorporated in the final revision.

Marquette University and its Department of Theology were supportive throughout the project, aiding me with assistantships and scholarships and finally with the Smith Family Scholarship, which enabled me to travel to India to complete my research in several of the Gandhi archives there. The librarians and curators of the Gandhi memorial museums, libraries, and archives at Madurai, Ahmedabad, and New Delhi were very cooperative in supplying me with all their archival materials. So also were the people at the Jawaharlal Nehru Memorial Library Archives, and those at the office of the Collected Works of Mahatma Gandhi, New Delhi. For interviews given to me, I am grateful to Indira Gandhi, Morarji Desai, Pyarelal Nayar, C. N. Patel, T. K. Mahadevan, and Professor K. Swaminathan.

The Archdiocese of Milwaukee and its officials helped me by providing a residence during the four or so years of my doctoral studies. Retired Archbishop Cousins took a personal interest in me and my work. Three parishes hosted me during my stay in Milwaukee: St. Mary Help of Christians, St. Barbara's, and St. Wenceslaus. To the people and pastors of these parishes I owe heartfelt thanks. I must single out Father Donald Braun of St. Wenceslaus parish for his most generous welcome, hospitality, help with the typing of the earlier drafts, and other acts of service and kindness, which are too many to enumerate.

Many other American and Indian friends and dear ones have helped me with their encouragement, good wishes, and prayers. I must be content to thank them all globally rather than by name.

1

Gandhi's Locus Theologicus:
The Historical Setting

Karl Marx has pointed out that human ideas are shaped by the socio-economic and political conditions in which humans live. "Life is not determined by consciousness, but consciousness by life." Marx's analytical insight is part of a continuum reaching back to the scholastic axiom about the primacy of life over philosophy. It is used as a hermeneutic principle by contemporary theologians such as Johann Metz[1] and Matthew L. Lamb[2] and will be assumed as an operating principle in this work.

In his sociology of knowledge Karl Mannheim refines Marx's position to postulate that no mode of thought can be understood unless its social origin is understood.[3] Modern biblical scholarship and theology recognize this primacy in their acceptance of the *Sitz im Leben* as an interpretive principle. Mannheim adds a second principle to his sociology of knowledge, related to the first, namely, that given their relation to the conditions of their origin or production, ideas and modes of thought change in meaning as their carriers, the social bodies or institutions, undergo significant historical change.[4] These principles have an immediate bearing on the parameters of theological reflection.

From the Middle Ages, according to François Houtart of Louvain University, the *locus theologicus*, or the starting point of theological reflection, was the religious group itself, as this was supposed to be the privileged location of the presence of God. Such orientation was possible because of the dominant status of the religious group, which could therefore treat the rest of society as profane. Today, however, the locus of theology has changed. It has come progressively to bear on human beings in the context of society.[5] In other words, the sociology of knowledge has become integral to, or integrated with, the process of theological reflection, particularly as practiced by political theologians and theologians of liberation. Religion's function of furnish-

1

ing a complete ideology for society has progressively decreased and political thought has become autonomous. Insofar as theology has failed to take this autonomy of human beings and society into account in its own reflective processes, it has treated the social process of emancipation as atheistic. This attitude might have been tolerable in an age that did not recognize the multiple causality of every social phenomenon, but it is not acceptable today.[6]

Referring to the birth and evolution of the theology of liberation, Houtart says that it occurs in a defined situation of alienation or dependence, such as in regions regarded as "peripheral," in countries that depend economically, politically, and culturally on the Western world. In countries where these social conditions become most extreme, theologians, who by profession and status do not belong to the most oppressed classes, have perceived, analyzed, and taken upon themselves the condition of the oppressed. Nor is this an isolated phenomenon in time. Always in history religious people have spoken out vigorously against the abuse of power and have denounced intolerable situations. But what is new in the contemporary movement is the utilization of a specifically analytical intervention—an analysis that extends from the perception of misery and poverty to the mechanisms and social system at the root of such situations.[7] Not only has the development of the social sciences illumined these situations, but they have themselves become a theological locus. In other words, the social situations out of which liberation theology arises must be considered as "a place of encounter between God and man, a preferential place because of their determinative influence on all human life."[8]

Although Gandhi's theology reflects his social situation in history, he does not diminish religion's function of furnishing a holistic ideology for society. His religion was his inspiration in a lifelong devotion to liberation—a liberation that would extend to all his fellow humans. Liberation, or the establishment of *swaraj* (self-determination), was for Gandhi the concrete encounter of human beings with God in society and the concretization of the kingdom of God in history. To see religion primarily as an agent of oppression, as Marx does, or to dismiss liberation theology as a new form of atheism is to overlook the fact of Gandhi.

In Gandhi's theology of liberation, the test of theological orthodoxy is a liberating orthopraxis. Gandhi inspired major economic, social, political, and cultural movements in India's struggle for liberation. Hence a discussion of his theology, a theology that takes social reality as its point of departure, must start with a description of that reality.

This study must first take one through the history of the struggle that shaped Gandhi's life and theology—a struggle in turn that was given shape by Gandhi's life and thought. The Indian mind has been generally thought of as lacking historical consciousness, and the Indian religions as nature-based rather than history-based. Gandhi's theology, born of his historical consciousness, should serve as a refutation of that charge.

INDIA'S STRUGGLE FOR FREEDOM:
THE PRE-GANDHIAN PHASE

Gandhi sums up the beginnings of British power in India approximately in these terms: the British East India Company, a royally chartered joint stock company, by its own intentions and intrigues, and through the lack of national self-respect and cohesion of the Indian people and princes, successfully transformed itself in the course of 150 years, by fair means and foul, from a trading company into a colonial empire, until India's Sepoy Mutiny of 1857 and the Royal Proclamation of 1858 put an end to the company's political existence and its rule over India.[9]

The mutiny was not a war of independence; it was largely a military outbreak of which some disaffected princes and landlords availed themselves. Only one of the provincial armies rebelled. There was neither a single leader nor the unity of purpose or consciousness to make it a national movement. Its effects, however, were far-reaching, making it a turning point in Indian history. Despite the company's protests, the British crown in 1858 took the possession and rule of India completely and exclusively into its own hands. The governor-general became viceroy. The army was thoroughly reorganized and the civilians disarmed. The Indian princely states, though still retaining sovereignty, had to recognize the paramountcy of the British crown. Understandably, hostile feelings were engendered and lingered on for many years.*

The subjugation became even more pronounced in 1877, when Queen Victoria assumed the title "empress of India." At once, the Indian states became part of the British empire, and, the peoples of the states, including their rulers, were classed as vassals of the British sovereign.

A British cabinet minister with a parliamentary council was appointed the secretary of state for India. By dint of his own independent action, subsequent legislation,† and the paucity of knowledge and interest evinced by the parliamentarians, the secretary's authority over the government in India be-

---

*W. H. Russell, the *Times* (London) correspondent in India, rightly observed in his *Diary* that "the mutinies have produced too much hatred and ill-feeling between the two races to render any more change of the rulers a remedy for the evils which affect India, of which those angry sentiments are the most serious exposition. . . . Many years must elapse ere the evil passions excited by these disturbances expire; perhaps confidence will never be restored; and, if so, our reign in India will be maintained at the cost of suffering which it is fearful to contemplate" (quoted in Majumdar, *An Advanced History of India*, pp. 782–83). For the difference that the mutiny made in the writing or telling of India's history before and after the event (the monumental classical works critical of British rule before the mutiny and the apologetic textbooks that did not care to tell the Indian side of the story at all), see the preface of R. C. Majumdar, ed., *History and Culture of the Indian People*, vol. 11, pp. xxiii–xxxiii.

†The Act of 1869 made a law of that precedent by limiting the term of office of the council members to ten years, which was renewable at the pleasure of the secretary of state for India.

came practically unlimited. The establishment of direct telegraphic connection between India and England facilitated this control, making the viceroy in effect an agent of the secretary of state. The viceroy, in turn, dominated the members of his council and maintained control over the provinces. Authority was highly centralized and was seen as flowing from the top downward. This was particularly true in the matters of financial administration, in spite of the limited familiarity of the government in India with conditions in the provinces, and the consequent frictions between the central and the local governments.

It was in response to this executive predominance that the Indian National Congress, which first met in 1885, demanded the expansion of legislative councils to additional provinces, the inclusion of elected members to the legislative councils, and the granting of additional powers to the councils, such as the right to discuss the budget and the right to receive answers to questions on matters of public interest. The Act of 1892 conceded parts of these demands, giving the legislature some control over the executive, and paving the way for similar reforms, that were destined to give India a large measure of control over its own administration.

A welcome change from centralization was the emergence of local self-government. Although self-government had been part of the tradition of ancient India, it had been bypassed during the breakup of the Mogul empire. The East India Company rulers had tried unsuccessfully to revive it. Under the crown, local self-government on a British model was first introduced in the Bombay presidency in 1868, and was given great stimulus by the government in India's Resolution of 1870. Other presidencies followed the Bombay example on the district level. The principle of election, however, had not yet been introduced. Viceroy Lord Ripon endeavored to remove this defect, but his attempt to increase the political involvement of the people was ill-received by the secretary of state as well as by local administrators and ultimately met with only limited success.

In the centralized financial administration under the crown's rule, customs duty was a principal source of revenue, and duty on imported cotton goods accounted for two-thirds of all customs duty. When the starting of the textile mills in India affected textile import prices, and the English textile magnates complained, for their sake all customs duties were lifted. This strained India's economy and a 5 percent import duty was reimposed on British textiles. But in order to equalize competition the Indian textile industry was made to pay an excise duty of 5 percent as well. Thus the British industry, protected by the crown, prospered at the expense of the Indian industry.

The centralization of administrators, all ultimately answering to the secretary of state, gave rise to an all-powerful bureaucracy in India headed by the members of the Indian civil service. Although able and honest, these civil servants became the virtual "owners of India," feeling so superior by virtue of their power over the people that they created a gulf between the rulers and the ruled.*

Despite Queen Victoria's Proclamation of 1858, which opened imperial service to Indians and English alike, Indians were effectively excluded from the Indian civil service. Although a system of open competitive examinations for these posts had been introduced in 1853 and reaffirmed in 1858, the exams were held exclusively in England in Queen's English. This hardly gave equal opportunity to Indians wishing to compete for these jobs.†

A national movement of educated Indians was formed to agitate for the rights to which Indian people were entitled. It proposed that "whatever might be our differences in respect of race and language, or social and religious institutions, the people of India could combine and unite for the attainment of their common political ends." The movement was initiated with the civil service agitation and continued with agitations against the Arms Act and the Vernacular Press Act of Lord Lytton, acts that sought to limit the possession of arms and to control the vernacular press. All three agitations were responding to an apparent attempt to curb the growth of a nationalist India, revealing the reactionary character of the regime of the secretary of state, Lord Salisbury. Agitation against such reactionary measures helped to shape the political life of India and make it conscious of its own strength. Thus in 1883 Bengal's Surendranath Banerji organized the Indian National Conference to help develop India's national and political aspirations, setting as a goal not merely more responsible jobs for Indians but the eventual subjection of the entire administration to popular control through representative institutions.

In the same year, Allan Octavian Hume, a retired civil servant, organized with official approval an association for the moral, social, and political regeneration of the people of India, called the Indian National Congress. The congress, which eventually would provide a forum from which Gandhi would guide the country to liberation, met for the first time in Bombay in 1885. It continued to meet once a year in a number of the larger cities, with ever larger delegations from the country, fulfilling well the goal that Hume had set for it in his opening manifesto:

---

*W. S. Blunt observed (in reference to the period following the Sepoy Mutiny) that "the Anglo-Indian official of the Company's days loved India in a way no Queen's official dreams of doing now; and loving it, he served it better" (quoted by R. C. Majumdar in *An Advanced History of India*, p. 855).

†In spite of the promises contained in the Charter Act of 1833 and the queen's Proclamation of 1858 and the Indian Civil Service Act of 1861, a growing reluctance became apparent on the part of the British government to admit Indians in any large numbers to the civil service. This failure to fulfill the already-made pledges is admitted by British statesmen themselves. Lord Houghton agreed that "the declaration which stated that the Government of India would be conducted without reference to differences of race, was magnificent but had hitherto been futile." The governor-general, Lord Lytton, stated in a confidential dispatch on the subject that "all means were taken of breaking to the heart the words of promise they had uttered to the ear" (quoted by R. C. Majumdar in *An Advanced History of India*, p. 889).

Directly to enable all earnest labourers in the National cause to become personally known to each other, to discuss and decide upon the political operations to be undertaken during the ensuing year; and indirectly, this Conference will form the germ of a Native Parliament, and, if properly conducted, will in a few years constitute an unanswerable reply to the assertion that India is unfit for any form of representative institution.

Until the end of the nineteenth century, the congress, with great dignity and moderation, was engaged in criticizing government policy and demanding reforms that would ensure national prosperity, abolish poverty and oppression, and introduce representative forms of government. Specifically, it petitioned the government for the following: establishment of representative councils in provincial and central governments; increased availability of technical and general education; reduction of military expenditure and military training of Indians; separation of judicial and executive functions in the administration of criminal justice; and wider employment of Indians in higher offices in the public service.

Although the congress submitted these demands for consideration as petitions accompanied with sincere protestations of loyalty to the crown and trust in the liberalism and sense of justice of the British statesmen, the government did not see fit to acknowledge the justice and fairness of the Indian claims. The viceroy and other high officials, who had taken part in the deliberations of the congress in its beginnings, began to look with suspicion and disfavor on the congress and its policies, regarding it as an irrelevant body made up of a "microscopic minority" of educated Indians, who had no right to represent or speak for the vast masses of the country. As Hume stated, "The National Congress had endeavoured to instruct the Government, but the Government had refused to be instructed." Disappointed at this, the congress turned to constitutional means of agitation, aiming to influence public opinion in England and India through public meetings and publications.*

A section of the congress began to lose its faith in the efficacy of the congress as a whole if it were limited to this program of action. No longer believing in restraint, they advocated action instead of petitions. Their leader was Bal Gangadhar Tilak, a Maratha Brahmin. Through his paper, *Kesari*, he preached the political ideals of self-help and national revival among the masses, which would later contribute to the growth of the radical wing within the congress.

If enthusiasm for the congress program was not undivided from within, support for it at the mass level was even more fragmented. It was especially

*A weekly paper called *India* was started in England. This method did show results even against the government in India's resistance and countermeasures. The India Councils Act of 1892 bore the traces of the demands of the congress for representative government.

out of favor among the Indian Muslims, whose history is one of the sources of the complexity of India's struggle for liberation. The congress's plea for representative government had little appeal for the Muslims, since they comprised a minority totaling only one-fourth of the population. Furthermore, the British regime in India tended to accentuate Hindu-Muslim differences by showing political favoritism to the Muslims. In 1905 Lord Curzon divided the Bengal presidency into East and West Bengal. East Bengal was predominantly Muslim, and the West was Hindu. The Bengalis sought unsuccessfully through national education, the promotion of *swadeshi* (indigenous) products, and the boycott of British goods to pressure the government into reversing this decision. The congress of 1906 backed their protests, advocating "the system of government obtaining in self-governing British colonies" as its goal. Eventually, however, Nawab Salimulla, of Dacca, set up a permanent Muslim political organization, called the Muslim League, in opposition to the congress's nationalism and in support of the division of Bengal.

In 1909 the government introduced some constitutional changes in the Minto-Morley reforms. These reforms minimally provided for the association of qualified Indians with the government in deciding matters of public interest and introduced or expanded representation in legislative councils. The most significant innovation of the reforms was the delineation of a separate communal constituency for the representation of the Muslims in the councils.* Lord Minto's wife wrote in her diary that British officialdom hailed this act as "nothing less than the pulling back of 62 millions of people from joining the ranks of seditious opposition"—namely, the congress.

The introduction of communal representation was in effect an introduction of "a cardinal problem and ground of controversy at every revision of the Indian electoral system," which would eventually result in the partition of India and Pakistan. Thus the 1909 act fell short of Indian expectations,† leaving in its wake still a great deal of political discontent. Such, briefly, was the political condition of India when Gandhi made his debut on the scene.

---

*One seat on the viceroy's executive council was reserved for an Indian member. New provinces had their executive council expanded to four members. Even though the Reforms Act did not provide for the inclusion of Indian members in provincial executive councils, in practice a beginning was made of it. More importantly, the act changed the composition and functions of the legislative councils. The central legislature had its membership raised from sixteen to sixty. Twenty-eight of these were ex-officio members, five were nominated from official and nonofficial ranks; the other twenty-seven were elected by other elected bodies, such as landowners, Muslims, provincial legislative councils, and the chambers of commerce of Bombay and Calcutta. Responsibility thus was to the government of the king rather than to the people.

†Lord Morley, the secretary of state, plainly admitted this in the House of Lords when he said, in 1908, "If it could be said that this chapter of reforms led directly or indirectly to the establishment of a parliamentary system in India, I, for one, would have nothing at all to do with it." (Quoted by R. C. Majumdar, *An Advanced History of India*, p. 915.)

INDIA'S STRUGGLE FOR FREEDOM:
THE GANDHIAN PHASE

Gandhi's Early Life (1869–91)

Mohandas Karamchand Gandhi was born in 1869 at the port town of Porbandar, in the state of Gujarat, in western India. He was the youngest child born into a moderately wealthy, vegetarian family of the bania, or merchant, caste. The family religion was Vaishnavism, one of the two mainstreams of theistic Hinduism, with Vishnu, the second member of the Hindu triad, as the personal high god.

India in 1869 was made up of about six hundred princely states and some eleven provinces directly administered by English officials. For three generations, to the time of Mohandas's father, the Gandhis had been prime ministers in several of the western states.[10]

According to the autobiography of the Mahatma, as he was later known, his father was a man who exhibited the qualities of love for his clan, truthfulness, bravery, and generosity, and, judging by the fact that he married for the fourth time when he was over forty, some weakness for the pleasures of the flesh. Mohandas also remarked on his father's incorruptibility, strict impartiality, loyalty to the state, unambitiousness with regard to riches, knowledge of practical affairs, and the kind of familiarity with religious culture that was accessible only through frequent visits to temples and attendance at religious discourses.[11] The outstanding impression his deeply religious mother left on the Mahatma was that of saintliness marked by prayers, daily visits to the Vaishnava temple, and frequent and prolonged fasts connected to vows.[12]

Mohan (as Mohandas was often called) was a serious, thoughtful boy, who placed great value on devotion to one's family and on truthfulness. The man who in his adult life would speak of God as truth assumed this value in his formative years. While yet a freshman in high school, Mohandas was so truthful that, even at his teacher's prompting at the time of inspection, he could not bring himself to copy the correct spelling of a test word from his neighbor.[13] The legend of Shravana's parental devotion and of Harishchandra's truthfulness, which Gandhi saw performed on stage, provided a touchstone for his most strongly held beliefs. He wrote:

I must have acted Harishchandra to myself times without number. "Why should not all be truthful like Harishchandra?" was the question I asked myself day and night. To follow truth and to go through all the ordeal Harishchandra went through was the one ideal it inspired in me. I literally believed in the story of Harishchandra. The thought of it all often made me weep. My common sense tells me today that Harishchandra could not have been a historical character. Still, both Harishchandra and Shravana are living realities for me.[14]

The family was for Gandhi a model of the polis. Devotion to the family was to be extended to the larger family of the political community, regulated by the familial virtue of suffering love. Gandhi's desire to emulate Shravana and Harishchandra would be echoed in his later attitude toward Christ.

Married at thirteen, the later liberator felt himself torn between his youthful openness to experience and a strong sense of family tradition. Influenced by the then current wave of social reform, he was convinced by a sturdy Muslim friend to try eating meat to become strong "so that we might defeat the English and make India free."[15] Mohandas knew what freedom meant, though he had not yet heard the word *swaraj*. But he had qualms about the secrecy of meat-eating, insofar as secrecy was already perceived as a departure from truth.[16] The concern for truthfulness and the wish not to lie to his parents made him abjure his meat-eating "reform."[17] This decision was not made lightly. The clash between his passion for freedom, on the one hand, and his commitment to truthfulness, on the other, shook him to the core. He became disconsolate to the point of contemplating suicide, going so far as to prepare himself for it by prayer and a visit to a temple before he abandoned the idea.[18]

The occasion of a voluntary confession to his father, which resulted in Mohan's experience of his father's vicariously suffering love, perfected Gandhi's sense of contrition and repentance by the trust, forgiveness, and reconciliation that it engendered. The boy had taken a bit of gold from his brother to compensate for a debt that the latter owed. In his written confession, Mohan promised amendment and asked for an adequate punishment, begging that the father not punish himself. His father read it with "pearl-drops" trickling down his cheeks. Mohan also cried. The Mahatma wrote:

Those pearl-drops of love cleansed my heart and washed my sin away. . . . This was, for me, an object lesson in *Ahimsa*. Then I could read in it nothing more than a father's love, but today I know that it was pure *Ahimsa*. When such *Ahimsa* becomes all-embracing, it transforms everything it touches. There is no limit to its power.[19]

This incident became in his adult years the model of *ahimsa* (non-violent and vicariously suffering love), which he sought to apply to the resolution of social, religious, political, and economic conflicts on both national and international scales.

In religious literature the *Ramayana* and the *Bhagavat* impressed Mohandas favorably, while the *Manusmriti*, with its story of creation, inclined him, rather, to atheism. It did not provide a model for his idea of *ahimsa*. The conviction of morality as the basis of religion, and truth as the substance of all morality, took deep root in him, so that truth became his sole objective; he grew in its dimensions every day, with the result that his definition of truth kept widening. A didactic stanza in his native Gujarati, inculcating the return of good for evil, became his passionate guiding principle.[20]

While outward manifestations of religion such as temple worship, with its pomp and glitter and reported immorality, held little interest for Mohandas, he was profoundly influenced by contact with religious persons of various faiths. These included a servant-nurse, Rambha, from whom he learned the power and efficaciousness of the *Ramanama*, or the name of Rama (he was to die with that name on his lips when he was hit by an assassin's bullets), Jain monks, and Muslim and Parsi (Zoroastrian) visitors, who would hold religious conversations with Mohan's father.

The roots of many of Gandhi's later beliefs can be traced to these times. Rama, one of the nine past *avatars*, or incarnations, of Vishnu, is the model of every family virtue. Gandhi's prayer life became tied to God as Rama. Jainism, a religion of Buddhist times found now only in western India, incorporates *anekandavada* (the many-sidedness of truth) as its main epistemological position, and *ahimsa* (noninjury to sentient beings) as its principle ethical doctrine. Fasting unto death was an ancient custom among Jain monks. These aspects of Jainism were to be assimilated into Gandhi's life and applied to his theory and practice of conflict resolution. Gandhi could thus be said to have grown, like Hinduism itself, in a climate of religious dialogue. His father's respect for all religions inculcated in Mohandas "a toleration for all faiths" from which Christianity alone was excluded for, as his father once said, "pouring abuse on Hindus and their gods"[21] and for changing the lifestyle of converts.

Having finished high school, Mohandas obtained his brother's support and his mother's permission to go to London for legal studies. His mother's consent was obtained under oath of abstinence from meat, wine, and women. While these oaths were originally an external imposition, voluntary vows were to become part of his public life at the service of liberation. Defying the religious objections of other members of his caste to his going overseas, and excommunication from his subcaste, Gandhi was determined to carry out his plan.[22] He was eighteen when he sailed for England.

Despite much pressure to the contrary, Mohandas held to the vow of vegetarianism he had made to his mother. He had been so hungry for a hearty meal that in reaction to his first meal in London, in a vegetarian restaurant, he declared, "God had come to my aid." Later he was to say, "To the hungry millions, God dare not appear except as food." Having been a vegetarian by necessity so far, he made vegetarianism his mission for the rest of his three-year stay in London.[23] The later missionary of liberation, and of many other causes subsumed by liberation, was first proved in the mission field of a land of beef-eating English.

His obligations as a law student did not preclude Gandhi's further exploration of religious ideas. He became acquainted with a group of theosophists who introduced him to Madame Blavatsky, founder of theosophism, and Mrs. Annie Besant, who had just then joined the Theosophical Society. Invited to join the society, young Gandhi declined the invitation: "With my meagre knowledge of my own religion I do not want to belong to any religious body.''[24] It was in the company of the English theosophists that Mohandas first read the *Bhagavad Gita*. He was deeply impressed by it. Subsequently he would regard it as "the book *par excellence* for the knowledge of truth," and an invaluable help in his moments of gloom. A good Christian contact put the Bible into Gandhi's hands. He read it all and was especially impressed by the Sermon on the Mount, writing that it "went straight to my heart." Its doctrine of nonresistance and nonretaliation to evil delighted him "beyond measure" and reinforced Shamal Bhatt's Gujarati poem on the subject.

Gandhi's young mind tried to unify the teaching of the *Gita*, Edwin Arnold's *Light of Asia* (being a work on the life and teaching of the Buddha), and the Sermon on the Mount. Renunciation began to appear to him as the highest form of religion. From Carlyle's *On Heroes and Hero-Worship*, Gandhi learned about Prophet Muhammad's "greatness and bravery and austere living." He had also read some books about atheism and attended the funeral of a well-known British atheist, Charles Bradlaugh. But having "already crossed the Sahara of atheism," Gandhi was strengthened in his aversion to and "prejudice" against atheism by his religious readings as well as by the conduct of some atheists whom he happened to observe.[25] Unable to read more on religion and religions for the present amid his legal studies, he resolved to do so later. He had been exposed to Christ at the biblical source and had commenced a spiritual dialogue that was to have a formative influence both on his choice of strategy to resolve the national conflicts that awaited him and on the religious spirit and language in which his mission would be carried out.

Three years of legal studies went by quickly. Gandhi passed his examinations, was called to the bar on June 10, 1891, enrolled in the High Court on the 11th, and on the 12th he sailed for home, feeling neither confident nor competent to practice law.[26] He had learned nothing of the Indian law—he did not even know how to draft a plaint—and doubted that he would be able to earn his living by the profession.[27]

Gandhi in South Africa: The Birth of Satyagraha (1891–1914)

The London-returned barrister was received with ceremonial baths of purification in Gujarat's sacred rivers. His debut in the legal profession in India, however, was a disaster. The rescue came in an invitation to go to South Africa as a legal interpreter to the Porbander-based Dada Abdulla Company.[28] Gandhi accepted the invitation and embarked on a journey that was to have a profound impact on the course of his later life.

While traveling by train from Durban to Pretoria, Gandhi experienced his first incidents of racial prejudice. The young Indian was evicted from the first-class compartment of his train, was refused a seat inside a stagecoach, and was struck by the coach driver. Once in Pretoria he was denied room in the hotels. Mohandas was quick to learn that the treatment he received was typical of treatment meted out to all Indians in South Africa because of color or racial prejudice.[29] Tempted to go back to India rather than face such insults and injury, Gandhi decided, rather, to complete the work that had brought him to South Africa and to do all he could to undo the evil system before his return to India. This commitment was the mainspring of all his future political action and religious thought. He was later to refer to the time at which he made this commitment as the most creative moment in his life.

The case in which he had been called to assist involved a lawsuit over a sum of forty thousand pounds sterling, between two Indian Muslim merchants who were kinsmen. Gandhi successfully negotiated an out-of-court arbitration with terms so favorable to both the winning and the losing parties that they retained their kinship relations intact. The success of this settlement boosted Gandhi's self-confidence and justified his belief in arbitration as a valuable alternative to conflict resolution through the legal framework, since arbitration retained personal communication between the conflicting parties. Much of his legal career in South Africa was to be devoted to conflict solving through arbitration or out-of-court compromise settlements. He thought he gained by it—both money and his soul.[30]

His stay in Pretoria in connection with the lawsuit just mentioned enabled Gandhi to make a deep study of the social, economic, and political condition of the Indians in the Transvaal and the Orange Free State. This study proved to be of "invaluable service" in developing his social program and techniques as well as for his professional career as an attorney.[31]

Indian laborers had been taken to South Africa since 1860 on indenture or contract work for five-year periods, with the option of returning on free passage to India when the contract period was over. Housing and a small pay were assured during indenture. After their work contracts expired, many Indians decided to settle in South Africa and to pursue agriculture or other small trades. But those who opted to stay did not find it easy. They encountered opposition from the whites, who, because of color prejudice and fear of economic competition, took every opportunity to make life difficult and humiliating for the Indians.

By a special bill passed in 1888, all Indians remaining in the Orange Free State had been deprived of all their rights, except the right to serve in menial capacities. Merchants were obliged to leave with nominal compensation and no legal remedy. In the Transvaal, Indians had to pay a poll tax of three pounds to enter the state, could own no property except in segregated areas, and had no franchise. In addition, as colored people, they were denied access even to public footpaths and denied the right of outdoor movement after 9:00 P.M. without a permit. Gandhi himself was once kicked off a footpath onto the road by a policeman without notice or warning.[32]

In Natal differences of religion, culture, race, psychology, lifestyle, and levels of business aspiration contributed to the antagonism of the whites to the Indians. Contrary to the contract of indenture, the Europeans proposed forcibly to repatriate the laborers so that the indenture would terminate in India. The government in India was not likely to accept this. Legislation was proposed stipulating (1) that the indentured laborers should return to India on the expiry of their indenture or that they should sign a fresh indenture every two years with an increment in pay; and (2) that in case of their refusing both alternatives, they should pay an annual tax of twenty-five pounds. The spirit of these proposals was one of fear and antagonism working itself out through either enslavement or eviction, violating in both cases the terms of the original agreement. Lord Elgin, the viceroy in India, slashed the poll tax to three pounds, but he was still breaching the spirit of his trusteeship in compromising the interests of the Natal Indians. When the average income of a working Indian was not more than fourteen shillings a month, a three-pound-a-year poll tax was an inhuman exaction. The Natal Indian Congress, established by Gandhi, organized a fierce campaign against it.[33]

Gandhi's method of overcoming these hardships imposed on his people was an extension of his strategy in the Dada Abdulla case—namely, the utilization of the suffering caused to the weaker party in evoking the goodwill of the dominant side. For this purpose, on the one hand, Gandhi promoted the education of Indians through the Natal Indian Congress; on the other, he made written appeals to the British in both South Africa and England, in which he acquainted them with the situation of the Indians from their own perspective. Two of Gandhi's pamphlets, "An Appeal to Every Briton in South Africa" and "The Indian Franchise—An Appeal," won the Indians many friends and active sympathizers and placed before the South African Indians a clearly defined line of action.[34]

While on a visit to India to take his wife and children to South Africa, Gandhi wrote letters to several newspapers in India to inform and educate readers about the status of Indians in South Africa and to influence governmental action in support of them. These actions had some unexpected repercussions. A summary of a long article by Gandhi published with editorial comments in *The Pioneer* of Allahabad was cabled by Reuters to England. The Reuters office in London cabled a summary of that summary to Natal. On his return to Natal, Gandhi was attacked by a white mob.[35] But for rescue and escort by police in disguise, Gandhi might have been killed. Joseph Chamberlain, the British secretary of state for the colonies, cabled the Natal government to prosecute Gandhi's assailants. But, as in lesser incidents previously, Gandhi refused to have his assailants prosecuted.[36] The news of this magnanimity won Gandhi and the Indian community new prestige.

Still, new bills were introduced in the Natal Legislative Assembly to impose trade restrictions on Indian merchants as well as stringent immigration restrictions on all Indians. Gandhi and the Natal Indian Congress appealed to the colonial secretary to mediate a settlement. On his refusal to intervene, the bills became law.

In spite of these setbacks, Gandhi retained his loyalty to Britain. During the Boer War, in 1899, he organized an ambulance corps of 1,100 Durban Indians, and persuaded the government to accept it at the service of the imperial army. Pushing aside his sympathy for the Boer cause,[37] Gandhi wished to demonstrate the loyalty of the Indians to the empire and the Indians' own courage, to counteract the average English person's belief that the Indian was "a coward, incapable of taking risks or looking beyond his immediate self-interest." The services he and the corps rendered, often within the firing line, won further recognition for Gandhi and the Indian community.[38]

During the South African phase of Gandhi's life, his religious attitudes and the pattern of his response to religiously motivated initiatives of others became stabilized. But that stability did not involve closure to truth or to a new light on any question.

During the first half of his twenty-three year stay in South Africa, persistent efforts were made to convert him to Christianity. One Michael Coates, a Quaker, would give Gandhi Christian literature to read, and Gandhi would give him the weekly diary of his spiritual journal; they would then discuss the impressions that the books had made on Gandhi. But the upshot of all his reading was that while the ethical side of these writings appealed to him, the apologetic and doctrinal, or dogmatic, parts left him unmoved.[39]

Nonetheless, the successful barrister continued his earnest search into religion. For a time he was asking: Which is the true religion? But soon he gave this up as a false supposition: there could be no such thing as one true religion, all others being false.[40] On the personal side there was reason for prejudice. His Christian friends were rather aggressive in their initiatives, showing scant regard for non-Christian religions and their practices. Friends and associates of various Christian denominations presented their own opposing interpretations of Christianity as exclusive paths to *the* saving truth. Coates, for instance, declared the futility of human effort alone as a means to salvation, but he did not totally disregard good works. The Plymouth Brethren, on the other hand, left no role for moral effort in life and doctrine on the ground that Christ had atoned for all sins. Despite disagreement with some of these ideas and the abrupt end of some valued friendships, Gandhi was not prejudiced against Christianity. He gave an assurance to A. W. Baker, Abdulla's attorney and a Protestant lay preacher who took him to prayer meetings, that "nothing could prevent me from embracing Christianity should I feel the call."[41]

In fact, Gandhi did not feel called to convert to Christianity:

> The pious lives of Christians did not give me anything that the lives of men of other faiths had failed to give. I had seen in other lives just the same reformation that I had heard of among Christians. Philosophically there was nothing extra-ordinary in Christian principles. From the point of view of sacrifice, it seemed to me that the Hindus greatly surpassed the Christians. It was impossible for me to regard Christianity as a perfect religion or the greatest of all religions. It was impossible for me to believe that I could go to heaven or attain salvation only by becoming a Christian.[42]

This shocked his friends when he shared it with them. But they gave him no satisfactory answers to his mental "churning." He had serious questions with regard to the Bible and its accepted interpretation, namely, concerning the nature of Christ and of his redemption. Moreover, the Buddha, with his universal compassion, was more appealing to Gandhi than was Christ.[43]

The openness of Gandhi's mind and the earnestness of his search are clear from the religious correspondence he carried on with Hindu authorities in India and with Christian authors in England, as well as from the discussion of his dilemma with Kalicharan Banerji, a prominent Christian congressman, at Calcutta in 1901.[44] At that time Gandhi, who was thirty-two years old, was seeking to convince himself of the objective truth of Christianity. But even Kalicharan Banerji had failed to convince him of that.[45] Gandhi also met with prominent Brahmos, read Brahmo literature, visited Hindu religious institutions, and met Sister Nivedita with "her overflowing love for Hinduism."[46]

The works of two authors helped to crystallize Gandhi's beliefs. Gandhi was drawn to *The Perfect Way* by Edward Maitland, "a repudiation of the current Christian belief," as well as his *New Interpretation of the Bible*. Both these books seemed to support Gandhi's own native Hindu faith. Another decisive influence was Tolstoy, whose *Gospel in Brief*, *What to Do*, and *The Kingdom of God Is within You* Gandhi read voraciously. Of the last book he said that it "overwhelmed me" and "left an abiding impression on me." His further comment on the book is revealing: "Before the independent thinking, profound morality, and the truthfulness of this book, all the books given me by Mr. Coates seemed to pale into insignificance."[47]

Gandhi also carried on a correspondence with the Jain ascetic, poet, and diamond merchant, Raychandbhai, of Bombay. In answer to Gandhi's questioning, Raychandbhai had written to this effect: "On a dispassionate view of the question, I am convinced that no other religion has the subtle and profound thought of Hinduism, its vision of the soul, or its charity."[48]

Finally, Gandhi says of his comparative study of religions: "I took a path my Christian friends had not intended for me."[49] That path led him back to Hinduism—a religion that was undogmatic and open enough in its spiritual vision and charity to embrace all other faiths as alternative absolutes for the people born into them. He returned to Hinduism with an open mind, however, asking himself what the inspiration of the Vedas meant and, if they were inspired, whether the Bible and the Qur'an could not be inspired as well.[50]

Late in 1901, Gandhi judged his work in South Africa to be done. He had attained personal, financial, and professional success and had donated his services for the betterment of the Indian community. Leaving for the use of the community the gifts of gold and diamonds his compatriots and clients had showered on him, he left for India, with a promise to return if his services were required.[51]

In India, Gandhi became a missionary for the South African Indians. On their behalf he moved a resolution in the Calcutta session of the Indian National Congress. He had just established a successful law practice in Rajkot and Bombay when he was recalled to South Africa. Gandhi recognized in this event a special divine intervention in his life that thwarted his own plans. "God has never allowed any of my own plans to stand. He has disposed of them in his own way."[52]

Gandhi's recall to South Africa was for the purpose of leading the South African Indian deputation to Joseph Chamberlain, the secretary of state for the colonies, who was to visit the country shortly. The Indians hoped for redress of their grievances through this channel. However, a newly created Asiatic Department was reviving all the old Boer laws against the Indians in the Transvaal, and Gandhi was effectively excluded from the deputation to the secretary. Chamberlain, rather than intervening on behalf of the Indians, asked them to placate the Europeans if they wanted to continue to live there.[53] A long struggle seemed to lie ahead, and Gandhi settled in Johannesburg as a Supreme Court attorney.[54]

Gandhi's religious attitudes became increasingly well-defined. Contacts with theosophists, whose literature was replete with Hindu influence, confirmed many of his ideas. He learned the *Gita* by heart, and it became for him "a dictionary of daily reference" and an "infallible guide of conduct." A visit to a Trappist monastery made a deep impression. The love of service and the faith in God that he observed there, together with the *Gita*'s message of detachment or nonpossessiveness, led him to change some financial plans. He canceled his life-insurance policy and, at the cost of a rift with his brother, earmarked all his savings for community service. His concept of religion and brotherhood enlarged to include all life and all people.[55]

The movement of South African Indians gained new strength when, with Gandhi's support in June 1903, *Indian Opinion* commenced publication in Durban. Though he was not its first editor, Gandhi had the primary responsibility for its publication and contributed to almost all of its editorial columns. All of the major changes in his personal life were reflected in the journal. It would later provide the forum for the principles and practice of *satyagraha*.

About a year after its inception, Gandhi took over financial responsibility for *Indian Opinion*, which had been running at a loss. His writing had won him a Jewish friend and convert, Henry Polak, who was himself a professional journalist.[56] Polak introduced Gandhi to John Ruskin's *Unto This Last*, a book that cast a magic spell on Gandhi and brought about "an instantaneous and practical transformation" in his life. He later translated the book into Gujarati, with the title *Sarvodaya* (The Welfare of All), an inspired formulation of the goal of the good life and of the ideal society. As well as confirming Gandhi's philosophical convictions, Ruskin's book gave him some practical ideas. Inspired by its exaltation of manual labor, Gandhi conceived a plan to put *Indian Opinion* on its feet. He bought a one-hundred-acre orchard at Phoenix near Durban, where the press was relocated in an egalitarian, quasi-monastic settlement, run by cooperative labor. Polak joined the settlement.[57]

At this point *Indian Opinion* reflected Gandhi's belief in a constitutional mode of opposition, based on faith in the British constitution and in the British empire as a family of nations. *Indian Opinion* was dedicated to bringing the Indian and European subjects of King Edward VII closer together, educating public opinion, removing causes for misunderstanding, and showing the Indians the path of duty while securing their rights.[58]

From 1905 on there were deep changes in the personal life of Gandhi as well as in the Indian community in South Africa. Gandhi's life was marked by austere simplicity and bodily labor. After consulting his wife, Kasturbai, he took the vow of *brahmacharya*, or perpetual celibacy:

I had been wedded to a monogamous ideal ever since my marriage, faithfulness to my wife being part of the love of truth. But it was in South Africa that I came to realize the importance of observing *brahmacharya* even with respect to my wife. I cannot definitely say what circumstances or what book it was, that set my thoughts in that direction, but I have a recollection that the predominant factor was the influence of Raychandbhai—himself married. . . . The final resolution could only be made as late as 1906. Satyagraha had not then been started. I had not the least notion of its coming. I was practising in Johannesburg at the time of the Zulu "Rebellion" in Natal, which came soon after the Boer War. . . . During the difficult marches that had then to be performed, the idea flashed upon me that if I wanted to devote myself to the service of the community in this manner, I must relinquish the desire for children and wealth and live the life of a *vanaprastha*—of one retired from household cares.[59]

Later he wrote to his brother, "I do not claim anything as mine. All that I have is being utilized for public purposes. I have no desire for worldly enjoyments of any type whatever."[60]

In 1906 the draft Asiatic Ordinance became law, requiring Indians to register and be fingerprinted, despite their prior voluntary registration. Their freedoms of entry, residence, locomotion, and livelihood had already been abridged. The registration was intended to set them apart from the rest of the population and, eventually, to drive them out of the Transvaal. Gandhi condemned it as "a crime against humanity" and asked the Indians to refuse obedience to the "Black Act" and to submit to imprisonment for their disobedience. At a mass meeting on September 11, 1906, Gandhi led some 3,000 Indians in a vow, with God as witness, pledging disobedience to the law. In his autobiography, Gandhi later reflected that "some new principle had come into being" as an alternative to constitutional agitation. It was to be christened *satyagraha*.[61]

Gandhi's concept of this new way of conducting the struggle was influenced, as had been his search for religion, by readings from diverse sources. An important influence was Salter's *Ethical Religion*, parts of which he summarized in the Gujarati columns of *Indian Opinion*, upholding the voluntary and disinterested character of moral action, the immutability and transcendence of the moral law over all temporal law, and the worthlessness of an ethical idea that was not translated into action.[62]

Gandhi rejected the term "passive resistance," as narrowly construed, as representing the weapon of the weak, characterized by hatred, and finally capable of manifesting itself as violence.[63] He insisted that the struggle was to remain peaceful. "Indians in the Transvaal will stagger humanity without shedding a drop of blood."[64] He also saw the actions of the Indians as Christian in manner.[65] His concept was of an ethical and spiritual struggle, for which he found support in Thoreau's essay on "Civil Disobedience," and he characterized it as "really not resistance but a policy of communal suffering."[66]

In 1907 Gandhi set up the Passive Resistance Association to carry out the resolutions of disobedience drafted in September 1906.[67] New tactics were announced. The Indians would be fined for defiance of the law. They would accept jail in lieu of the fines. If licenses were denied they would trade without them. The very movement was to be an ethical education.

It was clear that no existing term was adequate to describe this new movement. Gandhi's second cousin, Maganlal, suggested combining two Sanskrit words, *sat* (truth) and *agraha* (firmness or force), into the term *sadagraha*. This was changed to *satyagraha*, a more easily comprehensible form, meaning the force of truth, the firmness of truth; or the power of the soul. Though the term was new, Gandhi believed that the conduct of *satyagraha*, or "soul-force," was as old as the human race, represented in its purest form by Jesus Christ, Daniel, and Socrates. He had faith that "a *satyagrahi* will shine the brighter and grow the more courageous the more he is crushed."[68]

The campaign against the Transvaal Registration Act was successful. Registration offices were systematically, peacefully, and successfully picketed. Despite the government's repeated extension of the deadline for registering, less than 5 percent took out "the bond of slavery." Signatures were collected to demonstrate Indian opposition to the law. Gandhi denounced the evils of the law through public meetings and newspaper campaigns, until more and more white-controlled newspapers condemned the government and wished success to the Indians.[69]

Eventually, the Transvaal government of General Smuts decided to prosecute Gandhi and other leaders. Gandhi and the defendants pleaded not guilty, so that the court could hear from their own mouths what they had to say.[70] These trials brought more publicity to the movement than had all the past petitions and deputations and compelled the attention of the imperial government.

Gandhi was ordered to leave the Transvaal in forty-eight hours for refusing to register under the Act. The motivation was to drive out the educated Indians—the "ring leaders" of disaffection. With Thambi Naidoo and Leung Quinn, Gandhi disobeyed the sentence and was resentenced to two months in jail for disobedience. At a private meeting Smuts had assured Gandhi that he would repeal the Asiatic Registration Act in return for voluntary registration, which would secure the government's purposes. Risking his life at the hands of an Afghan immigrant, who struck him down for it, Gandhi voluntarily registered himself. Smuts began to make reservations on his compromise and to insist unrelentingly on the educated Asians' leaving the province. Gandhi saw this as depriving the people of their natural leaders and of the community's "organic growth." The specter of the obnoxious law was revived when Smuts confirmed that it was to be retained in the statute book. *Satyagraha* was resumed.

Indians courted arrest by disobeying rules and laws relating to trade permits and certificates of registration, by entering the colony without identification, and, on the breakdown of other negotiations, by making a bonfire of all the voluntary certificates of registration in a mass rally.[71] Jail sentences were counted in the thousands. Gandhi himself was sentenced to prison two more times.

Gandhi grasped the Transvaal struggle as bearing on India's own struggle, goals, and method.[72] "In fighting the battle," he wrote to Polak in India, "we are presenting the Indian Motherland with a disciplined army of the future; an army that will be able to give a good account of itself against any amount of brute force that may be matched against it."[73] To Count Leo Tolstoy, "the best and the brightest exponent of the doctrine," Gandhi wrote: "In my opinion, this struggle of the Indians in the Transvaal is the greatest of modern times. . . . If it succeeds, it will be not only a triumph of religion, love and truth over irreligion, hatred and falsehood, but it is highly likely to serve as an example to the millions in India and to people in other parts of the world, who may be down-trodden."[74]

In his seminal book *Hind Swaraj*, which was written in 1908, Gandhi had attacked modern industrial civilization as materialistic, soulless, and atheistic, and condemned the legal and medical professions as cooperating to maintain and continue the exploitation of the masses. He had upheld the ancient Indian civilization, and its ideal of simple living with high thinking, for continued implementation in order to reassert the spiritual as well as political freedom of India. Following his own advice, and in order to meet the demands of the intensified struggle, Gandhi started the Tolstoy Farm near Johannesburg in 1910; he settled on the farm, having given up the legal profession once and for all. The farm was modeled on the Phoenix settlement near Durban except that the residents of the Tolstoy Farm were mostly participants in the struggle undergoing further discipline for the same; they lived a simple communal life organized on a cooperative pattern of self-help, manual labor, and regulated habits of food, dress, and sex.

In January 1911, the government in India announced its decision to prohibit, as of July, the indenture and emigration of Indian laborers to Natal. Gandhi negotiated with General Smuts on the fate of resident Indians in South Africa. General Smuts proved a hard bargainer, always conceding less than he promised. Gandhi, for his part, fought for every inch of the ground promised, in keeping with his principles of justice.[75]

The provisional settlement of 1911 between Gandhi and Smuts stipulated that Indian immigrants not be subjected to discriminatory disabilites. But the new immigration bill adversely affected their existing rights and imposed fresh liabilities by building racism into the law. Gandhi saw it as a deliberate attempt to oust the Asian population of South Africa. Moreover, a Cape Supreme Court verdict in 1913 ruled that Indian marriages performed according to non-Christian rites or not registered before a marriage officer could not be recognized in the Union of South Africa. In effect the decision reduced Hindu and Muslim wives to the status of concubines and their children to that of illegitimate offspring. Indian religious sentiment was deeply outraged.

To remedy the anomaly of this judgment and the other disabilities, Gandhi demanded modification of the marriage laws of the Union, amendment to the immigration bill so as to restore existing rights, abolition of the three-pound tax, and removal of the racial taint in the Transvaal laws, initiating a spirit of liberalism. Unionwide resistance to existing laws of discrimination was held out if these just demands were not met. Though the government relented somewhat in agreeing to amend the immigration bill as desired, it refused to acknowledge legally marriages performed in India according to Hindu and Muslim rites and customs. The government demanded marriage-registration certificates. In India these were neither necessary nor well-kept, and hence unproducible. The government's concessions and amendments were inadequate, such as abolishing the three-pound tax on women while discriminating against men. Despite Gandhi's readiness to give more time so as to avoid precipitating a confrontation, the administrative measures and amendment of laws requisite for removing the legal and economic disabilities of the Indians were not forthcoming. The British Indian Association gave the government notice of passive resistance. In Gandhi's words, ". . . as an un-represented and voiceless community which has been so much misunderstood in the past and which is labouring under a curious but strong race prejudice, it can only defend its honour and status by a process of sacrifice and self-suffering."[76]

In addition to earlier forms of protest, passive resistance was now offered to all those laws that had no natural or moral basis. Women, including Kas-turbai Gandhi, joined the agitation and courted arrest. Indian workers in Newcastle coal mines joined and struck against the three-pound tax, to be joined by workers in railways, sugar mills, docks, and corporations. India's viceroy, Lord Hardinge, openly expressed his sympathies for the passive re-sisters and sent a commission to report on South Africa. The Smuts-Gandhi settlement was reached, leading to the passing of the Indians' Relief Act on June 26, 1914. Years of struggle had finally brought results. The hated three-pound tax was abolished altogether. Indian marriages received legal recognition. The system of indentured immigration from India was ended.

Legislation curtailing the economic rights of Indians was removed. Gandhi listed among the gains of these efforts the new spirit of conciliation resulting from the hardships, sufferings, and sacrifices of the passive resisters. "The struggle has more than proved the immense superiority of right over might, of soul-force over brute-force, of love and reason over hate and passion."[77]

Though subsequent events were to show that the racial problem in South Africa were far from solved,[78] Gandhi had invented and perfected there the philosophy and technique of *satyagraha*, which was eventually to lead to the liberation of his motherland and the end of the age of imperialism in India.* The mission that had prolonged his stay in South Africa for over two decades being now completed, Gandhi left the country that had become for him "a sacred and dear land, next only to my motherland,"[79] "where the greatest spiritual treasures were to be found for the comforting and uplifting of the whole world."[80]

Gandhi in India (1914–48)

Once in India, Gandhi traveled extensively in the country, meeting eminent men and acquainting himself with the political situation and the living conditions of the masses. Looked upon as Mahatma, or Great Soul, he established an ashram in Ahmedabad. He completed one of his prior commitments, convincing the government to abolish all indentured emigration of Indians to South Africa by July 1916. Then he set his energies to the problems of his people in their homeland.

The first opportunity for trying out *satyagraha* in India was in the Champaran district of Bihar where the tenant farmers had been reduced to great poverty and degradation at the hands of the indigo planters. In 1917 the already much-hailed Mahatma went to Champaran to investigate their grievances. There was an attempt by planters and divisional police officials to evict him from the area by serving executive orders on him to leave the territory.

---

*Robert A. Huttenbach states that the government of the Union of South Africa had no intention of abating the pressure on the Indian population. The Transvaal Asiatic Land and Trading Amendment Act of 1919 severely limited the rights of Indians to own fixed property. The Asiatic Inquiry Commission of 1920 recommended the old plan of voluntary repatriation to India and the establishment of segregated areas in towns to which Indians would be limited in trade and business. Natal Indians were denied franchise in municipal election from 1924. The Areas Reservation and Immigration and Registration (Further Provisions) bill of 1925 strengthened all the foregoing white practices and sought to enforce another registration of all Indians in South Africa, thereby to restrict any further immigration. On the basis of these facts, Huttenbach points out that Gandhi's optimism was not well founded (*Gandhi in South Africa: British Imperialism and the Indian Question*, pp. 334–36). It would seem that, after these events, Gandhi reevaluated his previous optimism in much the same light as Huttenbach has done. Therein Gandhi anticipated his critic. This may have been a reason for his considering a return to South Africa in 1926. In further fairness to Gandhi, we must note, with Stanley Windass, that amid continuing governmental acts of repression, "the leaders of the disenfranchised majority have shown extraordinary patience in pursuing their just aims for many years by non-violent means, taking their inspiration both from Christianity and from Gandhi" (foreword to P. Regamey, O.P., *Non-Violence and the Christian Conscience*, p. 27).

Following the pattern established in his South African years, Gandhi chose to disobey the orders and to plead guilty to disobedience, in obedience to a higher moral law of duty and conscience. The action brought results. Intervention from the viceroy, the governor, and the collector served to dismiss the case and to place Gandhi on a governmental commission of inquiry into the Champaran farmers' grievances, eventually ending in redress. The task took several months. Gandhi later claimed that it was "no exaggeration, but the literal truth, to say that in this meeting with the peasants I was face to face with God, Ahimsa and Truth."[81]

Gandhi also intervened in a major labor dispute in Ahmedabad. The millworkers of the textile city of Ahmedabad were very low paid and demanded a raise. The millowners resisted and ordered a lockout. Gandhi called for a strike until either the workers' demand was met or the case was submitted to arbitration. The millowners rejected arbitration. Gandhi decided to initiate a fast, an action that he would repeat on many occasions with far-reaching results in the future. The fast inspired both millworkers and millowners to negotiate peacefully, and a settlement was reached.[82]

The next testing ground was Kheda, a district in near-famine condition. Under the Land Revenue Rules, the cultivators could obtain full suspension of revenue assessment for the year if the crop amounted to not more than 25 percent of the normal yield. The official estimate of the crop did not tally with that of the farmers. When prayers and petitions for suspension failed, Gandhi advised resorting to *satyagraha*—refusal to pay the dues and submitting to penalty. Finally the revenue authorities compromised their demand by conceding suspension to poor farmers if the well-to-do paid their dues. This was not a real victory for Gandhi or *satyagraha*, since the government, not the people, decided who was poor and who was not, with the result that few farmers got the benefit of the compromise. Yet the peasants were awakened to their strength, their capacity for suffering, and their ability to take their destiny into their own hands. Kheda was not a perfect *satyagraha*, but more was to come.[83]

Distressed by the absence of genuine communal friendliness between Hindus and Muslims, Gandhi was committed to fostering harmony between the two groups. He saw this situation from the perspective of his South African days as the testing ground for *ahimsa*. His own friendship toward Muslims was so genuine that he was invited to address the Muslim League in 1917. The Muslims were engaged in an effort to save the khilafat (caliphate), the center of the Muslim world, which was jeopardized by the defeat of Turkey. When two Muslim leaders, the brothers Mohamed and Shaukat Ali, were jailed for agitating on the future of the khilafat, Gandhi pleaded for their release. He was also instrumental in setting the Muslim leaders on a course of non-cooperation with the government.[84]

Gandhi attended the Delhi War Conference in 1917, being invited and persuaded to do so by the viceroy, Lord Chelmsford, and he supported the resolution of the conference to aid the British war effort. Then, in the face of challenges from his supporters, he set out on the laborious job of recruiting for the armed forces. His reasons for such a course of action, held forth in his published letter to the viceroy, were pragmatic. India's wish to be a partner in the empire demanded that it support the latter in the hour of its need; the interests of India's *swaraj* (self-determination) were bound up with the empire's *swaraj*. He referred to his actions in Champaran and Kheda as his "direct, definite and special contribution to the War." Cooperation in the war effort therefore did not mean surrender of *satyagraha* to tyranny. In short, the cooperation was an act of faith, hope, love, and trust in England's sense of justice and fair play.[85] Gandhi very nearly ruined his health and constitution in his campaigns of recruitment, and was close to death's door when World War I ended.[86]

The Noncooperation Movement

While recovering from his illness, Gandhi was startled by the report of the Rowlatt Committee, a group appointed to study the question of Indian sedition. This report recommended the perpetuation of the extraordinary wartime powers repressing freedom of speech and the press and authorizing imprisonment without trial or the due process of law. As the viceroy did not withdraw the bill, Gandhi organized a *Satyagraha Sabha* (*Satyagraha* Association) in Bombay to go into action in case the bill became law. He also attended the debate on the Rowlatt bill in India's Imperial Legislative Council. Although the Indian member of the council opposed it, Gandhi judged the debate as but a formality to give legality to the government's predetermination. The Rowlatt bill became a legal act. Gandhi called upon the country to observe a twenty-four-hour general *hartal* (strike) and to devote the day to self-purification through fasting and prayer. Virtually all of India observed the *hartal* on April 6, 1919. At his Bombay public meeting that day, Gandhi called for civil disobedience in regard to the state's salt monopoly and the sale of "proscribed literature," that is, his own *Hind Swaraj* and *Sarvodaya*.[87]

Invited by local leaders to proceed to Delhi and Amritsar amid great popular excitement, Gandhi was forbidden by the government to enter the Punjab. On April 10 he was sent back a prisoner to Bombay, where he was set free. People were frenzied at the news of his arrest. The commissioner of police warned Gandhi that he would lose control of the people: "We, police officers, know better than you the effect of your teaching on the people. Disobedience of law will quickly appeal to them; it is beyond them to understand the duty of keeping peaceful."[88] Addressing a public meeting the same day, Gandhi instructed his listeners on the duty of nonviolence and the other limitations of *satyagraha*, and on his own unwillingness to launch the movement except under those limitations and conditions.[89]

There was violence in Ahmedabad and Amritsar. At a rumor of the arrest of their leader, Anasuyabehn, the Ahmedabad millworkers had committed arson. Telegraph wires were cut, and there were casualties among both officials and rioters. On April 13 Gandhi acknowledged himself guilty of precipitating the violence in Ahmedabad, imposing on himself a three-day fast. He appealed to the people to confess their guilt and fast for one day, while calling on the government to condone the crimes. Neither side accepted his suggestion.[90]

Addressing a public meeting in Nadiad, near Ahmedabad, Gandhi confessed to his audience his "Himalayan miscalculation" in having launched civil disobedience at Kheda. The miscalculation consisted of calling to disobedience people who had not learned to obey the laws of society with their intellect and free will as a sacred duty. Only a person who had learned this integral and consecrated obedience can distinguish the just laws from the unjust and acquire the right and duty of disobeying the unjust laws in certain well-defined circumstances. Gandhi admitted that he had erred in failing to observe this necessary limitation. On April 18 he suspended civil disobedience.

Gandhi set out to educate and prepare people for civil disobedience through training in obedience. Experience proved this to be a slow and laborious process. He instructed a core of volunteers who in turn would educate the masses; and he reached people directly through his writings. Through *Young India* and the Gujarati *Navajivan*, of which he was invited to be the editor, Gandhi educated the subscribing literate population and, in some measure, even the government.[91]

The worst turn of events occurred in the Punjab, where the lieutenant-governor, Sir Michael O'Dwyer, had already exasperated the province by forcibly recruiting soldiers and collecting funds during the war, ruthlessly suppressing rights through imprisonment of hundreds, stifling the press, and insulting the educated intelligentsia. The *hartal* of April 6, 1919, was quiet and uneventful. The news of Gandhi's arrest on April 10, however, caused a protest in Lahore. A peaceful procession of a few hundred students was stopped and fired upon for not moving away. A meeting at the Badshahi mosque likewise met with fire. Gunfire was also used against another crowd of over ten thousand people. Three local leaders who went to complain to the magistrate were deported. The killing of a calf led to destruction of much public property in Gujranwalla. Alleged police excess sparked mass violence, burning of government buildings, and the beating to death of two European soldiers.

In the Punjab capital of Amritsar, the deportation of two local leaders and news of Gandhi's arrest led to protest marches. Despite the fact that the marches were peaceful, the protesters were fired upon and twenty were killed. The infuriated crowd murdered five Europeans, committed arson, and beat a medical missionary, a Miss Sherwood, unconscious. On April 11 General Reginald Dyer arrived in Amritsar, and the next day he established de facto martial law. This law prohibited all meetings and gatherings, though it is not clear how widespread awareness of the law was. On April 13, the same day Gandhi was announcing his fast, a public meeting took place drawing a crowd estimated at six thousand to ten thousand. Without giving any warning or trying to disperse the crowd, Dyer's troops opened fire. Dyer later reported that his action was deliberate and calculated to strike terror into the whole of the Punjab, and that to have dispersed the crowd without firing on it would have denigrated him as a defender of law and order.[92] According to official estimates, five hundred Indians lay dead—one thousand according to the subsequent investigation by the congress. Dyer imposed a strict curfew, with the result that the wounded could not be retrieved and the bodies of the dead could not be buried.

Martial law was officially proclaimed in Amritsar on April 15. The martial law regime was a reign of terror characterized by acts of brutality unbecoming any civilized nation. Under Dyer's orders every person passing through the street on which Miss Sherwood had been assaulted was ordered to crawl past the spot where she had been attacked. The alleged assailants of Sherwood were publicly flogged and tried afterward. The Martial Law Commission tried about three hundred people on major charges, sentencing fifty-one to death, forty-eight to deportation, about eighty to seven years in prison, and others to lesser prison terms. There was aerial bombardment of any gathering within the state.

The government in India attempted for eight months to veil the horrors perpetrated on the Punjab, which had supplied more soldiers than any other state during Word War I. But news did leak out to the rest of India. Horror and indignation swept through the country.* Even under such provocation, Gandhi did not resume civil disobedience. The government, however, introduced and passed a bill of indemnity to protect the civil and military officials in the Punjab from the just and legal consequences of their action, and afterward appointed a committee of inquiry into the acts of persons whom the viceroy had already pardoned. Prior to organization of the viceroy's committee of inquiry, headed by Sir William W. Hunter, the congress leaders had appointed their own inquiry committee of six men, headed by Gandhi.

The Congress Inquiry Committee, while condemning mass excesses, found the government to be the chief culprit. The theory of rebellion, war, or conspiracy to overthrow the government was proved hollow. The martial-law proclamation and prolongation was, therefore, found unjustified. Nearly twelve hundred lives had been lost, and three times that many wounded. The viceroy was censured for ignoring the pleas and complaints of individuals and public bodies, for keeping the tales of horror from the public and the imperial government, for preventing the public from ascertaining the facts, for refusing to postpone death sentences pronounced by martial-law tribunals except after he was forced to do so by the secretary of state in Whitehall, and for endorsing the action of the Punjab government without any inquiry. The

---

*Poet Rabindranath Tagore relinquished his knighthood in protest, "giving voice to the protest of the millions . . . surprised into a dumb anguish of terror" because "the universal agony of indignation roused in the hearts of our people has been ignored by our rulers—possibly congratulating themselves for imparting what they imagine as salutary lessons. . . ."

congress demanded, therefore, his removal from office and the dismissal of
O'Dwyer, Dyer, and five other English and Indian officers.

The Hunter committee report was divided into a majority and a minority
report. Both agreed on the *satyagraha* movement as the cause of the outbreak, justifying the subsequent firing on mobs. On Dyer's action the judgments differed. The majority considered his firing without warning and for
so long "a grave error of judgment." The minority report took a more critical view of the whole event, branding it as inhuman and un-British. Both
reports exonerated the government of India from all blame. The majority
saw the outbreak as a rebellion and thus agreed that martial law was justified.
The minority stated that martial law was imposed as a punitive measure after
the crisis was over and denounced it as unconstitutional.

While a few Englishmen condemned the action of the government in India,
the government of Britain pronounced in the House of Commons only a mild
censure on Dyer, removing him from active service, and absolved O'Dwyer
and Chelmsford from all guilt. The House of Lords passed a resolution de-
ploring the removal of Dyer from the army as unjust.*

> It is difficult to say which outraged the Indian feelings more, the brutal
> acts of Dyer and other officials, or the approval of their conduct by the
> Englishmen in general, both in India and Britain. In any case, the Pun-
> jab atrocities created a river of blood between India and Britain which
> could not be bridged. The relation between the Indians and the British
> could never again be what it was before 1919. No other event since
> 1857–58 created such bad blood between the two.[93]

There was a limited attempt at improving the political situation of the Indians. The Government of India Act of 1919, based on the report on Indian
constitutional reforms by Secretary of State Montagu and Viceroy Chelmsford, provided for increased representation of Indians in the government.
Although the activist leader C. R. Das asserted that the Reforms Act was
inadequate and demanded that steps be taken toward self-determination for
India, Gandhi advised that the Reforms Act was "an earnest of the intention
of the British people to do justice to India," and that India's duty therefore
was "to settle down quietly to work so as to make them [the reforms] a
success." It was Gandhi who prevailed with the Amritsar session of the congress. The acceptance of his advice was a yardstick of the hold he had secured
not only on the masses, with his personality and saintly life, but also on the

---

*Worse still, the House of Lords acclaimed Dyer a hero and raised public subscriptions to
present him a purse. The English public and newspapers never repudiated Dyer's inhumanity or
the callous attitude of the House of Lords. English people in India hailed Dyer as the savior of
the British empire. European associations all over India protested the Commons' action and the
Lords' failure to reinstate Dyer. They supported the fund appeal for General Dyer started by
London's *Morning Post* and organized a memorial to him in India! The English women in India
started a Dyer Appreciation Fund at Mussorie and presented him with a sword and 20,000
pounds.

educated and politically conscious classes of India. "In that assembly of veteran nationalist leaders who had distinguished themselves in various fields of life and had a long record of public service in India behind them, Gandhi, a comparatively new figure in the congress, easily established his position as a leader of the first rank."[94]

The result was that the Amritsar session authorized Gandhi to prepare a new draft constitution for the congress. Gandhi's new constitution defined the goal of the congress simply as *swaraj*, rather than "self-government within the British empire," as stated in the old constitution. This change helped to accommodate the radicals, whose political ideal was complete independence. Neither long usage nor general vogue having given the term any very precise connotation, Gandhi left it deliberately vague so that users could see in it their own interpretation. For himself, Gandhi defined *swaraj* as "self-government within the Empire, if possible, and outside, if necessary."Concerning the means for achieving this goal, Gandhi substituted the words "all peaceful and legitimate means" for the old "constitutional means." This again could be accepted by both moderates and radicals. Gandhi also initiated within the congress a system of committees. These ranged from village committees to the representative All-India Congress Committee (A.I.C.C.) to the national executive or Congress Working Committee (C.W.C.). This gave the congress contact with, and the support of, the masses, which it needed to become a representative national organization.[95]

Despite his loyalty to Britain, Gandhi was becoming increasingly impatient with Britain's treatment of his fellow Indians. He was particularly disheartened by the British government's failure to redeem its promise to the Muslims of India regarding Turkey and the khilafat. In June 1920, as head of the Khilafat Committee, Gandhi wrote to the viceroy warning him of noncooperation with the government if Britain would not honor its promise to keep the Turkish Ottoman empire intact. On August 1, 1920, the noncooperation movement was launched with a *hartal* and Gandhi's return of all his war medals. A special session of the congress was held at Calcutta on September 4, in which Gandhi introduced a resolution of noncooperation as a means to call attention to the plight of the Muslims, to protest the self-righteously unrepentant attitude of the British government and people with regard to the terrorism in the Punjab, and to establish *swaraj* as the only effective way to vindicate national honor and prevent the repetition of similar wrongs in the future.

Gandhi and the congress called for: (1) surrender of titles and honorary offices and nominated seats in local bodies; (2) refusal to attend functions held by government officials or in their honor; (3) gradual withdrawal of children from schools and colleges owned, aided, or controlled by the government, and establishment of national schools and colleges; (4) gradual boycott of British courts by lawyers and litigants and the establishment of private arbitration courts; (5) boycott of recruitment for service in Mesopotamia; (6) withdrawal of candidates for election to the reformed councils and refusal by voters to vote for independent candidates; and (7) boycott of foreign goods.

In advocating the boycott of foreign goods, Gandhi introduced the concept of *swadeshi*, or the use of indigenous products to promote national pride. He advocated reliance on *khadi* (hand-spun cloth) as opposed to fabric imported from abroad.

> Inasmuch as Non-co-operation has been conceived as a measure of discipline and self-sacrifice without which no nation can make real progress, and inasmuch as an opportunity should be given in a very first stage of Non-co-operation to every man, woman and child, for such discipline and self-sacrifice, this Congress advises adoption of *Swadeshi* in piece-goods on a vast scale, and inasmuch as the existing mills of India with indigenous capital and control do not manufacture sufficient yarn and sufficient cloth for the requirements of the Nation, and are not likely to do so for a long time to come, the Congress advises immediate stimulation for further manufacture on a large scale by means of reviving hand-spinning in every home and hand-weaving on the part of the millions of weavers who have abandoned their ancient and honourable calling for want of encouragement.[96]

The resolution of noncooperation was carried by over a two-thirds majority, and it was approved at the Nagpur regular session of the congress in December 1920 by almost all of the fourteen thousand delegates. Gandhi toured the country popularizing the program.

Success of the program, however, was only partial, despite the enthusiasm that it generated. The boycott of councils was a failure, since all the seats were filled up by noncongressmen; all that the congress could do was to demonstrate the nonrepresentative character of the legislative councils elected under the new constitution. Thousands of Indians were accused of sedition and put in jail. The boycott of honors was insignificant in volume. Students in large numbers did give up their studies and become full-time national volunteer workers; yet the movement never gained enough strength or momentum to have any serious effect on existing institutions. The significance of the program could be measured, however, in a new zeal and spirit in India's struggle for freedom.

On November 17 a *hartal* was announced to boycott the visit of the Prince of Wales. This prompted a huge bonfire of foreign cloth in Bombay. The peaceful protest degenerated, however, into a scene of mob violence on the part of Bombay's millhands. Gandhi denounced the violence and fasted until it abated. Except for the incidents in Bombay, the November 17 *hartal* passed successfully and peacefully. In Calcutta it was so successful that both *The Statesman* and the *Englishman* stated that congress volunteers had taken possession of the city and the government had abdicated. Within twenty-four hours the government declared the congress and the Khilafat Committee unlawful. Prohibitive orders were imposed in Bengal, and other provincial governments followed that lead. The viceroy asked the congress leaders to give up noncooperation in return for restoration of civil liberties and proposed a Round Table Conference of representatives of the government and the congress to settle the future constitution of India. But Gandhi's demand for the release of the Ali brothers, coupled with his agreement to meet at a Round Table Conference, caught the viceroy off guard. When Gandhi's response arrived, the government changed its mind. According to C. R. Das, "The chance of a lifetime had been lost."[97]

With about forty thousand congress workers in jail, the 1921 session of congress in Ahmedabad urged the continuance of the noncooperation movement with greater vigor and advised all congressworkers to spearhead civil disobedience as soon as the masses were sufficiently trained in the nonviolent method. Gandhi sent an ultimatum to the viceroy demanding the restoration of civil liberties to the nonviolent imprisoned, as well as humane treatment for all prisoners, holding out civil disobedience as the alternative to a declaration of a change of policy within seven days. This was a bold and unprecedented step in India's history, which only a person of Gandhi's stature could conceive. The government failed to act.

Gandhi proceeded to the district of Bardoli, intending to lead its village residents in a display of total civil disobedience. This was to be a dramatic gesture of the effectiveness of mass protest against the government. "The whole of India watched the great battle in a spirit of animated suspense. But the battle was lost before it had begun." News of a dastardly crime committed by the people of Chauri Chaura, Uttar Pradesh, forced Gandhi to call a halt at the critical moment. When the police, who had opened fire on a procession, had shut themselves in their station for want of ammunition, a mob had set fire to the building, later throwing the hacked bodies of the constables into the fire. On the appeal of prominent leaders, Gandhi suspended the civil disobedience movement. Bardoli was a turning point in the history of the freedom struggle. "It put a stop not only to civil disobedience, but practically to the whole program of Non-co-operation which involved any defiance to Government, laying down instead a constructive program which aroused very little enthusiasm."[98]

The British government, which had held back on arresting Gandhi through all the previous turmoil, now decided to bring him to trial. On March 10, 1922, Gandhi was arrested for "exciting disaffection toward His Majesty's Government as established by law in India." As testified to by his letters both before and after the event, Gandhi anticipated his arrest and welcomed it with relief. The outbreak of violence in many parts of India despite his earnest appeals for peace had disturbed him to his depths. Admitting personal responsibility, he stated at his trial that "it is impossible to dissociate myself from the diabolical crimes of Chauri Chaura or the mad outrages in Bombay and Madras."[99] But he had either to submit to a system that, in his view, had done irreparable harm to his country or to risk the mad fury of his people bursting forth when they understood the truth from his lips.[100] In the dilemma of having to live *ahimsa* in a world of *himsa*, he had chosen to risk letting loose his nation's fury and was humbled to see his worst fears come true. "I have now a more vivid sense of truth and of my own littleness than I had a year ago," he wrote.[101]

The trial was a forceful challenge to the moral justification of the British rule. In it Gandhi traced the history of his change "from a staunch loyalist and cooperator" to "an uncompromising disaffectionist and non-cooperator,"[102] holding it "to be a virtue to be disaffected towards a Government which, in its totality, has done more harm to India than any previous system"[103] politically and economically.[104] Gandhi ended his statement by calling on the judge to resign and refuse to cooperate with the law, if he saw its evil, or else to inflict the severest penalty.[105] The defendant was sentenced to six years' simple imprisonment.

In prison Gandhi spent his time reading, meditating, and working at the spinning wheel. He carried on correspondence and wrote thirty chapters of *Satyagraha in South Africa*.

Released before the end of his term, in February 1924, Gandhi came out confirmed, by reflection in solitude, in his attitudes toward religion, politics, and modern civilization, only to find India less responsive to his message than when he went in. The harmony forged by the noncooperation movement was in shambles and dissolving into communal riots; noncooperation itself was set aside by the congress when it permitted its members to enter the legislative and executive councils. Those who, led by veteran intellectuals like Motilal Nehru and C. R. Das, had entered the councils, had formed the *Swaraj* party within the congress, bitterly opposed by others who were described as No-changers. Gandhi, who respected the *Swaraj* party leaders, took time to state his disapproval of the party's program of obstruction from within as retarding the nation's progress toward *swaraj* and accommodating violence in its pressure tactics. But accepting council entry as a settled fact and therefore a necessary evil, he began work to secure unity and cooperation between the two camps.[106] He also devoted energy toward reconciling the warring religions of India and antagonistic factions within Hinduism[107] and Sikhism.[108]

To cleanse the social atmosphere of fanatical interreligious riots, desecrations, and killings, Gandhi undertook in September, at Mohamed Ali's house in Delhi, a purificatory fast of twenty-one days—to purify himself of traces of violence so as to regain the power to appeal to the people. "Defeated and helpless, I must submit my petition to His court."[109] "Had I not been instrumental in bringing into being the vast energy of the people? I must find the remedy if the energy proved self-destructive."[110] The fast set the climate for the Unity Conference, which deplored and condemned the increasing strife as contrary to religion, and appointed arbitrators to settle Hindu-Muslim disputes and to frame a plan for the protection of minorities.

The Constructive Program

Elected president of the congress for 1925, Gandhi accepted the honor despite his awareness of the gulf between his ideas and the events that had transpired. The intellect of the country seemed not to understand his mode of thought and action.[111] Admitting that his noncooperation movement had not worked, he was ready to try a different approach. He formulated the Constructive Program, a plan to take positive action in three areas: the strengthening of *khadi*, the promotion of Hindu-Muslim unity, and the removal of untouchability.[112] Rather than demonstrating against the British government, the Indian people would purify themselves from within. *Swaraj* would follow naturally. In due course global history would impinge upon Gandhi's program as first Europe and then countries around the world were drawn into World War II.

Khadi. With the *swaraj* party rehabilitated at the Patna session of the Congress Working Committee, politics became the focus of the congress, with emphasis shifting to economic issues. Gandhi promoted the idea of *khadi* (hand-spinning; homespun cloth) for its spiritual and practical values. Every member of the congress was to wear only *khadi*, and each was to engage in spinning for an hour a day, if possible. Self-sufficiency in cloth production would provide work for otherwise jobless Indians and keep Indian revenues from leaving the country.

The All-India Spinners' Association was formed, and the *swadeshi* movement was intensified through a wider and better-organized use of the *charkha* (spinning wheel). Gandhi asked both Hindus and Muslims to support the *khadi* movement by plying the *charkha*. He also tried to convince the millowners to foster the boycott of foreign cloth by standardizing their prices and lowering their profits. When the negotiations with millowners did not bear fruit, Gandhi reminded them of the power of *satyagraha* and asked them not to stand in the way of the national cause.[113]

National Aspirations and Hindu-Muslim Relations. The frustration caused by the suspension of civil disobedience had adversely affected the relations between Hindus and Muslims. There was no common program to bring them together. The transformation of Turkey into a secular state under Kemal Atatürk brought an end to the khilafat movement. Scheming persons were sowing discord between the two communities. A series of communal riots, which (except for occasional intervals) were to be an almost regular feature of Indian political life, broke out in 1923.

The situation had become so complex that Gandhi thought it wise to do nothing about it, temporarily, until he could come up with a workable solution.[114] He toured the affected areas to ascertain the facts and to try to help solve the communal problem of religions and castes.

In 1926 Gandhi voluntarily retired from public work to rest in the confines of his ashram. Problems of the Indians in South Africa involving new racial legislation contrary to the Smuts-Gandhi agreement engaged much of his energy.[115] He assured the South African Indian deputation of his willingness to return to South Africa if it should prove necessary. But he turned down invitations to visit America, China, and Finland, saying, "If there is any power in my message it would be felt without the physical contact."[116]

During this time of political alienation, the Mahatma found his peace and rest in God: "No man need ever feel lonely who feels the living presence of God near him and in him. Whatever peace I have found, has been found by increasing faith in the hand of God being in everything. Calamities then cease to be calamities. They test our faith and steadfastness."[117] For months Gandhi kept his silence on the work of the legislatures and on Hindu-Muslim quarrels, devoting himself to the promotion of the rest of the Constructive Program. His writings continued to educate the nation in nonviolence and to assure it that India's greatest contribution to human happiness would be to attain its freedom by peaceful and truthful means, even while events seemed to contradict this eventuality. His own service to India was his contribution to humanity. For, "One who serves another selflessly and without any attachment serves all."[118] Service was impossible without self-sacrifice, as salvation was impossible without suffering. Hence the nation had to be prepared to suffer for its cause.[119]

The finest fruit of Gandhi's sabbatical year was his *Discourses on the* Gita, a series of talks reflecting his own meditation on that religious classic. His interpretation of the *Gita* was *adyatmic*, that of mystagogy or mystical spirituality.[120] From the *Gita* Gandhi stored spiritual energy that would sustain him in the struggles to come.

Touring South India and Ceylon late in 1927 to popularize and raise funds for *khadi* work, Gandhi spoke out against the Brahmin–non-Brahmin schism as well as the prevalent form of *varnashrama*. He envisioned a social system free of the taint of untouchability.[121] Answering the criticism that this was utopianism, he replied that it was given to individuals to live their utopias without waiting for acceptance by society.[122]

In 1928 the government announced that a statutory commission of seven parliamentarians, headed by Sir John Simon, would be visiting India to report on the working of the Reforms Act of 1919; their purpose was to determine what further action might be necessary to extend, modify, or restrict the degree of responsible government then in existence. Ostensibly the Simon Commission's timing, two years ahead of the date originally set, was a concession to Indian political opinion. But a sinister motive was attributed to the British move on two accounts. The year 1929 was to be an election year in England, in which the liberal Labour party, which was sympathetic to India's aspirations, was expected to win. Therefore the current move was thought to be designed to prevent Labour's prospective concessions to India, which might adversely affect British interests. The second consideration was the exclusion of the Indians from the statutory commission. The viceroy, Lord Irwin, in announcing the commission, was at pains to defend its composition: "The desire, natural and legitimate, of the Indian members to see India a self-governing nation, could hardly fail to colour their judgment of her present capacity to sustain the role!" This was not to deny totally the right of the Indians to contribute their solutions to the constitutional problem; they could deposit their ideas with the Simon Commission. The announcement of the Simon Commission was received with deep disappointment and indignation by influential political leaders in India, and they unanimously decided to boycott the commission,[123] although Gandhi did not actively associate himself with the boycott in order not to bring the masses into the movement and "possibly embarrass the promoters."[124]

The most significant event of this period from Gandhi's perspective was the Bardoli *satyagraha*, resumed six years after its abandonment because of the Chauri Chaura affair. The precipitating incident was the announcement of an excessive increase in the land revenue assessment. The cultivators asked for an imperial tribunal to examine the issue, but the government was intransigent. The farmers refused to remit the revenue. Sensing challenge to its authority, the government attempted to crush the spirit of the peasantry, resorting to wholesale arrests, intimidation, and seizure and auctioning of livestock and property. The cultivators, led by Vallabhbhai Patel, remained peacefully defiant. Gandhi guided the movement from a distance by building up public opinion in favor of the people's case. Though local and limited, this *satyagraha* was an important step toward *swaraj*, as it provided training in "disciplined and peaceful resistance" and "corporate suffering."[125] The government agreed to come to terms.

Gandhi also wrote a series of articles on education at this time, exposing the hollowness of the prevailing system and spelling out his own ideas of a village-based and village-oriented education. Students had to be instructed not only in the texts of the classics, such as the *Ramayana* and the *Mahabharata*, but in "their modern spiritual meaning."[126] It is a sign of the deeper inwardness gained during his retreat that Gandhi recognized nothing as possessing spiritual or moral value "apart from work and action,"[127] and recognized no religion that could not be reduced to economic terms and no economics that could not be "reduced to terms of religion and spirituality."[128] At the death of C. R. Das, Gandhi could say, "A time comes in the life of every Indian when mere political battle jars on him and . . . he seeks to base everything on spiritual, lovingly moral foundations."[129]

Gandhi saw a connection between the existence of his ashram and the success of *satyagraha* at Bardoli.

The *satyagraha* derived its strength from the asceticism, constructive work, and discipline practiced in the ashram. The ashram enabled *satyagrahis* "to give battle on an extensive scale."[130] It was from there that Gandhi was to undertake the Salt March two years later. The ashram life and the Bardoli success became with him symbols and synonyms for "organic *swaraj*," "*Ramarajya*" or substantive *swaraj*. The constitutional or statutory *swaraj* for which the All-Parties Conference at Lucknow and the Nehru Report paved the way through formal self-government was important. Substantive *swaraj* was more important.[131]

Toward the end of 1928 Gandhi cautiously made his reentry into active political involvement by attending the Calcutta session of the congress, on Motilal Nehru's appeal.[132] He took a leading part in the deliberations, championing the overriding of an earlier Delhi resolution calling for complete independence in favor of the Nehru Report's recommendation of dominion status for India.[133] But in order to accommodate the youthful enthusiasm and revolutionary spirit of leaders like Jawaharlal Nehru and Subhas Bose, Gandhi agreed to set a deadline for action on his program. He proposed a two-year limit, but later agreed that if India had not attained *swaraj* within one year, by the end of 1929, the congress could declare independence and resort to mass agitation.[134]

In preparation for the struggle for *swaraj* envisaged by the Calcutta Congress, and as chairman of the Foreign-Cloth Boycott Committee formed by the Congress Working Committee according to his own plan, Gandhi wrote *khadi* propaganda and organized a foreign-cloth boycott. The boycott of foreign cloth was not merely a political weapon, but the economic counterpart of the promotion of *khadi* as a means of relieving the chronic unemployment in the country and attaining "*swaraj* in terms of the hungry millions."[135] The boycott was dramatized by public bonfires of foreign cloth, a form of protest revived from earlier years.

The Round Table Conferences. On October 31, 1929, the viceroy, Lord Irwin, issued an official statement that "it is implicit in the declaration of 1917 that the natural issue of India's Constitutional progress, as there contemplated, is the attainment of Dominion Status,"[136] and announced the British government's intention to call a round table conference in London to discuss a new constitution for India. Gandhi and other national leaders issued a statement cautiously welcoming the announcement. Gandhi wanted an assurance from the viceroy that the purpose of the conference was to frame a plan for a dominion constitution.[137] Lord Irwin was unable to give his assurance. It became clear that the agreed-upon deadline would not be met. The congress, then gathered at Lahore, proceeded to act upon the previous year's ultimatum and passed a resolution on December 31, 1929, proclaiming *purna swaraj* (complete independence) as the country's goal.

The continuing frustration of nationalist aspirations, along with deepening poverty, resulted in a rapid spread of violence and the growth of the terrorist party. Sensing the mounting impatience of nationalist India, and judging that "the spirit of violence must be dealt with by non-violent *action*" if the situation is to be at all saved," Gandhi made up his mind "to run the boldest risks"[138] and devised a plan of action to circumvent both the organized violence of foreign rule and the lawless and disorganized violence of secret crime.[139] A new form of organization would emerge in this campaign. The congress being divided on commitment to nonviolence, Gandhi did not want to run the campaign in its name; he would lead it himself or jointly with a few companions.[140] On February 15, 1930, the Congress Working Committee authorized Gandhi and those of his co-workers who believed in non-violence to start civil disobedience, and called upon all congressmen to extend full cooperation to the civil resisters. His prayer-meeting speech that day was a serious call to suffering and to the conversion of the ashram into a "lamp of sacrifice."[141] In a *Young India* article he then declared his intention "to start the movement only through the inmates of the ashram and those who have submitted to its discipline and assimilated the spirit of its method."[142]

In a dramatic move on March 12, 1930, Gandhi initiated a two-hundred-mile march to the sea. Ending at the seaport of Dandi, the Salt March was ostensibly a protest against the government's tax on so basic a necessity as salt, which Gandhi symbolized by extracting some salt from the sea. In fact, the effect of the march was much more far-reaching. During the three-week period of the march, supporters joined in mass meetings and protests all over the country. More than one hundred thousand arrests were made. Gandhi was arrested on May 5 and removed to Yerawda Jail, where for the most part he abstained from all political discussion, practicing the *Gita*'s doctrine of *anasakti* (detachment).

The first Round Table Conference proceeded without representation from the congress. It was based on the Simon Commission's recommendation of a federal constitution as the ultimate goal and full autonomy in the provinces, the governor having overriding powers to ensure internal security and the safety of all communities. While the British side was unwilling to concede dominion status and responsible government, the Indian side, representing princes and other eminent leaders, insisted on both. The princes agreed to federate with a self-governing and federal British India. A subcommittee on minorities agreed on the need to protect their interests and employment opportunities in federal and provincial services and to have elections rather than nominations for representative purposes. B. R. Ambedkar, the spokesman for the untouchables, asked that the depressed classes be considered a separate electorate, and other minorities made the same request. In this way each social or religious community hoped to maximize its power in the representative body. There was a proposal for a joint electorate of Muslims and Hindus, but agreement could not be reached and a separate electorate of Muslims was made a condition for agreement. Prime Minister Ramsay MacDonald, who presided, summed up the agreed recommendations of the conference: that the responsibility for the government of India should be placed upon legislatures, with such provisions as may be necessary to fulfill obligations to the princes and the minorities. As for the question of communal electorates, he asked the communities to come to an agreement among themselves. He expressed the wish to help in the implementation of the constitution with the cooperation of all, calling especially for the support of the congress.[143]

Though the congress, through its Working Committee, had refused to recognize the conference, the mediation of two Indian delegates to the conference helped to bring about negotiations between Gandhi and the viceroy. These meetings led to a compromise plan, the Gandhi-Irwin Pact. The pact was a provisional settlement in which the congress would accept as a constitutional framework the proposals of the first Round Table Conference and would agree to take part in further deliberations of the conference, while discontinuing civil disobedience. The government, for its part, would put an end to all executive and police harassments. Since it clearly violated the Lahore resolution of complete independence, Gandhi's pact caused much dissatisfaction; it was accepted, however, out of respect for the Mahatma.[144]

At the second Round Table Conference, Gandhi spoke in favor of wider adult franchise and against a separate electorate for the depressed classes; he felt that a separate electorate "would divide the Hindu community into armed camps," making untouchables remain untouchables in perpetuity, a condition that he vowed to resist with his life. Disagreeing sharply on this issue of communal representation, most Round Table delegates left the decision to the prime minister's arbitration. Gandhi agreed, on the condition that MacDonald make the decision as an individual rather than as the prime minister.[145] He suspected the government of working to prevent communal agreement between Hindus and Muslims, following a policy of "divide and rule."

Meanwhile, as Gandhi had feared it might, the provisional settlement began to break down. With the consent of the British Cabinet, the government in India had gone back on the Gandhi-Irwin Pact. Antagonisms had surfaced again between members of the congress and the government, and there had been a new wave of arrests. A request by Gandhi to discuss the government's repressive measures was denied by the viceroy. In January 1932, Gandhi and the congress decided that civil disobedience would be resumed.[146] The government responded by passing more repressive ordinances. Some ninety thousand congressmen were convicted and jailed, and Gandhi was arrested.

The factionalization of Indians by religion and class troubled Gandhi deeply. From Yerawda Jail he informed the British government that in the event of their decision to create a separate electorate for the depressed classes, "I must fast unto death. For me the contemplated step is not a method, it is part of my being. It is a call of conscience which I dare not disobey. . . ."[147] His subsequent six-day fast awoke the conscience of the country and marked the beginning of the breakdown of untouchability.

Gandhi's work thereafter was more social than directly political. The abolition of untouchability was his major concern. The congress and Gandhi were not in accord on either the content of *swaraj* or the means to its attainment.[148] Gandhi wanted mass civil disobedience given up by the congress in favor of individual civil disobedience; congress did not agree.[149] In 1934, Gandhi retired from active leadership of the congress.

Untouchability. The Government of India Act of 1935, passed by Parliament in July, set out a new constitution for India, which fell far short of meeting Indian hopes for true independence. The Indian Federation was to include elected representatives from the provinces, but it would also include appointed nominees from the princely states. The power of the legislators was to be further restricted by the overriding authority of the governors. Jawaharlal Nehru described the Indian Reforms Act as a "charter of slavery." Both the congress and the Muslim League decided not to work out the provincial autonomy granted by the Act. Such an unsatisfactory response on the part of the government in exchange for Gandhi's suspension of civil disobedience contributed to a widespread feeling of "despair and depression."[150]

Gandhi turned his attention to the Constructive Program for village uplift. He hoped to "bring about a silent revolution in the structure of society," by substituting the struggle for mutual service for the mere struggle for existence.[151] Although not officially a part of the congress, he continued to guide and direct its leaders, particularly Jawaharlal Nehru, even from his retirement. In 1936 Gandhi settled in Sevagram village, to live among the poor and "show them how to live" by personal example and service, rather than by preaching.[152] He worked to rid the village of disease and superstition; for Gandhi, these were substantive parts of *swaraj*.

Ramsay MacDonald's decision had upheld the idea of separate communal electorates, with untouchables each receiving one vote as Hindus and one extra vote. Untouchability now became a political issue. Ambedkar and other untouchable, or *harijan*, leaders attempted to detach the *harijans* from the Hindu society through mass conversion to another faith. Leaders of various religions in India were vying with one another, trying to entice the *harijans* into their folds. Gandhi felt it was a travesty of religion to seek to uproot from the *harijans*' minds such faith as they had in their ancestral religion. He deplored this practice as an unholy rivalry—a commercial spirit imported into religion by self-constituted leaders who were bartering the religious freedom of the *harijans*. Gandhi felt that evaluating religion in terms of politics and economics made a mockery of religious values; the right course would have been to evaluate politics and economics in terms of religion.[153] Despite his agreement with Ambedkar that Hinduism was to be condemned for the practice of untouchability, Gandhi maintained his faith in Hinduism. Rather than disavowing his religion, he would work within it to eradicate the practice that he found so abhorrent.

The question of Gandhi's possible conversion to Christianity or any other religion had long been resolved. He was and remained a Hindu, because Hinduism was not inconsistent with his moral sense or spiritual growth. Of all the religions he had examined, he had found Hinduism to be the most tolerant. Its "freedom from dogma" had a strong appeal to him "in as much as it gives the votary the largest scope for self-expression. Not being an exclusive religion, it enables the followers of that faith not merely to respect all other religions, but it also enables them to admire and assimilate whatever may be good in the other faiths. Non-violence is common to all religions, but it has found the highest expression and application in Hinduism."

In India during the religious and political struggles of the 1920s through 1940s, Gandhi spoke and wrote much on Christianity and Christian missionary work. Concurrent with his presence on the Indian political scene was his involvement in the course of missionary thought and the theology of religions. Prominent evangelists and missionaries in India and abroad discussed questions of mission with him and discussed his views among themselves, his interchange with them remaining amicable, though often critical: "Up till now [1939] they have come as teachers and preachers with queer notions about India and India's great religions. We have been described as a nation of superstitious heathens, knowing nothing, denying God. We are a brood of Satan. . . . To me this is a negation of the spirit of Christ.'' Gandhi welcomed missionaries if they came as fellow-seekers in India's quest, accepting India's religion as true, though, like all religions, imperfect by reason of its human tradition. But if the missionaries came as preachers of the "true Gospel" to a people wandering in darkness, so far as he was concerned they could have no place.[154]

Gandhi believed that "the soul of religion is one, but it is encased in a multitude of forms. The latter will persist to the end of time." There was a need not for one religion, but for mutual respect and tolerance for the devotees of different religions,[155] for truth existed within every one of the great religions.[156]

Addressing a Christian audience at the Leonard Theological College in Jubbulpore in 1933, Gandhi had called for Christian cooperation in the *harijan* uplift and the removal of untouchability, with the honest recognition of Hinduism as a gift of God and not of Satan, and hence without ulterior motives of religious propaganda and conversion.[157] Christian life was to be its own evangelism. "There is no desire to speak when one lives the truth. Truth is most economical of words. There is thus no truer or other evangelism than life."[158]

From the end of 1936 on, some progress was made on the question of untouchability. Gandhi saw the sins of the past being rectified as the temples were opened to *harijans* for the first time in Travancore and elsewhere.[159] The congress session of that year was exclusively concerned with the parliamentary program established by the 1935 act. Since the total electorate was only 10 percent of the population (35 million out of 350 million), and mostly confined to cities, Gandhi was concerned with ways of awakening the millions in the villages to the consciousness of their strength, so that violence and even civil disobedience would become unnecessary.[160] It was evident to him that there could be no complete independence (*purna swaraj*) without the participation of the masses. They were to be "taught to know what they should want and how to obtain it in the shape of sanitation and hygiene, improvement of material conditions and social relations."[161] Against the people's "hopeless unwillingness . . . to better their lot" and their tendency to "hug their ignorance and dirt as they do their untouchability," the program required deep personal commitment and missionary dedication.[162]

Though the congress secured absolute majorities of six of the eleven provinces in the general election, Nehru vehemently opposed any plan to accept office under the "slave constitution" in preference to "our Constituent Assembly."There was also pressure on the congress in the opposite direction, both from within and without. Opinion was divided as to whether cooperation or noncooperation was the best way to resist the act. Anxious to prevent a split within, and in hopes of "the creation . . . of a situation that would transfer all power to the people," Gandhi was inclined toward cooperation or acceptance of office by the congress, so as to strengthen it.[163] The congress approved Gandhi's plan for cooperation, on condition that the British Raj (administration) give assurance that the governor would abide by the advice of the council of ministers and not use his special powers of interference. The British Raj rejected the demand and appointed puppet interim ministries, which could carry on the administration for six months without legislative backing. Thanks to Gandhi's persuasive mediation between the congress and the government, both sides reinterpreted and toned down earlier statements and demands, and congress councils of ministers assumed office in late 1937 in seven provinces.

Justifying the change from noncooperation to cooperation with the government, Gandhi pointed to the difference between 1930 and 1937. In his own words, Gandhi "never made a fetish of consistency."[164] As "a worshipper of truth" and "a servant of the people," he could not but be affected by the prevailing atmosphere and feeling for parliamentary democracy; and, he pointed out, the congress's cooperation entailed cooperation by the government as well.[165] Gandhi was aware, however, that the council program was "full of temptations" and capable of waking "the brute in man."[166] Writing in the weekly magazine *Harijan*, he not only insisted that the council remain an organization of truth and nonviolence; he also instructed the new rulers in simplicity of lifestyle and administration,[167] reminding them of their responsibility on behalf of "the true welfare of the starving millions."[168] The congress must hold power not tightly, but lightly; not as a prize, but as an avenue to service,[169] its moral authority derived from the goodwill of the people whom it sought to represent and serve.[170] In this spirit he invited courteous, open, and well-informed criticism of these officials as a duty.[171]

In the persisting "storm signals" of violence and labor unrest in cities like Ahmedabad and Kanpur, where there were large Muslim concentrations, Gandhi saw symptoms of the congressmen's lack of faith in truth, nonviolence, and the Constructive Program; he warned them that without "that political faith in the means, office-acceptance may prove to be a trap."[172] There was a widening gap between the congress and the Muslim League, as well as between Gandhi and the Muslim leader M. A. Jinnah. Gandhi noted a diminishment of nationalist spirit in Jinnah.[173] Jinnah replied by decrying "the amount of vilification, misrepresentation and falsehood that is daily spread about me" in the congress press. The growing distrust ended in communal riots in Allahabad, which the government quelled with the use of the army. This to Gandhi was "as if the Congress had lost and the British had won."[174] He told congress, through his *Harijan* columns, to face the "naked truth" of its unfitness as yet to substitute for the British authority, pointing out that it did not yet represent all of India.

The year 1938 was a time of social, political, and economic unrest in India. Radicals within the congress were inciting peasants to violence in an attempt to abolish the land revenue system. There was insubordination, lack of discipline, and open violence among congressmen, and corruption in the congress administration at various levels.[175] Gandhi advocated an all-India political party, with control over all of the provinces in order to prevent the political fragmentation of the country.

The struggle of the people of the princely states for responsible government intensified. With the encouragement and military support of the paramount British power, the princes tried to crush the movement. Gandhi called on them to concede to the people's demands, which were legitimate, and to become trustees themselves for the people, taking an earned commission for their labors.[176] In so doing, they would have nothing to fear from their resident subjects, in whom the supreme power actually resided.[177] In the states whose rulers met popular aspirations halfway, Gandhi asked the people's organizations to moderate their demands.[178]

Gandhi also "plunged into the European waters" with the Munich agreement of September 1938, which he called "peace without honour." He called on the Czechs to offer nonviolent resistance, without bitterness, to the Nazis,[179] since in order to be human, people had to cease to be brutal. Gandhi condemned Japan's depredations in China and Nazi Germany's persecution of the Jews. Nor did Zionism meet with his approval. While he admired and sympathized with the Jews, his sense of justice demanded that they not carve out a national homeland by displacing the proud Palestinian Arabs, but make their homes in the countries in which they lived.[180] From the "chosen race," whose gifts he extolled, he expected nothing less than exemplary nonviolence.[181]

The election of Subhas Chandra Bose of Bengal in 1938 to the presidency of the congress was seen as a rejection of earlier congress policies under Gandhi's guidance. Bose insisted on a six-month ultimatum to the British government, after which time mass action would be initiated. Gandhi persisted in his belief that the atmosphere was not yet right for nonviolent mass action.[182] In such a context any action would discredit the congress and bring disaster to its struggle for independence.[183] He felt that he had been overconfident and hasty in launching his previous civil disobedience campaigns.[184] Therefore, he advised suspension of disobedience in the states, while reminding the princes that they would eventually have to yield to the "reign of law" over their personal rule.[185]

World War II: Prelude to Swaraj. With the outbreak of World War II the constitutional experiment in provincial autonomy ended abruptly. The national leadership was faced with a dilemma: to support the British war effort would be to help preserve imperialism, but refusal of cooperation would appear to be support of the fascist powers. Gandhi was horrified by the war on moral grounds. On the other hand, he could not entertain the prospect of a liberated India against that of a defeated England and France.[186] Holding Hitler responsible for the war, and sympathizing wholly with the Allies, Gandhi saw it as a war between Hitlerite totalitarianism and such democracy as the West had evolved.[187] He asked for the congress's unconditional moral support for the British,[188] with the stipulation that if the war was fought to a finish it would be the duty of the congress to see that no humiliation was heaped on the vanquished.[189] To acquire this moral authority, the congress itself would have to adopt nonviolence as a matter of religio-political belief and social practice.

The congress, as representative of the whole country, did not subscribe to nonviolence as a principle of conduct. Neither did it offer unconditional moral support to the British, because it did not put much faith in the British claim of fighting for democracy. As a condition for such moral support, the congress wanted the British government to declare its war aims and to explain how these objectives applied to India.[190] The viceroy reiterated the British government's intention to help India "attain its due place among our Dominions"; promised modifications in the Government of India Act of 1935 after "consultation with representatives of several communities, parties, and interests in India, and with the Indian princes"; and offered to set up such a consultative group.[191] This reply was profoundly disappointing to Gandhi.

The British Parliament rejected the congress's demand for full democracy and the "right of self-determination by framing their own constitution through a Constituent Assembly without external interference."[192] The British were more concerned with the protection of some sectional interests than with the evolving of a constitution with full mass participation to create a just and unified society in India. Even though the congress's planned constituent assembly was to be "by agreement in regard to Communal representation,"[193] the British played up the minority problem. Continuing to hold India in subjection, they evaded the question of the propriety and sincerity of the Congress's plea for the minorities.[194]

Congress therefore refused to cooperate in the war effort. Even so, Gandhi pressed the congress not to embarrass Britain in the prosecution of the war.[195] To avoid embarrassing Britain himself, Gandhi abstained from civil disobedience.[196]

Gandhi sensed that while unity was the need of the hour, his refusal of civil disobedience had widened the gap between himself and the Congress Working Committee. He pointed out that ruling out civil disobedience was not to rule out all action. The resignation of the congress ministers was a way of noncooperative action, and he felt confident that congress could come up with other suitable ways to deal with the crisis within its self-imposed limits.[197] As to his own thoughts, "More will be revealed to me from day to day, as my plans have always been. . . . I must act in obedience to the still small voice."[198] The solution Gandhi came up with was individual *satyagraha* in the form of preaching against involvement in the war. This plan gained widespread support, eventually leading to arrests in the thousands.

Churchill's speech to the House of Commons, stating that the terms and goals of the Atlantic Charter did not apply to India, fueled Indian distrust of Britain.[199] Singapore fell to Japan. Pressured by President Franklin D. Roosevelt to settle matters with India, Churchill demurred until the fall of

Rangoon. When Japan was knocking on India's doors, Churchill sent Sir Stafford Cripps to settle differences with the country. Cripps's draft declaration included proposals of "a new Indian Union which will have the full status of a Dominion"; a constitution-making body to be set up "immediately upon the cessation of hostilities"; the implementation of the constitution forthwith, allowing those states or provinces that were unprepared to accept the new constitution to frame constitutions of their own giving them "the same full status as the Indian Union"; a treaty to be signed between the British government and the constitution-making body to cover matters arising out of the transfer of responsibility, particularly relating to the protection of all minorities; and finally, in the intervening period, the retention of India's defense control by Britain and collaboration between India's people and the government in all else. The leaders of all principal factions were invited immediately to participate in the counsels of India, of the British Commonwealth, and of the United Nations. These proposals pleased no group or party completely, all of them finding aspects that were unacceptable. In the last analysis, the shaking of India's implicit faith in Britain by Churchill's earlier statement in Parliament and the pressure under which Churchill himself was acting had foredoomed the Cripps mission to failure.[200]

The failure of the Cripps mission veered Gandhi's position toward a mass movement once again with a novel but ill-defined scheme to ask the British to quit India. Gandhi hypothesized that the British presence and power were serving as the bait for the threatened Japanese attack on India.[201] He believed that with the British quitting India in an orderly and dignified way Japan would not want to invade India, and, even if an invasion were to take place, India would be able to meet it with nonviolent noncooperation. Nehru and other Indian leaders also felt strongly about the need for independence; but whereas Gandhi wanted India to be free in order to be able to use nonviolence against Japan, they wanted India to be free in order to fight Japan. On July 14, 1942, the Congress Working Committee, meeting at Wardha, passed a resolution calling for immediate independence for India. If this demand was refused, there would be no choice but a campaign of civil disobedience. The A.I.C.C. approved the "Quit India" resolution on August 8, subsequently being advised by Gandhi that action should not be initiated for two or three weeks—until he had had one additional opportunity to negotiate with the viceroy.

Gandhi never had the chance to carry on those negotiations. He was arrested on August 9 and imprisoned at the palace of the Aga Khan at Yerawda, near Poona. Most of the other congress leaders, as well as Gandhi's wife, were jailed along with him. If the government hoped by this means to crush the movement, they soon learned their miscalculation of the popular feeling and the hold the congress had on it.[202] Gandhi's arrest ended any possibility of a nonviolent campaign. The Indian people, frustrated and leaderless, turned to violence. Government buildings were set on fire, telegraph lines were destroyed, and a number of British officials were attacked and killed. The viceroy, Lord Linlithgow, wanted Gandhi to take responsibility for the violence. Gandhi pointed out that it would not have occurred but for his arrest, placing the blame on the unresponsiveness of the government. To protest the charge that he was responsible for the violence, Gandhi undertook a twenty-one-day fast, from February 10 to March 2, 1943.

The Muslim League and the Hindu communal organization, the Mahasabha, were at large while the entire congress leadership was in jail. The Muslim League was obsessed with the idea of partition of India and the formation of a separate Muslim nation, later to be called Pakistan. The Hindu Mahasabha, however, was firmly determined to preserve the unity of India, to achieve freedom with a strong central government, and to deny to any province, community, or group the right to secede. Both were threatening "direct action" for their goals.[203] Gandhi, who had been refused interviews by Viceroy Linlithgow and by his successor, Lord Wavell, was released from jail by the latter in May 1944, because he was suffering from malaria. Gandhi's offer in July, for cooperation in the war effort in return for a declaration of immediate independence, was rejected by the secretary of state in Parliament as an unpromising approach to the problem.

Gandhi felt the need to carry on discussions with the Muslim leader, M. A. Jinnah. Although Jinnah had previously participated in negotiations with Chakravarty Rajagopalachari on the question of the partitioning of India as a basis for settlement with the Muslims, he (Jinnah) had turned down Rajaji's plan as offering "a shadow and a husk, a maimed, mutilated and moth-eaten Pakistan." Now he was ready to discuss the issue with Gandhi. That these two men even considered the idea of partition infuriated the Hindu and Sikh minorities in the Punjab and the Hindus in Bengal. Vinayak Damodar Savarkar, of the Hindu Mahasabha, warned, echoing Hindu sentiment everywhere, that "The Indian provinces were not the private properties of Gandhiji and Rajaji so that they could make a gift of them to anyone they liked."[204] The two negotiators differed on the questions of the basis of partition, its timing, and the treaty relations that would be in effect following partition. Jinnah's theory of Hindus and Muslims in India being two nations, and Gandhi's theory of their being a large family, though one that could divide at will, were mutually exclusive. Jinnah wanted partition before freedom, and Gandhi wanted it after freedom. Gandhi conceded Pakistan only for Muslims in the six Muslim-majority provinces, while Jinnah wanted the territories of the non-Muslim minorities in addition to those six provinces. Gandhi wanted a confederation between the federations of India and Pakistan, while Jinnah rejected any delegation to a common central authority. Ultimately Gandhi and Jinnah failed to reach any agreement. This convinced Viceroy Wavell that the initiative for the settlement of the problem between Hindus and Muslims must come from His Majesty's government.[205]

In June 1945 the government convened an all-parties conference in Simla to discuss the formation of a national government under the viceroy, which could effect a united front of resistance to Japan. This was to provide the transition to the postwar government and constitution, without, however, prejudging those issues. The conference was unsuccessful because of Jinnah's insistence that the Muslim League have the exclusive right to nominate any Muslims to positions in the government. Jinnah then used the failure of the conference as a case in point in his demand for the creation of Pakistan.[206]

Swaraj in Bloodshed and Division. Just before World War II ended with the surrender of Japan on August 15, 1945, the Labour Party, which had a more genuine sympathy for the Indian cause than the Conservatives, had come into power in Britain. Clement Attlee was named prime minister and Lord Pethic-Lawrence became the secretary of state for India. The very first political act of the Labour government was to hold a general election in India, the first one in ten years, to promote the early realization of full self-government in India and to choose the legislators who would draft the constitution. The elections were scheduled for the winter of 1945.[207] In spite of the breakdown of the congress organization owing to the imprisonment of all its leaders and the government's sequestration of its funds, the congress won the highest percentage of votes among the general electorate while the Muslim League gained the support of most of the Muslim constituencies. The provincial elections confirmed the pattern of the elections to the central legislature, indicating that the congress and the Muslim League were the only parties of significance in the country. But the Muslim League did not have an absolute majority in any of the four provinces that were to form Pakistan and could form a ministry in only two, Bengal and Sind—in the latter by the governor's intervention rather than by parliamentary convention. The Hindu Mahasabha had not contested the elections, and large sections of the depressed classes supported the congress.[208] The viceroy, Lord Wavell, announced on January 28, 1946, that he would form a new executive council. He informed the secretary of state for India of his plan to go ahead without Jinnah if the latter did not want to join; he also stated that, though Pakistan had to be conceded, the large non-Muslim population in East Punjab and West Bengal could not be forced into Pakistan against their will.[209]

While accepting the viceroy's proposal, His Majesty's government announced a plan to send three cabinet ministers to India to seek, in association with the viceroy, an agreement with the leaders of Indian opinion on the principles and procedures relating to the constitutional issue. The announcement was well received throughout India. At last independence seemed to be certain.[210] In his announcement the prime minister stated, "We are mindful of the rights of the minorities, and the minorities should be able to live free from fear. On the other hand, we cannot allow a minority to place their veto on the advance of the majority."[211] Jinnah demurred, claiming that the Muslims were not a "minority," but a "nation," and holding out his threat that if only a single constitution-making body was set up, the Muslim League would refuse to cooperate with it.[212]

After listening to the opposed viewpoints of all parties and interests, the cabinet mission, headed by Lord Pethic-Lawrence, announced its criticism of the various plans proposed, and presented its own plan. The division of India was ruled out as geographically, economically, and militarily unsound. The plan set forth by the cabinet mission called for a voluntary alliance of various federating units with a minimum of centralized powers, limited only to foreign affairs, defense, and communications. A constituent assembly based on total populations of the provinces was to be elected, subsuming communal representation within the representation of the total population. All major communal decisions had to be approved by majorities of all the voters as well as by majorities of the Hindu and Muslim communities.[213]

Gandhi welcomed the cabinet mission's plan, while the Sikhs and the congress opposed the compulsion inherent in the initial grouping of provinces. The congress was concerned with the status of the interim government in relation to the governor-general.[214] On June 6, 1946, the council of the Muslim League accepted the cabinet mission's proposals and authorized Jinnah to negotiate with the viceroy concerning the interim government.[215]

After much backsliding by both the congress and the Muslim League on the interpretation of the freedom or the compulsion of a province to remain in or out of a group, and due to the Muslim League's unrelenting demand for a sovereign Pakistan, the congress-majority interim government was dissolved.[216] Jinnah had expanded his demands at each step of the negotiations. Now he called for "direct action" to protest the congress's formation of government without the Muslim League. Riots broke out in Calcutta. Jinnah denied ever having agreed to the constituent assembly and asked the Muslim League to boycott it.[217] The British government absolved itself of responsibility to back up a constitution framed without the Muslim League's participation.[218] The assembly, however, met on December 9, 1946, and formed committees to deal with various parts of the constitution, kept open vacancies for the Muslim League members, and chose Dr. Rajendra Prasad as its president.[219]

Amid these tensions the British government announced its intention in February 1947 to quit India by June 1948. Viscount Mountbatten, appointed to the office of viceroy of India, was to arrange for the transfer of authority to whatever responsible Indian party or parties might be ready for it.[220]

While the proclamation evoked great enthusiasm all over India, the Muslim League resorted to its plan for "direct action," precipitating violence throughout the Punjab, which soon extended to the North-West Frontier Province.[221] Gandhi attempted to contain the outburst in Bengal. The Hindus and Sikhs of the West, who had wanted a united India, now saw its unworkability and accepted the inevitability of the partition of Punjab and Bengal.[222] Lord Mountbatten announced the formation of two dominions and two constituent assemblies with the partition of Bengal and the Punjab, a referendum in the North-West Frontier Province to determine which division it wanted to join, and a boundary commission to demarcate Hindu from Muslim districts.[223] Though Hindus and nationalist Indians deplored the prospect of the vivisection of India, both the congress and the Muslim League agreed to it as the only workable alternative under the circumstances.[224]

The Indian Independence Bill, passed without dissent by Parliament on July 1, 1947, fixed August 15, 1947, as the date for the transfer of power. Accordingly, at midnight on August 14, a special session of the constituent assembly declared the independence of India. Jinnah was appointed the first governor-general of Pakistan, and Lord Mountbatten became the first governor-general of the new Indian dominion in the British Commonwealth.[225]

Gandhi, who had brought about the "miracle" of Calcutta, from fire and sword to much Hindu-Muslim fraternizing, spent the day in that city in fasting and prayer.[226] Later he returned to Delhi on his mission to "do or die" for Hindu-Muslim unity, amid continuing riots accompanying the transfer of population across the boundaries of India and Pakistan.[227] On January 30, 1948, while on the way to address a prayer meeting near Birla House, Gandhi was shot by a fanatical Hindu nationalist and died on the spot, with "Rama"—the name of God—on his lips.[228]

2

Liberation as Swaraj

DEFINING *SWARAJ*

Swaraj is Gandhi's Indian term for liberation. It occurs hundreds of times throughout his talks and writings. Although its coinage was not his own, he effectively established it as the Indian term connoting liberation, freedom, independence, self-determination, self-government, autonomy.[1] Gandhi advanced many reasons for the choice of this word, most of which were truthfulness to history and accessibility to the masses:

> I submit that swaraj is an all-satisfying goal for all time. We the English-educated Indians often unconsciously made the terrible mistake of thinking that the microscopic minority of English-speaking Indians is the whole of India. I defy anyone to give for independence a common Indian word intelligible to the masses. Our goal at any rate may be known by an indigenous word understood of the three hundred millions. And we have such a word in "swaraj" first used in the name of the nation by Dadabhai Naoroji.* It is infinitely greater than and includes independence. It is a vital word. It has been sanctified by the noble sacrifices of thousands of Indians. It is a word which, if it has not penetrated the remotest corner of India, has at least got the largest currency of any similar word. It is a sacrilege to displace that word by a foreign importation of doubtful value. . . . Personally, I crave not for "independence," which I do not understand, but I long for freedom from the English yoke.[2]

Gandhi, in his nonelitist concern, drew upon the idiom of the masses in attaching a sacred or religious character to the popular term *swaraj*.

While popularizing the word himself, Gandhi was painstakingly honest in giving credit to those who had introduced it before him. Addressing the Gujarat Political Conference on November 3, 1917, he said:

*In his presidential address at the Calcutta Congress in 1906, Dadabhai used the word *swaraj* as a synonym for "self-government." He did not coin the word, which was far older in Indian usage.

47

The air of the country is thick with cries of swaraj. It is due to Mrs. Besant* that swaraj is on the lips of hundreds of thousands of men and women. What was unknown to most men and women only two years ago has, by her consummate tact and her indefatigable efforts, become common property for them. There cannot be the slightest doubt that her name will take the first rank in history among those who inspired us with the hope that swaraj was attainable at no distant date. Swaraj was, and is, the goal of the Congress. The idea did not originate with her. But the credit of presenting it to us as a goal realizable in the immediate future belongs to that lady alone. For that we could hardly thank her enough.[3]

Gandhi's preference for *swaraj* over other words to express the idea of independence for India lay in its speficically Indian connotations and context. "Independence," "freedon," and "liberation"—all terms used by Gandhi and all embodied in the concept of *swaraj*—also carried Western connotations that were not strictly applicable to India's situation.

The only competition as an alternative expression for *swaraj* is *moksha*, as an equivalent of the Christian term "salvation," although Gandhi's usage of *moksha* is richer in connotation. Gandhian *moksha* is not limited to either this world or the next, but is a continuum through history and beyond. "Salvation," for Gandhi, is far more comprehensive than is the Christian concept of it. For Gandhi *moksha* was broad enough to encompass the concretely historical, political, and incarnate liberation connoted by *swaraj*. That Gandhi's theology is actualized in political terms accounts for the fact that he chose to focus specifically on *swaraj* rather than *moksha*. Thus the choice of *swaraj* over against *moksha* is as significant in Gandhi's theology as is choice of "liberation" over against "salvation" in the post-Medellín theology of Latin America.

In this chapter our concern will be with the concept of *swaraj* as found in Gandhi's writings. From this survey of Gandhian thought we can, in the following chapter, explore the theological implications of *swaraj*.

ORIGINS OF THE CONCEPT

The concept of *swaraj* first began to appear in Gandhi's writings in 1908, six years before his return to India from South Africa. In his last article on *sarvodaya* (the welfare of all) in his South African *Indian Opinion* weekly of July 18, 1908, he appended a few thoughts on *swaraj*, which read like a simple preview of the ideas that were to find a fuller treatment in his book *Hind Swaraj*. Noting that from one side one hears the cry of "*swarajya*" (*swaraj*) and from another the cry for quick accumulation of wealth through indus-

---

*Annie Besant (1847–1933), British theosophist, orator, writer. She founded the Theosophical Society in 1907, established the Indian Home Rule League in 1916, presided over the Indian National Congress in 1917, edited *New India* (a daily) and *The Commonweal* (a weekly). She wrote several books including *The Religious Problem in India*.

trialization, Gandhi reflected, "Our people hardly understand what swar-ajya means." He sensed from contemporary events in India that what passed for *swarajya* was in fact not *swarajya*:

> Real swarajya consists in restraint. He alone is capable of this who leads a moral life, does not cheat anyone, does not forsake truth and does his duty to his parents, his wife, his children, his servant and his neighbor. Such a man will enjoy swarajya wherever he may happen to live. A nation that has many such men always enjoys swarajya.

Gandhi saw it as wrong for one nation to rule over another. British rule in India was such an evil. But it would be fallacious to think that any very great advantage would accrue to the Indians just by the exit of the British from India. The disunity, immorality, and ignorance of the Indians, which had facilitated British rule over India, were the real enemies. Exulting over violence done to the British showed ignorance and a lack of understanding of *swarajya*. No more could violence usher in *swarajya* than could wealth, as Ruskin had shown. India's demand for *swarajya* was just, but it had to be achieved by righteous means, including industry of the right kind. Indians had to transmute themselves by leading lives of virtue, so that India could be transformed again into a golden land. Truth, *satya*, was the philosophers' stone that would bring about this transmutation. If every Indian followed truth always, India would achieve *swarajya* as a matter of course.[4]

Gandhi supported the efforts of the Indian National Congress to work toward "home rule" (also known as "dominion status," which meant complete internal autonomy under British sovereignty). Under national leaders such as Dadabhai Naoroji (sometimes referred to as the Grand Old Man of India)[5] and G. K. Gokhale,* congress petitioned the government for a system of internal autonomy under British sovereignty, based on the Canadian model. The demand for the abrogation of the partition of Bengal† catalyzed efforts for home rule, strengthening the importance of *swaraj*. The criterion of judgment about every advance, political change, or reform was to be whether it aided or impeded the nation's march toward *swaraj*.[6]

---

*Gokhale was a distinguished Indian leader, statesman, educator, and reformer around the turn of the century. Gandhi writes of him in *Hind Swaraj* (chap. 1) that in order to serve the nation, he gave up a lucrative career, embraced poverty, and gave twenty years of his life to national work. He founded and presided over the Servants of India Society and was instrumental through his assiduous efforts in ending the system of emigration of indentured laborers from India to South Africa. Within the Indian National Congress, he was the leader of the moderates, as Bal Ganga-dar Tilak and C. R. Das were leaders of the extremists. Gandhi considered Gokhale as his political guru.

†The viceroy, Lord Curzon, had divided Bengal into East and West in 1905, allegedly for ad-ministrative convenience. The East was predominantly Muslim and the West predominantly Hindu. Nationalist Indians looked upon the act as a sinister British design to divide India on the basis of religion in order to continue to rule over it. Hence the demands for the abrogation of the division. The demand was complied with by the king-emperor, George V, on the occasion of his coronation *durbar* in Delhi in the first year of Lord Hardinge's viceroyalty (1910).

The protest of the partition of Bengal had also divided the congress into moderates and extremists, each group distrustful of the other. Gandhi allied himself with the moderates. Despite an impatience that he shared with the extremists, or revolutionaries, Gandhi was aware that his meaning of *swaraj* differed from theirs. For them, *swaraj* was "to drive the English out of India," but to retain the English system of administrative practice, military power, and national glory. Gandhi confessed to his difficulty in understanding such a *swaraj*: it was not true *swaraj*, the *swaraj* that he wanted.[7]

Gandhi was critical of the British parliamentary system as a system of party pressure-politics lacking in internal discipline on the part of the electors and the elected alike. People and politicians were made to waver in their loyalty, influenced to too great an extent by a partisan and dishonest press. Gandhi knew, however, that these faults were not peculiar to the English, but were products of modern civilization.[8]

SWARAJ VS. MODERN CIVILIZATION

In 1909 Gandhi published his Gujarati-language *Hind Swaraj*,[9] which is a short, systematic presentation of his concept of *swaraj* at the time of its writing.* It would be five years before Gandhi would return to India, and four additional years before he had enough familiarity with actual political conditions there to modify his ideas and begin to put them into practice. Yet the work is important as the basis of all subsequent conceptualizations of *swaraj*.

Hind Swaraj saw the enemy of *swaraj* as all of modern civilization. It describes modern civilization—which finds expression in comforts, possessions, free self-expression, fast locomotion, automation of work, mechanization of life, monetization of values, and degradation of quality—as a disease in need of a cure.[10] Civilization does not put much stock in morality or religion, but, ignoring them, makes a religion of mechanization. This is irreligion, involving enslavement of men and women to labor in hazardous conditions. Modern civilization is destructive of humanity and of itself. In religious terms, it is satanic, ushering in a Black Age.[11]

How then could a country as infected and diseased by civilization as England take India and retain it? Gandhi's answer is sociological history:

> The English have not taken India; we have given it to them. They are not in India because of their strength, but because we keep them. . . .
> They came to our country originally for purposes of trade. Recall the Company Bahadur? Who made it Bahadur? They had not the slightest

---

*Gandhi's preface to *Hind Swaraj* (*CW* 10:7) reads: "These views are mine, and yet not mine. They are mine because I hope to act according to them. They are almost a part of my being. But yet they are not mine, because I lay no claim to originality. They have been formed after reading several books. That which I dimly felt received support from these books." Gandhi adds: "The views I venture to place before the reader are, needless to say, held by many Indians not touched by what is known as civilization, but I ask the reader to believe me when I tell him that they are also held by thousands of Europeans. Those who wish to dive deep and have time, may read certain books themselves."

intention at the time of establishing a Kingdom. Who assisted the Company officers? Who was tempted at the sight of their silver? Who bought their goods? History testifies that we did all this. In order to become rich all at once, we welcomed the Company's officers with open arms. We assisted them. . . . When our Princes fought among themselves they sought the assistance of Company Bahadur. That corporation was versed alike in commerce and war. It was unhampered by questions of morality. Its object was to increase its commerce and to make money. It accepted our assistance and increased the number of its warehouses. To protect the latter it employed an army which was utilized by us also. Is it not then useless to blame the English for what we did at that time? The Hindus and the Mohamedans were at daggers drawn. This, too, gave the Company its opportunity and thus we created the circumstances that gave the Company its control over India. Hence it is truer to say that we gave India to the English than that India was lost.

The causes that gave them India enable them to retain it. Some Englishmen state that they took and they hold India by the sword. Both these statements are wrong. The sword is entirely useless for holding India. We alone keep them. . . . They hold whatever dominions they have for the sake of their commerce. Their army and their navy are intended to protect it. . . . Many problems can be solved by remembering that money is their God. Then it follows that we keep the English in India for our base self-interest. We like their commerce; they please us by their subtle methods and get what they want from us.To blame them for this is to perpetuate their power. We further strengthen their hold by quarreling among ourselves.[12]

Gandhi's concept of nationality would encompass all of the existing religious groups. "Inborn enmity" between Hindus and Muslims was a phrase invented by the common enemy—the English. History falsified that phrase, for Hindus had flourished under Muslim sovereigns and vice versa. There had indeed been fights and settlements for peace. The English, however, had accentuated tensions between the two groups through their politics and diplomacy. Gandhi believed that Hindus should strive to foster Muslim trust in the Hindu community. There would always be conflicts, but they should be settled outside the foreign court and judicial system.[13]

Lawyers and the British court system were enslaving India by accentuating Hindu-Muslim dissensions and confirming English authority. Thus the legal profession taught an immorality from which few were saved.[14]

The medical profession, too, had played a role in enslaving India to the English. Gandhi saw that profession as contributing to the moral debasement of society by setting a premium on indulgence rather than self-control. Medical facilities induced sin rather than virtue. Lack of self-restraint was not conducive to national service. Study of Western medicine, motivated as it was in many cases by the desire to become rich by charging exorbitant fees, could only deepen India's slavery. The population was cooperating with this enslavement and moral debasement in the name of bodily health.[15]

Civilization, cured of all these ills, is that mode of conduct that points out to people the path of duty: observance of morality and mastery over mind and passions. "So doing, we know ourselves. The Gujarati equivalent for civilization means good conduct." Gandhi saw Indian civilization as true civilization, with roots that were basically sound. That was the reason for its survival while all other ancient civilizations had disappeared. In India saints were still ranked higher than kings. Courts, lawyers, and doctors were subordinate to the people. Common people, untouched by modern civilization, continued to live independently and to enjoy a natural form of *swaraj*. As opposed to the atheistic and immoral Western civilization, Indian civilization was God-centered and ethical. As many writers had pointed out, India had nothing to learn from other civilizations. To change such a state of affairs would be to act as sinners and enemies of the country. Therefore Indians must cling to Indian civilization.[16]

Indian civilization was still strong enough to survive shocks. Only those Indians who were Western-civilized were really enslaved. If they became free, India would become free. It was in the hands of the Indian people to accomplish this:

> It is Swaraj when we learn to rule ourselves. It is, therefore, in the palm of our hands. Do not consider this Swaraj to be like a dream. There is no idea of sitting still. The Swaraj that I wish to picture is such that, after we have once realized it, we shall endeavour to the end of our life-time to persuade others to do likewise. But such Swaraj has to be experienced, by each one for himself. One drowning man will never save another. Slaves ourselves, it would be a mere pretension to think of freeing others. Now you will have seen that it is not necessary for us to have as our goal the expulsion of the English. If the English become Indianized, we can accommodate them. If they wish to remain in India along with their civilization, there is no room for them. It lies with us to bring about such a state of things.[17]

Good intentions and philosophy are insufficient for *swaraj*. Strategy and method are so potent as to effect a change in the goals and philosophy, as happened in the Italian unification: having overthrown foreign slavery, Italy was left with slavery to Italian princes.[18] India should not be a slave to Indian princes. To arm India would postpone *swaraj*, and any *swaraj* won with arms would not be Indian. The way of assassination is not the way of *swaraj*, for means modify and constitute the end.[19]

Despite its intentions, English education had become a means of enslavement of the Indian nation, since foreignness was enslaving. "It is we, the English-knowing Indians, that have enslaved India." Educationally, it would be progress to drive Western civilization out of India. Thereafter, all progress and decline, reform and reaction will be within the Indian civilization itself.[20]

Industrialization had also contributed to the enslavement of India. The capitalist, driven by selfish motivation, profited unduly from the labors of the working people, who lived in poverty. For *swaraj*, the evil of industrialization had to be eradicated.[21]

In the quest for *swaraj*, Gandhi beseeched the extremists and moderates to work together. Both groups must renounce tyranny, whether foreign or indigenous. As conscious nationalists, they must give up foreign language, imported cloth, professions, and wealth, and devote themselves and all their energies to indigenous practices. They would create their own industries, on a small scale, in a religious spirit of both repentance and reform. Through simple living and voluntary suffering, they would undo the evils of the past, and bring about the birth of a new and free India, to serve as a spiritual leader in the world.

Gandhi would submit to the English the conditions under which they might remain in India. These were submitted not as demands, but rather, as bespeaking India's state-of-mind—as one of readiness to suffer for the realization of these aspirations. Gandhi would ask the English to become servants of India by stopping the drain of India's wealth, putting an end to military spending, halting the flow of foreign cloth, accepting Indian civilization, not imposing on India anything contrary to its religions, learning Hindi, and restoring ancient Indian schools and courts. Subject to these conditions, the English could stay on. Otherwise, they must quit—to the detriment of England, India, and the world.

Gandhi concluded *Hind Swaraj* with four important observations: (1) real home rule is self-rule or self-control; (2) the way to it is passive resistance: that is, soul-force or love-force; (3) in order to exert this force, *swadeshi* (indigenousness) in every sense is necessary; and (4) Indian actions should be determined by a sense of duty; after the English leave India, Indians must not continue the harmful things the English did. Gandhi observed that Indians have used the term *swaraj* without understanding its significance. Having thus presented his own understanding of *swaraj* Gandhi stated: "My conscience testifies that my life henceforth is dedicated to its attainment."[22]

SUBSEQUENT MODIFICATIONS OF GANDHI'S *SWARAJ* CONCEPT

While the concepts contained in *Hind Swaraj* became known to the literate public in India, the practical impact of Gandhi's ideas was not immediately significant. Only after Gandhi returned to India from South Africa and fully familiarized himself with the political scene* did he gain prominence in na-

*Gokhale had advised Gandhi to abstain from active politics until he had thoroughly familiarized himself with the Indian political situation. Gandhi abided by this advice for nearly four years, by which time he was fully familiar with the situation.

tional politics and start implementing his ideas. Gandhi's travels throughout the country and first-hand observation of conditions added to his understanding of what *swaraj* meant to the Indian masses. With that knowledge he could expound and implement *swaraj*.

At the Gujarat Political Conference held at Godhara in November 1917,[23] Gandhi publicly outlined his program for *swaraj*. The ideas are generally those of *Hind Swaraj* in a modified form. The manner of presentation was positive and absolute, rather than comparative, as in *Hind Swaraj*. An exception is his discussion of *satyagraha* and *duragraha*. He translates them respectively as soul-force or love-force, and brute-force. *Satyagraha*, as love-force, resisting *duragraha*, or physical force, means complete independence, which is the consummation of *swaraj*. But *swaraj* through *duragraha*, or at the sacrifice of truth, is useless and harmful and will ultimately lead to ruin.

A seeming contradiction to this belief in nonviolence was Gandhi's dictate that India should support the British war effort in World War I. He would have a different perspective in World War II, but in World War I Gandhi believed it was both morally right and pragmatic for Indian soldiers to fight along with the British. This view was consistent with his current elucidation of the principles underlying *swaraj*. He saw no inherent contradiction between *satyagraha* and warfare. Gandhi's image of *swaraj* at this time assumed that India would remain within the British empire. Rather than enraging Britain by refusing to join in the war effort, India would fight along with Britain, thus establishing an atmosphere of respect in which eventually *swaraj* could be attained.*[24]

---

*Gandhi's principles underlying *swaraj* at this time can be summarized as follows:

(i) *Swaraj* was a performance of duty automatically conferring a corresponding right, in this case, of dominion status, without distinction of race in the empire in whose defense Indians fought World War I. (ii) It was thus a consecration based on the hope of a better future. (iii) Help to defend the empire in time of war would not include cooperation in the tyranny of its officials or representatives, as inconsistent with British justice. (iv) Obstruction, though legitimate, would enrage the British in their hour of trial; cooperation would not only disarm them, but make India strong and confident. (v) A volunteer force would be called a national army rather than a government army. (vi) War was an opportunity to get the military training without which *swaraj* would be useless. (vii) Cooperation was the opposite of vindictiveness, for which there is no room in *satyagraha*. It was the duty of a nation seeking equal partnership to defend the partner in its war as well. (viii) Rights won by taking advantage of the empire's weakness were likely to be lost when the empire regained its strength, and prospective partners should not embarass each other. (ix) Distrust of the other is basically distrust of oneself and, as such, a sign of weakness rather than strength. (x) Search for *swaraj* in hostility to the empire would enable the empire to use its Indian friends (the princes, the rich, and the *sepoys*) against *swaraj* itself. (xi) Preparation for *swaraj* must not be based on the goodness or weakness of statesmen, but on the nation's fitness and strength. (xii) Honesty begets honesty and sympathy begets sympathy. Truth conquers, and our truthfulness should make us confident of success. (xiii) Even if the government refused army commissions to Indians, it was the *duty* of Indians to enter the army. (xiv) Maintaining a link with Britain was more beneficial to India, Britain, and the world than severing it. (xv) Despite the vices of the English, a tendency to domineer over and forget the self-respect of subject nations, they bore loyalty to equals. This should inspire faith in England to respect India, which respected itself.

Gandhi remained committed to the "internal dimension of *swaraj*." His view of *swaraj* assumed "the capacity of the people of India to enforce their demands," as opposed to the viceroy's view that "swaraj must come from the British Parliament, unless it comes through the sword."[25] Gandhi was once asked a question which at best showed a misunderstanding of his intentions and at worst imputed to him selfish ambition: Who would rule under *swaraj* after his death? Gandhi's answer was at once illuminating and disarming: "Swaraj means one's own rule. Everyone has to rule over himself. When all have learned to rule over themselves, then it will be rule by all, by the people. My living or dying is irrelevant to the issue."[26]

Gandhi described *swaraj* in terms of self-control.[27] *Swaraj* would come about when each Indian ended his or her submission to enslavement. Reflecting on the national noncooperation program he inaugurated in 1920, he wrote:

The foundation stone of swaraj was laid when non-co-operation was started. The slave who stops saluting his master, is he not freed from that very day? Let the master kick him, abuse him, hang him. The slave has stopped saluting. He has realized that he was a slave. What does he care if the master does not acknowledge him a free man? His strength increases with the latter's resistance, because it is a challenge to him.[28]

It was impossible to define *swaraj* narrowly. The only definition that could be attached to it was "that status of India which her people desire at a given moment." If asked what India desired, Gandhi would say he did not know. He could only say:

I would have her desire truthful relations between Hindus and Mussalmans, bread for the masses and removal of untouchability. That is how I would define swaraj at the present moment. I give that definition because I claim to be a practical man. I know that we want political independence of England. It will not be attained without the three things mentioned by me. . . .[29]

In answering a political caricature of *Hind Swaraj* as "Gandhi-Raj," Gandhi gave his own authentic hermeneutic of *Hind Swaraj*, while also indicating the political concessions he had made to the social reality:

It is a clever piece of caricature permissible in Western warfare. It is only suggestively false. Let me say what I mean. In the first instance, India is not striving to establish "Gandhi-Raj." It is in dead earnest to establish swaraj and would gladly and legitimately sacrifice Gandhi for the sake of winning swaraj. "Gandhi-Raj" is an ideal condition, and in that condition all the five negatives will represent a true picture, but under swaraj nobody ever dreams, certainly I do not dream, of no railways, no hospitals, no machinery, no army and navy, no laws and no lawcourts. On the contrary, there will be railways; only they will not be intended for military or for the economic exploitation of India, but they will be used for promoting internal trade and will make the lives of third-class passengers fairly comfortable. . . . Nobody anticipates complete absence of diseases during swaraj; there will therefore certainly be hospitals, but one hopes that the hospitals will then be intended more for those who suffer from accidents than from self-indulgence. Machinery there certainly will be in the shape of a spinning wheel, which is after all a delicate piece of machinery, but I have no doubt that several factories will grow up in India under swaraj intended for the benefit of the people, not as now for draining the masses dry. I do not know of the navy, but I do know that the army of India of the future will not consist of hirelings to be utilized for keeping India under subjection and for depriving other nations of their liberty, but it would be largely cut down, will consist largely of volunteers and will be utilized for policing India. There will be law and lawcourts also under swaraj, but they will be custodians of the people's liberty, not—as they now are—instruments in the hands of a bureaucracy which has emasculated and is intent upon further emasculating a whole nation. Lastly, whilst it will be optional for everybody who chooses to go about in a *langoti* [loincloth] and sleep in the open, let me hope that it will not be necessary, as it is today, for millions to go about with a dirty rag which serves for a *langoti* for want of the means to buy sufficient clothing and to rest their weary and starved bodies in the open for want of a roof. It is not right therefore to tear some ideas expressed in *Indian Home Rule* from their proper setting, caricature them and put them before the people as if I was preaching these ideas for anybody's acceptance.[30]

As Gandhi was ever ready to learn from experience, he likewise conceived *swaraj* in the same spirit. In answer to admirers and followers who tended to become too dependent on him, he called upon them to imbibe the spirit of bold experimentation in *swaraj*. *Swaraj* was a way of government by tests, trials, and mistakes. It was better that India was undone through its own mistakes than that it should avoid them through the perpetual guidance of one man. Therefore Gandhi even seriously asked himself whether it would not be in the best interests of the country for him to retire altogether from public activity and simply devote himself to spinning and weaving in his ashram. In any case, he strongly advised his friends and fellow workers never to accept his word as law. While he would never refuse to give advice, he wished that it should be sparingly sought.[31]

Gandhi's conception of *swaraj* was thus a democratic one, based on the will of the people. He specified its political structure in terms of people's representatives, elected by something very close to the universal adult franchise.* There was no place for elitism: "Real swaraj will come not by the acquisition of authority by a few, but by the acquisition of the capacity by all to resist authority when it is abused. In other words, *swaraj* is to be attained by educating the masses to a sense of their capacity to regulate and control authority."[32] Indeed, democracy was so intrinsic and essential an aspect of *swaraj* and so much a part of the very definition of it, that he considered it tautological to speak of "democratic swaraj."[33]

Why did Gandhi attach such importance to *swaraj* and agitation for it? Without *swaraj* India was helpless, lacking even the strength to protest exploitation by the British beyond the passing of resolutions. Insofar as India was removed from *swaraj*, Indians were removed from their own personhood. Not only therefore was "swaraj our birth-right," but it was "our sacred duty to win it."[34]

According to Gandhi's concept of *swaraj* in the 1920s, India would still remain within the empire, but the connection would be maintained by choice, not by necessity. He took issue with those who could not think of India's future without the British connection.[35] Full *swaraj* meant partnership, and a partnership had no meaning if one part was too weak to dissolve it.[36] Moreover, a necessary connection with the empire would imply that *swaraj* was a grant from the British Parliament, whereas Gandhi's concept of *swaraj* was that of an inner condition that India itself would assume.

The least that *swaraj* should mean was a capacity, even under dominion status, to declare independence at will. So long as India did not achieve that capacity, it could have no *swaraj*. But Gandhi wanted the meaning of *swaraj* to grow with the growth of national consciousness and aspirations: Indians of his time might be satisfied with dominion status; future generations might not be so satisfied. This was the message that Gandhi sought to describe in the cryptic phrase, "swaraj within the Empire, if possible," without "if necessary." Ultimately, the real definition of *swaraj* would be determined by India's action, the means Indians adopted to achieve the goal. If Indians would but concentrate upon the means, *swaraj* would come about naturally.[37]

Specifically, Gandhi saw the road to *swaraj* in terms of progress in three areas: hand-spinning, the removal of untouchability, and Hindu-Muslim unity. These programs, which he referred to as the "pillars of swaraj,"[38] served as the internal organization for *swaraj*, while work in the legislative councils was the external organization.[39] Of the three goals, hand-spinning, which would lead to economic independence, was the most basic. Without an honest means of survival, the higher social freedoms were illusory. "It may be that all of us do not mean the same thing by swaraj," Gandhi wrote. "To me it has but one meaning; the eradication of the poverty of India and freedom for every man and woman. Ask the starving men and women of India. They say that their swaraj is their bread."[40]

*The qualifications proposed by Gandhi were that the person wishing to vote must take the trouble to register as a voter and must contribute manual labor to the service of the state.

SWARAJ AND THE SPINNING WHEEL

As well as believing that the *khadi* (hand-spinning)—or *khaddar* (spinning wheel)—movement was fundamental to the attainment of *swaraj* and its two other programs of Hindu-Muslim unity and the removal of untouchability, Gandhi believed that there were pragmatic reasons for placing the greatest emphasis on *khadi*:

> Swaraj can be peacefully attained only if the whole Indian mass work as with one will. . . . Such an effort presupposes national consciousness. This is possible only through the spinning-wheel. It is not remunerative enough for individuals. It is therefore not enough incentive for an individual selfishly inclined. It is however enough to raise at a bound the national prosperity in an appreciable manner. . . . Thus the spinning-wheel means national consciousness and a contribution by every individual to a definite constructive national work. If India can demonstrate her capacity for such an achievement by voluntary effort she is ready for political swaraj. . . . The economic prosperity of India must indirectly affect the course of her political history, even using the word "political" in its narrow sense. Lastly, when the exploitation of India by Lancashire ceases by reason of the ability of India through the wheel to clothe herself and consequently to exclude foreign cloth and therefore also Lancashire cloth, England will have lost the feverish anxiety at any cost to hold India under subjection.[41]

Khadi demanded from the population honest daily work. The work it involved was far more visible than work on the other two programs. In an India of thirty *crores* (tens of millions) of people scattered on a surface 1,900 miles long and 1,500 miles broad—in less than twenty cities but in 700,000 villages—the one program that could weld the whole mass together was *khadi*. *Khadi* required skillful organization and the combined efforts of all the people. To make *khadi* successful was to demonstrate India's capacity for self-government.[42] Furthermore, such organization could ultimately be seen as the first step in preparing for universal civil disobedience.[43]

SWARAJ AND THE REMOVAL OF UNTOUCHABILITY

The constructive programs were related among themselves as well as being components of *swaraj*. Thus the removal of untouchability and Hindu-Muslim unity were necessary because without them *khadi* could not be universalized. On a spiritual level, moreover, untouchability was incompatible with *swaraj*. A correspondent wrote to Gandhi that he was unable to understand the relation between untouchability and the establishment of *swaraj*. He argued that untouchability was only one of the many evils of Hindu society, even if it was perhaps a greater evil than others, but history knew of no society free from all evils. How then was untouchability an impediment to the attainment of *swaraj*? Why was Gandhi making its removal a prerequisite for *swaraj*? Could it not be set right after *swaraj*, if not voluntarily, at least by legislation? Gandhi replied:

> It is an abuse of language to say that we Hindus extend any toleration towards our *Panchama* [untouchable] brothers. We have degraded them and then have the audacity to use their very degradation against their rise. . . . Swaraj for me means freedom for the meanest of our countrymen. If the lot of the *Panchamas* is not improved when we are all suffering, it is not likely to be better under the intoxication of swaraj. If it is necessary for us to buy the peace with the Mussalmans as a condition of swaraj, it is equally necessary for us to give peace to the Panchama before we can, with any show of justice or self-respect, talk of swaraj. I am not interested in freeing India merely from English yoke. I am bent upon freeing India from any yoke whatever. . . . Hence for me the movement of swaraj is a movement of self-purification.[44]

Gandhi saw his work toward the removal of untouchability as an expiation and a penance. Hinduism had committed a great sin in giving sanction to this evil, and Gandhi sought *shuddhi* (purification) for himself and the Hindu religion.[45] Addressing himself to the suppressed classes, he described as self-interest this desire of his to rid himself of the sins his forefathers had committed against them. He went on to plead with them not to give up their religion.[46]

The removal of untouchability was essentially a Hindu question, and Hindus could not rightfully demand *swaraj* until they had restored the liberty of the suppressed classes. How could they protest enslavement by the British while they refused to recognize the humanity of their own people? As for the Hindu priests who were teaching that untouchability was a divine appointment, Gandhi asserted that he knew Hinduism well enough to know for certain that the priests were wrong. It was blasphemy to hold that God set apart any portion of humanity as untouchable. Furthermore, Hindus who were congressmen were obligated to work toward breaking down the barrier as quickly as possible.[47] Untouchability had no valid place in Hindu religion.[48] To say that a person was born untouchable was dishonest, immoral, and monstrous.[49] Untouchability was even more unethical than slavery. The tree of slavery had grown from the seed of untouchability.[50]

SWARAJ AND HINDU-MUSLIM COMMUNAL UNITY

Though Hindu-Muslim unity had reached a high point in the early 1920s during the khilafat movement, by the mid- and late twenties relations between the two dominant communities in India were strained. Hindu-Muslim riots broke out in many cities, and the political rift was widening.

Against the gradual gains in *khadi* and untouchability work, the disruption of communal unity was depressing to Gandhi. He despaired of achieving unity in the near future.[51] However, he had not given up faith in the ultimate possibility of that unity. For unity, he believed, is in human nature. Therefore, even if neither side made efforts to bring it about, time would do its work.[52] Gandhi's belief in Hindu-Muslim unity was absolute, and his commitment to achieving it was total. He was convinced that, along with *khadi* and the removal of untouchability, Hindu-Muslim unity was necessary for the attainment of *swaraj*.[53]

Yet after the riots of 1926 he had doubts about his ability to find a solution to the problem. At a public meeting in 1927 he said:

> I dare not touch the problem of Hindu-Muslim unity. It has passed out of human hands, and has been transferred to God's hands alone. . . . Let us ask for help from God, the All-Powerful, and tell Him that we, His tiny creatures, have failed to do what we ought to do, we hate one another, we distrust one another, we fly at one another's throat and we even become assassins. Let our heart's cry then ascend to His throne, and let us wash His feet with tears of blood and ask Him to purge our hearts of all hatred in us. We are disgracing His earth, His name and this sacred land by distrusting and fearing one another. Although we are sons and daughters of the same motherland, although we eat the same food, we have no room for one another. Let us ask God in all humility to give us sense, to give us wisdom.[54]

Gandhi described his attitude at this time as one of "indifference,"[55] but this indifference meant a sensitivity to the changed atmosphere and readiness for a new strategy to bring about unity, rather than a loss of faith in unity. He reminisced on the vast possibilities demonstrated by the Hindu-Muslim unity of 1920–21, and reflected on the positive gains even of the recent reversals: the violence, deceit, falsehood, and the like that marked the rupture between the two great communities were no doubt ugly signs, but they were also a demonstration of a crude self-consciousness. The noncooperation movement had catalyzed these tensions, but it would further serve to make it possible for them to be resolved.[56]

Gandhi's new strategy was a personal rather than a public approach:

> My interest and faith in Hindu-Muslim unity and unity among all the communities remain as strong as ever. My method of approach has changed. Whereas formerly I tried to achieve it by addressing meetings, joining in promoting and passing resolutions, now I have no faith in these devices. We have no atmosphere for them. In an atmosphere which is surcharged with distrust, fear and hopelessness, in my opinion these devices rather hinder than help heart-unity. I therefore rely upon prayer and such individual acts of friendship as are possible. Hence I

have lost all desire to attend meetings held for achieving unity. This
however does not mean that I disapprove of such attempts. On the
contrary, those who have faith in such meetings must hold them. I
should wish them all success.[57]

Consistent with his stance of nonparticipation in meetings and his desire to
serve in any way he could, in 1927, in consultation with the Hindu leader,
Pandit Malaviya,* Gandhi reformulated the congress resolution for Hindu-
Muslim unity. He set forth demands for each group:[58] Mussalmen should
forgo cow-slaughter, and Hindus should forgo music before mosques—
neither practice being a matter of religious obligation, and each offending the
sensibilities of the other group.[59] After the resolution was passed by congress,
Gandhi pleaded for its voluntary implementation in a spirit of mutual self-denial.

Gandhi went on to caution the Mussalmen and all other minorities not to
look to the government for the solution of their problems.[60] Intervention by a
third party weakens and humiliates both minority and majority and holds the
nation in bondage. Furthermore, Britain had fostered Hindu-Muslim enmity
by supporting a policy of communal electorates and had then used this lack of
unity as an argument for its position that India was not ready for *swaraj*.[61]

SWARAJ AND CIVIL DISOBEDIENCE

At the stroke of midnight, December 31, 1929, dominion status gave way
to complete independence as the immediate objective of the congress. The
secretary of state for India, Wedgewood Benn, made a statement to the effect
that India had already achieved a form of dominion status. He was referring
to the practice of representation of India at important functions by officials
nominated by the British government itself. For the congress and Gandhi,
this was not enough. The goal was complete independence, with the option of
voluntary partnership with Britain. Britain proceeded to inform the congress
that independence was illegal and that a resolution replacing dominion status
with independence would mean the death of the congress. "This threat made
it a sacred obligation for the Congress to incorporate complete independence
in the Congress creed. The Congress would not be worthy to represent
the nation if, for fear of consequences, it hesitated to enunciate the
nation's birthright." Thus if the meaning of *swaraj* had hitherto been in
doubt, it was now unequivocal; the new goal was *purna swaraj* (complete
independence).[62]

To the Constructive Program, Gandhi and the congress added a boycott of
the legislatures. Gandhi considered adding a boycott of the courts and of
government schools, but the mood of the country was not right. Hindu-

*Malaviya was the leader of Hindumahasabbha, the Hindu religious wing within the congress
and the general Hindu fold of India.

Muslim communal tensions and congress dissensions made it inopportune for any further disobedience to be offered at this time. Gandhi appealed to impatient patriots to join him in promoting the Constructive Program in an atmosphere of nonviolence. This would unify the country and help to set the stage for civil disobedience.[63] The opportunity for a dramatic act of civil disobedience came in 1930 with his successful Salt March, or march to the sea (see p. 35, above). This act touched Indians throughout the country and became a rallying point for *swaraj*.[64]

MASS EDUCATION AND INVOLVEMENT IN *SWARAJ*

Aware of the gap between the desire for *swaraj* and its achievement, Gandhi turned his attention to mass education. Even good government, whether by British officials or by Indian princes, could not be a substitute for self-government.[65] Self-government had to mean an awakening among the masses—an understanding among them of their true interests and the ability to serve those interests on their own. *Purna swaraj* had to mean harmony, freedom from aggression from within or without, and a progressive improvement in the economic condition of the masses. Some progress toward *swaraj* could be made through political power, but the more effective route was through *satyagraha*. Political power was only the shadow, not the substance, of freedom.[66]

Hence, to the already existing Constructive Program, Gandhi added national education, as well as the organization of both village and industrial laborers. Gandhi's shift in emphasis toward the masses of India was reflected in his own shift in residence from the city of Ahmedabad to the village of Sevagram. "The key to swaraj is not in the cities but in the villages, and so I have settled in a village."[67] Addressing a meeting of laborers in Ahmedabad, he stated: "I believed that the key to swaraj lay with the labourers; but I now feel that it is not with them alone. Swaraj will not come as long as our poverty is not wiped out. The magic cure for achieving this is . . . in the villages."[68]

To reach the masses, Gandhi sought to incorporate education into the movement for *swaraj*.[69] Some of Gandhi's closest disciples tended to confuse *swaraj* for India with Gandhi's rule over the country. Part of the program of education focused on correcting these misunderstandings. Thus Gandhi wrote to Nirmala Desai, one of the members of the ashram in Ahmedabad: "All of you seem to believe that swaraj means my rule. It will not be swaraj then. In swaraj, people who are known for their wisdom will rule." And to Pushpa Patel, he wrote, "If swaraj were to mean Gandhi's rule, it would be a curse. Swaraj means the rule of all and that would include Pushpa too."[70]

Much of Gandhi's program of education in *swaraj* dealt with nonviolence and truth. Gandhi pointed out that *swaraj* would not come about by way of falsehoods and violence, and that it would be a double wrong to indulge in them in the name of truth and nonviolence.[71] *Swaraj* of a people was the sum total of the *swaraj* of its individuals, and self-rule was exercised primarily in duties rather than rights. Duty fulfilled was the source of prestige and right; and people who obtain their rights as a result of performance of duty must exercise them only for the service of society.[72] Civil disobedience, or refusal of duty, therefore had to be very selective as a remedy for a diseased condition in society. By its nature it was temporary.[73] He wrote:

Let there be no mistake about my concept of swaraj. It is complete independence of alien control and complete economic independence. So at one end you have political independence, at the other the economic. It has two other ends. One of them is moral and social, the corresponding end is dharma, i.e., religion in the highest sense of the term. It includes Hinduism, Islam, Christianity, etc., but is superior to them all. You may recognize it by the name of Truth that pervades everything and will survive all destruction and all transformation. Moral and social uplift may be recognized by the term we are used to, i.e., non-violence. Let us call this the square of swaraj, which will be out of shape if any of its angles is untrue. In the language of the Congress we cannot achieve this political and economic freedom without truth and non-violence, in concrete terms without faith in God and hence moral and social elevation.[74]

THE DAWN OF *SWARAJ* AND THE END OF THE EMPIRE

Shortly after the outbreak of World War II, Gandhi launched his last attempt at establishing *swaraj* under British rule. He voiced a demand, through the Congress, for the convocation of a constituent assembly of representatives, elected on the basis of adult suffrage or an equivalent. True independence, or even dominion status, could mean nothing without self-determination by the people of India. The minorities represented in the assembly would be able to dictate their own safeguards. The princes of India would be free to join the assembly if they were elected by a vote of their own people. Neither the Congress nor the Muslim League would be allowed to obstruct the proceedings of such an elected group. Briefly Gandhi was asking the British government to make a declaration to convene, no later than the termination of the war, a constituent assembly of representatives, including princely states if possible, and without them if the princes did not agree.

When Britain's intentions for India after the war were announced they were disappointing both to Gandhi and to the Congress. The Congress responded by refusing to help Britain in the war effort. Gandhi's perspective on the subject was more complicated. The war was abhorrent to him in that it clashed with his belief in nonviolence; yet, he still maintained some loyalty to Britain and was committed to avoiding actions that would "embarrass" the British. Ultimately, however, he could not accept Britain's limited concessions to India and agreed with the Congress that India could not support the

war. If the war was in defense of freedom, Gandhi argued, only a free country could fight for it. India could not fight to defend a freedom that it did not
possess. He wrote in a letter dated May 23, 1940:

> What more can India as a subject country do than it is made to do! You
> do not suppose for one moment that they hesitate to take all they want
> from this country! The Congress has nothing but moral help to give.
> They have disabled India from doing more. . . . India as a subject coun-
> try cannot save Britain. India as a free country may. There is no want of
> will on my part. It is sheer want of ability.[75]

In 1942 Gandhi launched the Quit India campaign. He was arrested shortly
thereafter, setting off incidents of mass violence throughout India. In the
years after his release from jail, Gandhi's focus shifted from independence to
the relations between Hindus and Muslims in the face of the proposed establishment of Pakistan.

When the Labour party gained control of the British Parliament in 1945,
shortly before the end of the war, Britain announced its intention to grant
independence to India within three years. A general election was held in India
to choose a constitution-making body. This assembly met in 1946, but
without the participation of the Muslims, whose frustration in their demands
for a sovereign Pakistan had led to widespread riots. Gandhi saw the inevitability of the establishment of a separate Muslim state, but regarded it as a
"spiritual tragedy." The Indian Independence bill provided for the independence of India from Britain on August 15, 1947, and established an autonomous Pakistan.

Swaraj, when it came, left Gandhi desolate rather than jubilant. He was
disappointed that *satyagraha* in the pure form in which he had envisioned it
had degenerated into passive resistance, a form that allowed for violence.
Even though India had achieved through passive resistance its political
freedom, the enmity between Hindu and Muslim grieved Gandhi deeply. In a
letter to Madame Edmond Privat (known as "Bhakti") he decried "the humiliating spectacle of weak brother killing his weak brother thoughtlessly and
inhumanly."[76] Despite the obvious disappointment, however, there was hope
born of faith. He continued in the letter:

> I am only hoping and praying and I want all the friends here and in
> other parts of the world to hope and pray with me that this blood-bath
> will soon end and out of that, perhaps, inevitable butchery, will rise a
> new and robust India—not warlike, basely imitating the West in all its
> hideousness, but a new India bearing the best that the West has to give
> and becoming the hope not only of Asia and Africa, but the whole of
> the aching world.
> I must confess that this is hoping against hope, for, we are today
> swearing by the military and all that naked physical force implies. Our

statesmen have for two generations declaimed against the heavy expenditure on armaments under the British regime, but now that freedom from political serfdom has come, our military expenditure has increased and still threatens to increase and of this we are proud! There is not a voice raised against it in our legislative chambers. In spite, however, of the madness and the vain imitation of the tinsel of the West, the hope lingers in me and many others that India shall survive this death-dance and occupy the moral height that should belong to her after the training, however imperfect, in non-violence for an unbroken period of 32 years since 1915.[77]

Though historical events had precluded the ideal unfolding of liberation that Gandhi had envisioned, his efforts had been crucial in leading India to *swaraj*.

3

Gandhi's Theology of Swaraj

Gandhi's concept of *swaraj*, as has been seen in chapter 2, was built not merely on considerations of politics and economics, but on the broader ground of culture, religion, and civilization, which for him centered on God and the human spirit. Gandhi revolted from any civilization that was empirically godless and soulless or unconcerned about God and the human soul in its structural and functional aspects. There could be no autonomy apart from God-realization, or a God-oriented "self-realization." Politics, economics, religion, culture, and civilization in general were means to the full autonomy or liberation of human beings in God-realization. Thus God-realization was synonymous not only with seif-realization, but with the full realization of freedom or liberation. Gandhi was a theologian of politics and liberation, rather than a prophet of secularization.

To show Gandhi as a theologian of liberation, we must expose Gandhi's theology of *swaraj*, which was effectively his political theology. The theistic and spiritual orientation of his political action renders his theology of *swaraj* a theology of those programs of action for *swaraj*. Gandhi rarely theologized in the abstract; but theological considerations were intrinsic to his theories of politics and economics as well as to his politico-economic action.

THE ORIGINS OF GANDHI'S THEOLOGY OF *SWARAJ*

The Political Origin of Gandhi's Theology

Though Gandhi was deeply committed to the study of religion in his early years, his *Collected Works*, which date from 1884 onward, hardly contain a significant theological statement, until 1908, when Gandhi was forty years old. The statements that do appear in the first eight volumes of the *Collected Works* are those of a philosopher or historian of religion, rather than of a theologian. The one exception occurred in 1907 in a reference to the struggle of the Indians in South Africa against the Transvaal government: "Truth and justice were on our side. I believe God is always near me. He is never away from me. May you also act in this faith. Believe that God is near you and always follow the truth."[1] ("Our side" refers to the Indian side, as against the Transvaal government's side. The Indian side itself was composed of Hindus, Muslims, and Christians.) This statement illustrates both Gandhi's commitment to working for truth and justice in his community and the context of faith in which the events of his life took place. His belief in God underlies not just his theological statements but all of his thoughts and acts. Belief for Gandhi is an existential force; faith is inextricably bound up with conduct. Thus the events of his life are the actualization of his faith.

In 1908, speaking at a reception given in his honor, Gandhi addressed the Indian community in Johannesburg. To people who "suffer injustice and oppression and are denied their legitimate rights," Gandhi spoke about the true meaning of religion for those who have faith in God:

> Where there is God there is truth, and where there is truth there is God. I live in fear of God. I love truth only, and so God is with me. Even if the path of truth does not please the community it pleases God. Therefore I will do what pleases God, even if the community should turn against me.[2]

Initiating an early instance of civil disobedience, he told his Indian audience that, to protest their condition, their real duty was to suffer imprisonment. Echoing the Tamil Saivite poet Appar, Gandhi pointed out that "the servant of God will never consent to be the slave of any man." Separation from families, sacrifice of property, and other hardships would make the voice of truth heard. It was God, not the imperial government, who would secure for Indians their legitimate rights. Through God, the sight of their unjust suffering and sacrifice would stir their opponents' consciences. Thus would their enslavement be ended.[3]

In *Hind Swaraj*, Gandhi had referred to modern civilization as atheistic, and to ancient, true civilization as centered on God and his service, not that of the body and Mammon. Calling upon the Indian businessmen in South Africa to join the struggle against unfair laws against Indians, Gandhi spoke of the impossibility of serving both God and Mammon and of the need to embrace poverty for the sake of the war for justice.[4] In one of his statements he said:

> I have realized that those who wish to serve God cannot afford to pamper themselves or to run after luxury. Prayers do not come easily in an atmosphere of luxuries. Even if we do not ourselves share the luxuries, we cannot escape their natural influence. The energy that we spend in resisting that influence is at the cost of our devotional efforts.[5]

To stand firm in the truth was the essence of all religions, without which no religion would be true to itself.

The Indians' attempts to follow their religious beliefs, however, were being hampered by the government of the Transvaal. If the Indians clung to the truth and were not unduly attached to their wealth, they had nothing to fear from the despotic laws; the truth would vindicate them and set them free.[6] On the occasion of the hardships imposed upon some prominent Indians by the Transvaal government, Gandhi alluded to "the mysterious law of God" whereby the suffering of innocent people benefits and saves others.[7] He had confidence that "God is with those who follow the right. Since we follow the right, victory is bound to be ours."[8] When questioned about the achievements of *satyagraha* in South Africa, Gandhi listed as many as twenty-nine distinct gains from the campaigns. The first was the saving of the honor of India and the Indian identity. The last was that "by placing its trust in God, the community has demonstrated to the world the supreme value of religion." Gandhi added:

> The last mentioned is the foremost among them. A great campaign such as this could not have been waged without faith in God. He has been our only true support. If, through the struggle, we have learnt better to depend on Him alone, that is a sufficient gain in itself, and all else will follow as a matter of course.[9]

The Centrality of Gandhi's Politico-Theological Faith

Gandhi associated knowledge of God with the heart, rather than with reason: "Faith in God cannot be reasoned out. It does not come from the head but from the heart, and, things of the heart are spontaneous and instinctive."[10] Since feeling also pertained to the heart and could contaminate the source of God-knowledge, purity of heart was important for faith.[11] Faith was a source of strength and hope in the face of the social tragedy that India was going through. Consoling a Muslim over the national tragedy, Gandhi said:

> I share your grief. The whole thing is so sad. But I live in the hope based on God's promise that there is no such thing as eternal grief or eternal happiness in this world and that therefore every grief is followed by joy, if only one would wait and have faith. I have patience because I have faith and therefore refuse to weep over the tragedy going on [in] front of me.[12]

The immediacy of God in Gandhi's faith precluded any need for a mediator between himself and God.[13] It was intrinsic to his faith that God spoke to him, and that he heard God's voice. Gandhi readily admitted that he could not prove this, except by results. God would not be God if he allowed himself to be an object of proof by his creatures. But God did give his willing slave the power to pass through the fiercest of ordeals. In 1933, in a letter to his wife, Gandhi claimed that the fast he was undertaking was prompted by God,[14] who would therefore enable him to complete it. On another occasion he wrote that he had been hearing God's voice for more than a half-century, with an increasing audibility over the years.[15]

How certain was Gandhi of being led by God? Gandhi raised this question himself: "Who can know beyond doubt whether a certain step is inspired by God or by the Devil?" His answer was, "I only give probable cause of what is past and over." In other words, the answer had to be proved by time, that is, by the results, which is judgment in retrospect.[16]

In his numerous fasts, Gandhi's focus was on faith, not on the physical act of starving himself. The capacity for a fast was not sufficient qualification for undertaking one. A fast could never be a mechanical effort or mere imitation; it had to come from the depth of one's soul, in the context of a living faith in God.[17]

Faith in God is incompatible with certain attitudes and modes of behavior. It excludes dejection as want of faith. It likewise rules out the analysis of every act of God.[18] Faith is incompatible with evil deeds and violence.[19] It cannot exist where there is no fear of God.[20] As inner strength, and as the power behind nonviolence,[21] faith can be developed only by prayer.[22]

Faith and Works in Gandhi

Gandhi's faith was an active one—not merely cognitive or contemplative. Action was necessary to faith. His precept and his practice thus merged. Writing to a friend, Gangabehn Vaidya, May 1930, he said:

I keep myself busy and do not remain unoccupied even for a minute. That way alone can I have peace of mind. I can see God only through work. The Lord says that He is ever working without taking a moment's rest. How else, then, can we know Him except through work?

Gandhi's discourse number 42 on the *Gita* throws light on the nature of the work associated with faith. Gandhi identifies such action with *yajna* (sacrifice) and interprets it as "any work dedicated to God" that "helps me to attain *moksha*" (liberation). Gandhi (as well as the *Gita*) understands God's creative action to be liberative and unbinding. He further describes it, in his letter to Vaidya, as not mental or intellectual work, but bodily work:

Brahma did not ask human beings to multiply and prosper merely by working with their minds; what He meant was that they should do so through bodily *yajna*, by working with the body. Scriptures of other religions enjoin the same thing. The Bible says: "With the sweat of thy brow thou shalt earn thy bread." Thus bodily labour is our lot in life; it is best, then, to do it in the spirit of service and dedicate it to Shri Krishna. Anyone who works in that spirit all his life becomes free from evil and is delivered from all bonds.[23]

Bodily work, Gandhi believed, would keep the devotee humble, whereas mental work might encourage tendencies toward the development of an *asuri*, or proudly demonic, intelligence. Gandhi felt that this perspective also had practical importance in India, because of circumstances related to caste structure and to professional and economic injustices and inequalities.[24]

Within the context of a faith-in-action, and drawing from the *Gita*, upon which he was commenting, Gandhi saw God as both doer and nondoer, and the model for all who sought *moksha*.[25] He derived this personal synthesis from the *Gita*'s central message of *nishkama karma*, or selfless and unattached action,[26] as well as from the perspective of his own existential faith, in which God had never deserted him.[27]

Gandhi could also testify that the best and simplest means to self-realization, or to being with God, was to serve God's creatures.[28] He reasoned that God was incorporeal and not in need, whereas fellow humans were corporeal and in need. Service, therefore, was the measure of faith; and the country of India needed such service.[29] God had himself set the example of selfless service to his creatures, as though to say that there was no other way to serve him.[30] Even for someone who habitually listened to God's voice, there was the need for endless striving to see God face to face; hence there could be no room for backsliding from work as service.[31] Without work as service, prayer and professions of faith would be no more than words,[32] as could be seen in the failure of Christians, who believed in Jesus as the Prince of Peace, to work toward that much-needed peace.[33]

Within the framework of service as faith, Gandhi emphasized service to certain categories of persons: "The best and most understandable place where He [God] can be worshipped is a living creature. The service of the distressed, the crippled and the helpless among living things constitutes worship of God."[34] On the occasion of the earthquake in Quetta, Baluchistan, Gandhi wrote that such visitations should "humble us and prepare us to face our Maker whenever the call comes," and teach us to be ever ready to share the sufferings of our fellows whoever they may be."[35] Gandhi spoke of his own penance and suffering during his 1934 fast as the language of the heart, which was the only language intelligible to the masses and therefore the only means to identify with them at that time.[36] His quest for God was through self-realization in service to the villagers: "If I could persuade myself that I should find Him in the Himalayan cave, I would proceed there immediately. But I know that I cannot find Him apart from humanity."[37] He confessed that God appeared to him in many forms but was most evident in the poor, the oppressed, the frightened, the untouchables.[38]

Gandhi's Faith at Work in Satyagraha

Gandhi maintained that faith was the basis of *satyagraha*.[39] *Satyagraha* was based not on human efforts, but on unconquerable faith in God and his justice.[40] The potential for *satyagraha* having been derived from God, it would be impossible without a living faith in God. In other words, faith was the condition of the possibility of *satyagraha*.

Gandhi's reflections on *satyagraha* are couched in terms of conflict. On a practical level, the *satyagraha* movement began in conflict in 1906 when the Indians in the Transvaal refused to submit to the registration ordinance. But the word awakening Gandhi's faith in the presence of God in that struggle was spoken by a Muslim, Sheth Haji Habib.[41] On a spiritual level, Gandhi refers to *satyagraha* as a wrestling with evil in order to know God: "I shall never know God if I do not wrestle with and against evil even at the cost of life itself. I am fortified in the belief by my own humble and limited experience." Fighting injustice was as essential to *satyagraha* as was nonviolent love.[42]

Gandhi identified as hypothetical the conflict between love for God and love for humanity; such seeming disparity was in fact a conflict within the person, requiring an inner search and then purification. The idea of a divorce between the two loves was predicated on the base motives of self-love and self-gratification. Real love for humanity was impossible without love for God, Gandhi believed.[43]

This idea of the inner-conflictual character of faith finds confirmation in Gandhi's spiritual interpretation of the two greatest of the Indian epics, the *Ramayana* and the *Mahabharata*. Gandhi read them not as external and past histories, but as the ever-present inner history of every person. He did so particularly with reference to the epic wars, which provide the major themes for the poems.[44] In his interpretation of chapter 2 of the *Gita*, which is a part of the *Mahabharata* epic, for example, the war between the Pandavas and the Kauravas is seen as a shadow or symbol of the inner war between God and Satan, forces of good and evil.[45] The idea of a spiritual conflict between God and Satan could in turn be found externalized in the political conflict between India and the British government. In calling on the country to overthrow the British rule, Gandhi stated: ". . . So long as we do not succeed in overthrowing the Satanic Government that exists in the country, we are all participants in it."[46]

To Gandhi, *satyagraha* presupposed the living presence and guidance of God.[47] *Satyagraha* constituted the exploration, experimentation, discovery, and realization of the personal presence of God. At the time of one of his many arrests, Gandhi disclaimed his own guidance of the *satyagraha* movement in India and affirmed solely the guidance of God: "Let not my companions or the people at large be perturbed over my arrest, for it is not I but God who is guiding this movement. He ever dwells in the hearts of all and he will vouchsafe to us the right guidance if only we have faith in Him."[48] Hence, and since the movement came from God, the practical test by which to be sure that God was present in the movement was reconciliation, whereby people who were enemies to each other cease to be enemies and become friends of each other. "It is all the grace of God."[49]

The Subordination of Reason to Faith in Gandhi's Theology

Questions of theodicy or rational theology are minimal in Gandhi, his interests and concerns being with the ascetical and pastoral rather than the rational or speculative. Yet theoretical questions were of interest to him insofar as they were addressed to him by others or occurred to him in the context of the sacred texts which he was studying. Thus, to a reader of a book of philosophical atheism, he proposed the argument of the First Cause from the analogy of parenthood. Commenting on the *Gita*, he could speak of the negative character of theological language, or the defect of language which necessitates the negation, and of the basically idolatrous character of the religious imagination of even the iconoclast.[50] In the same context, he could discourse about God as doer and nondoer,[51] a point translatable in scholastic terms as the real relation between human and God and the logical relation between God and human. Likewise he could distinguish between *advaitism* and *Dwaitism* (theological monism and dualism) on the subtle basis of their methods: "The former derived evidence from God who alone exists and therefore contemplates identity between God and creation. The latter attempts to show that the two can be never one."[52]

From his religious and professional academic background Gandhi could examine criteria for the interpretation of religious texts in a pretheological realm intimately affecting the theological one. The hermeneutic criteria Gandhi lists are the five *yamas*:

> They are the fives rules of self-restraint. . . . First, *brahmacharya*, celibacy; the second is *satya*, truth; the third is *ahimsa*, absolute innocence, not even hurting a fly; the next condition is *asteya*, non-stealing, not merely not stealing in the ordinary sense in which the word is understood, but if you appropriate or even cast your greedy eyes on anything that is not your own, it becomes stealing. Lastly, *aparigraha*—a man, who wants to possess worldly riches, or other things, won't be fit really to understand the spirit. . . . These are the indispensable conditions. There are other conditions, but . . . these are the fundamental ones. . . .[53]

As other criteria Gandhi includes historical criticism, form criticism, and text criticism. He does not list these formally but applies them in his interpretation of texts. His emphasis, however, is on the ethical rather than the theoretical criteria of interpretation.

What mattered most to Gandhi was the effect of religious beliefs on the lives of the Indian people: "There is no doubt that mankind is affected largely by the way it looks upon God. So far as India is concerned the vast majority think of God as the Monitor within each one of us. Even the illiterate masses know that God is only one, that He is all-pervading, and therefore, is the witness of all our actions."[54]

Clearly, Gandhi's theology of *swaraj* is rooted in his political commitment to his community of oppressed people as the place of his encounter with God, and, further, in his putting that political faith to work and in his suffering for the cause of justice to the oppressed. Gandhi's theology was not born of speculative concerns. This brings us now to a consideration of his theology of practical, political means to God-realization.

GANDHI'S POLITICAL MEANS TO GOD-REALIZATION

Satyagraha was not only the faith of Gandhi at work, but, as he said explicitly, a means to God-realization, or the perfection of incarnation. *Satyagraha* was a means to be used in the political sphere, as a method for conflict resolution. There were also personal means to God-realization, which Gandhi employed in his own pilgrimage to truth.

God-realization, or becoming like God, is the human being's supreme end and the highest good; it raises the person above self and above the level of brute beasts.[55] When a person, idea, value, or experience takes hold of someone in his or her wholeness, Gandhi refers to this as "realization." Realization is therefore more than merely sensuous or notional knowledge. It includes the emotions, as well as the moral will and effort, thus bespeaking an overall transformation of one's personality. Not merely intellectual belief, it is based on a "heart-grasp" of the truth,[56] on a "search within": "For God you have to search within and find Him in His numberless works."[57] This is accomplished through prayer; for "prayer means being one with God."[58]

As guidelines in the quest for God-realization, Gandhi advocated the dual paths of nonviolence[59] and nonattachment.[60] He believed that fitness for God-realization would come particularly through a self-emptying, voluntary poverty—in becoming poor with the poor.[61] Such a way of life would also include identification with all of God's creatures[62] and service of all.[63]

An English Christian correspondent once challenged Gandhi's conformity with God's purpose:

> You have had your name blazoned abroad . . . as one of the greatest philosophers and sacrificial workers on earth. In India you have been proclaimed *the* Mahatma, and actually worshipped as one of the incarnations of India's many deities. . . . Your practice also of fasting when sin has been committed . . . has a tendency to make Indians believe that you can merit blessing which can be communicated to others, —but has anybody been loving and courageous enough to write and challenge you as to how personally you are going to attain atonement for your own sin? All your self-denials and fastings and prayer and good deeds cannot blot out one sin of your early days. For thirty or more years of your life you lived the carnal, self-life, seeking and following your own plans and ambitions without seeking to know God's purpose for your life or to honour His holy name. . . .[64]

Gandhi's answer manifested a humility characteristic of authentic contact with God at a level deeper than that exhibited by his overly zealous correspondent:

> Jesus atoned for the sins of those who accepted his teachings by being an infallible example to them. But the example was worth nothing to those who never troubled to change their lives. A regenerate outgrows the original alloy. I have made the frankest admission of my sins. But I do not carry their burden on my shoulders. If I am journeying Godward, as I feel I am, it is safe with me. For I feel the warmth of the sunshine of His presence. My austerities, fastings and prayers are, I know, of no value, if I rely upon them for reforming me. But they have an inestimable value, if they represent, as I hope they do, the yearnings of a soul striving to lay his weary head in the lap of his Maker.[65]

Even more important to Gandhi, however, than his personal means to God-realization was the political means to God-realization. Using the weapon of *satyagraha*, he devoted his life to working toward truth in the form of India's liberation. The strategy he used was twofold: noncooperation with the government and the Constructive Program.

The Theology of Noncooperation

During the 1920s the Indian struggle for independence was marked by "noncooperation." In a speech at Dibrugarh on August 25, 1921, Gandhi summed up noncooperation as follows:

> It is heinous to love a regime where untruth reigns, barbarities are perpetrated, and false despatches are sent. We therefore seek no justice from its courts and do not wish to have our children educated in its schools and colleges. This is called non-cooperation. We do not incite anyone to rioting. We can achieve swarajya prayerfully and peaceably and heal the wound of the Muslims.[66]

He pointed to the struggle of noncooperation as one of religion against irreligion;[67] as noncooperation "with sin, not the sinner; with Dyerism, not with Dyer";*[68] as noncooperation not with individuals but with their actions.[69] Thus noncooperation was a limited fight against a limited evil.

Challenged by fellow noncooperators as to the consistency of his position of noncooperation with a meeting he once had with the governor of Bombay, Gandhi elucidated the meaning of noncooperation in terms of self-denial and self-suffering:

---

*General Reginald Dyer. For his activities in the Punjab, see pp. 24–26, above.

Non-violent non-cooperation means renunciation of the benefits of a system with which we can non-cooperate. We therefore renounce the benefits of schools, courts, titles, legislatures and offices set up under the system. The most extensive and permanent part of our non-cooperation consists in the renunciation of foreign cloth which is the foundation for the vicious system that is crushing us to dust. . . . If then I go to any official for the purpose of seeking the benefits above-mentioned, I cooperate. Whereas if I go to the meanest official for the purpose of converting him, say to khaddar, or weaning him from his service, or persuading him to withdraw his children from Government schools, I fulfill my duty as a non-cooperator. I should fail if I did not go to him with that definite and direct purpose.[70]

One A. C. C. Harvey of the staff of Khalsa College, Amritsar, had written to Gandhi criticizing the policy of noncooperation as being wrong "in the light of the universal religion," not only negative and therefore barren, "not only politically wrong, but also *irreligious*, contrary to the will of God." He reminded Gandhi that he [Gandhi] had earlier persuaded the congress at Amritsar to adopt a "policy of moderation and cooperation."Never reluctant to admit that he had changed his mind, Gandhi replied with a justification of noncooperation on philosophical, pragmatic, and moral grounds:

I think that non-cooperation is a fundamental fact in God's plan, even as darkness is. There is no such thing as cooperation if there is no non-cooperation. If we give our cooperation for the prosecution of that which is good, we must withdraw it from that which is evil. I believe that the present British administration of India is not good but positively evil. . . . Non-cooperation . . . is the only alternative to an armed rebellion. It has been suggested that the object can be achieved by persuasion and argument. In my opinion which is based upon extensive experience, argument has only a limited place in an endeavour to persuade people. In deepest matters argument hopelessly fails. But whilst I feel so strongly about my position, let me assure you that my non-cooperation is itself designed to bring about cooperation.[71]

The Theology of the Constructive Program

Khadi *and* Charkha
It was Gandhi's claim that God appeared to him in thousands of forms. Sometimes he saw God in the *charkha* (spinning wheel), sometimes in the eradication of untouchability, sometimes in Hindu-Muslim unity.[72] The surest way to serve God was to serve the poor. The use of *khadi* was a way to serve the poor.[73] Therefore the use of *khadi* was the surest way of serving God. So spoke Gandhi to his *khadi* workers in July 1934.[74] Gandhi had dis-

covered God as Daridranarayan (God of the poor) through the *charkha*.[75] Furthermore, poverty was taking its toll of atheism among the slum-dwellers of Bombay. Implicitly, therefore, it was the duty of God-believers to serve the poor, who had been reduced to atheism.[76]

Addressing a public meeting at Kanadukathan, at which he was presented with a purse of money, Gandhi told the audience of *chettis* (merchants and moneylenders): "The greatest charity at the present moment that I can conceive for any Indian to do is undoubtedly to promote this khadi work."[77] Later on he wrote: "To those who are hungry and unemployed God can dare reveal Himself only as work and wages as the assurance of food." What the naked needed was not clothes, but work. To become their benefactor would be a sin, because that would only contribute to their ruination. Gandhi's *ahimsa* would not tolerate giving free food to a healthy person who did not put in honest labor. He would have closed down all charitable institutions and almshouses, blaming them for contributing to the vices of laziness, hypocrisy, and crime. Much of popular charity and almsgiving consisted of passing on leftovers and discarded things; Gandhi would rather have shared with the poor his best food and clothes by giving them work.[78]

Writing to his ashram women in 1926, Gandhi reminded them:

> Please remember that all of you are tied to Mother India with a cord of hand-spun yarn. If you give up spinning, you give up service too. Do not, therefore, neglect the spinning-wheel. Today Rama dwells in the spinning-wheel. The fire of starvation is raging all around. I do not see any other help against it except through the spinning-wheel. God always reveals Himself to us in some concrete shape. That is why we sing of Draupadi that for her God took the form of garments. Anyone who desires to see God today may see Him in the form of the spinning-wheel.[79]

The image of Rama dwelling in the spinning wheel is Gandhi's original way of suggesting a continuous *avatar*, or incarnation of God, accessible to all who would work at spinning. This idea became more explicit in a letter from Gandhi to Durga Desai in 1931: "God is no doubt the sole help of the poor, but the spinning-wheel is His hands and feet, and the poor man or woman who holds it holds God."[80]

The *charkha* was, for Gandhi—to use a Christian extrapolation—a sacrament of salvation in the concrete historical context. "After all we have to commune with God through some means or other. Why not through the charkha?" he asked.[81] Gandhi went on to advise Krishnachandra, who was one of his disciples:

> While plying the *takli* fix your mind on the thought that it is God who is doing it, that He is hidden in every fibre of the yarn. See Him with the inner eyes. Then spinning, which now seems secondary to you, will

become the primary thing. In the language of satyagraha the means become identified with the end.[82]

Gandhi's words are full of religious fervor, confirming even further the sacramentality of the *charkha* for him. To ply the *charkha* was "to examine its *infinite capacity* and to *reveal* it to the world" (italics added). This was a pursuit of more than mundane value; to follow it meant to live the teaching of the *Gita*. But it must be borne in mind that the fervor was never dissociated from the aspect of service to God and the poor.[83]

Swadeshi, or the movement to promote Indian products and national pride, served as the background for the program of *khadi* and *charkha*. A question by a Sikh correspondent provided an occasion for Gandhi to clarify some of the theological backing for the concept. The question bore on chanting the praise or name of God. Gandhi saw such chanting as the property of the soul (*atman*), and *swadeshi* as the *dharma* (natural law) attaching to the body. *Swadeshi* took precedence over and facilitated the praise of God. An Indian who, by refusing to use cloth woven by the hands of another Indian, thus cut the throat of his brother, was not fit to take the name of Ishvar and Allah. Through communion by means of the *charkha*, "Swadeshi is the power which takes us towards God, as it raises us higher." This raising was experienced as contemplation in the act of spinning itself, since spinning was a very restful activity, imitating God's own active rest and restful action.[84]

The Removal of Untouchability

As Gandhi himself admitted, untouchability was essentially a religious problem, and he therefore attempted its solution on the theological level. Basic to the theology of society and social order was Gandhi's concept of the equality of all before God. Gandhi examined various theological aspects of this idea of equality. His fundamental premise was that God is the creator of all, and he made all persons equal. Had he made any distinctions of high and low between person and person, they would have been visible, as are the distinctions between an elephant and an ant. But all human beings have the same appearance and the same desires. Furthermore, all people worship one God under different names. God the creator is one and the same for all. There are not different gods and creators of different people. Hence there cannot be inequality among creatures and worshipers of one God.[85] Neither can there be high and low within the order of creation:

> I do believe that there is only one religion in the world, but I also believe that although it is one mighty tree, it has many branches. . . . And even as all the branches take their sap from one source, even so all religions derive their essence from one fountain-source. Of course there can be only one God if there is one religion, and God who is one complete whole cannot have many branches. But He is invisible and indefinable and, one might literally say that He has as many names as there

are human beings on earth. No matter by what name we describe Him, He is the same without a second and if we are all children of the same Creator, naturally there cannot be any caste amongst us. We are one brotherhood and sisterhood, and there cannot be any distinction of high and low amongst us. There are no *savarnas* and *avarnas*, or all are *savarnas* or all are *avarnas*.[86]

The one creator God is Father, Father of all fathers. He does not, and cannot, treat some children as untouchables from birth and therefore as the lowest, while others are the highest.[87] As children of the household are equal and are treated as such by parents, so are all persons equal before God.[88] No mother treats her handicapped child unkindly or neglectfully; rather, she lavishes on that child her special care and affection. How much greater must be God's own love and concern for his handicapped children, and his justice toward them.[89]

Further, untouchability was inconsistent with sound religious and spiritual principles and practices. Religion advises us to consider ourselves as the lowest, and others as the highest. Untouchability, which is contrary to this view, was crushing the very soul of Indian religion and society.[90] Untouchability, with its implicit social caste system of inborn inequalities, was a social fact. On the basis of the theological truth, Gandhi went on to challenge the legitimacy of the social fact, to distinguish caste from *varnashrama* and to point out that *varnashrama* implied only a horizontal and not a vertical division:

> For me varnashrama does not mean a graded system of untouchability. I have explained what I mean by varnashrama. It does not mean to me grades at all. It is not a vertical division. It is a horizontal one. In my view, all varnas stand absolutely on the same plane, i.e., of equality. Hence there can be no question of untouchability. Varnadharma is a mighty economic law which, if we subscribe to it, would save us from the catastrophe that is in store for the world. I have sufficient warrant in Hindu scriptures for saying that Brahmins and scavengers are absolutely on a par in the eyes of God.[91]

God is above all social distinctions. He transcends them all. He is not, and should not be, morally implicated in the caste system. All individual selves are in essence one. Even such distinctions as man and woman lose all meaning before God.[92] Therefore untouchability was not from God. It was an institution devised by the Devil and put into practice by humans.[93] In an age of critical appraisal of all religions, that institution could no longer be justified; it had to be exorcised[94] as repugnant to the *Vedas* and the *Upanishads*.

With such theological criteria of judgment on untouchability, Gandhi's verdict on it could not but be one of guilt and condemnation. The verdict of guilty could be maintained and substantiated under many counts: First, it was a sin of disbelief in God, his goodness, and his fatherhood,[95] making him an "untouchable."[96] Second, it was a sin of irreligion, a prostitution of religious principles in the name of a satanic institution[97] made by human beings.[98] Third, it was a sin against Hindu religion in particular, spelling the death of Hinduism, since the two could not long survive together.[99] Last, it was a sin against the *harijans*, the children of God, the special servants of God, with whom he was specially present.[100]

Gandhi believed that it was mere superstition to think that God necessarily resides in special buildings that are called temples: "I tell you I know many temples in India in which God no more resides than in a brothel."[101] A temple is not merely an edifice of brick or marble, nor does it turn into a temple by the mere installation of the image of a deity. It becomes a temple only when life has been breathed into the image. Concomitantly, the worshipers have to consecrate their own lives and bodies to the worship of God.[102] Gandhi knew that some Hindus believed that a consecrated image in the temple would lose its sanctity by the *harijans*' entry into the temple, but that the majority were of the opinion that God himself would not come to dwell in the image until the *harijans* were admitted to the temples.[103]

Gandhi's own belief was that a temple barred to the *harijan* was not inhabited by God. If God is Vishwanath, Lord of the entire universe, to exclude one segment of society from entrance into the place of his presence was a contradiction of the meaning of the name of God. God could not be present, or forgiveness of sins obtained, in such a place. This applied to the holiest of the Hindu shrines, that of Kashi Vishwanath, as well as to every other Hindu temple.

Because of his close identification with the *harijans*, Gandhi himself was banned from many temples. He thanked God that the gates of the Guruvayur temple were closed to him.[104] Whereas temple closure had made the God of Hinduism nonexistent for the *harijans*,[105] the moral and theological consequence for Gandhi and his co-workers was that they became little temples themselves.[106] They abstained from visits to temples closed to *harijans*, and persuaded others to do likewise.[107]

The goal toward which Gandhi was working was nothing short of heart-conversion of the traditionalist Hindus to a deeper religion. He saw his efforts on behalf of the *harijans* as purely religious, without any political motivation. He wished therefore that this movement, "so grand and so pure, so religious and so humanitarian," not be exploited by anyone for political purposes. Rather than helping to bridge the already existing schisms, political activity would add to strife and divisiveness. So Gandhi proposed vicarious expiation of the evil of untouchability by methods that were pure.[108] He embarked on a number of fasts aimed at purifying himself and Hinduism of the taint of untouchability.[109] The opening of Hindu temples to *harijans* was such a fundamental matter of sin, repentance, and reparation that even if all *harijans* except one were converted to other religions it would have to be done. Even if it were demonstrated that the political or economic regeneration of the *harijans* would be enough to retain them in the Hindu fold, Gandhi would still insist upon opening the temples to them and removing every trace of inequality.[110]

In January 1937 some of the temples that had been closed to *harijans* were opened to them by royal decree; the Maharaja of Travancore proclaimed all the temples of Travancore open to all who called themselves Hindus, without the slightest reservation. Gandhi looked upon this royal act as an act of God. In speech after speech he stated: "Such an act could not be prompted by any purely worldly considerations. There must have been the spirit of God inspiring both the wise mother and brave son."*[111]

Gandhi told an audience in Kerala that he regarded himself as a *harijan* among the *harijans*, and that the title "Maharaja" could also be translated as *harijan*, or "servant of God." Gandhi called upon all high-caste people voluntarily to become *harijans* among the *harijans*, servants of God, letting all the world know by such action that by virtue of the royal proclamation there was none high and none low but all were equal in the eyes of God.[112] At a public meeting in Kottayam, Gandhi made a special appeal to Christians to join in the spirit of the proclamation and to sow peace and goodwill.

> I felt that I could not do justice to this great meeting, especially a meeting that is held in a Christian stronghold, unless I was prepared to utter a truth I held dear as life itself. We all consciously or unconsciously pine and strive for peace on earth and goodwill amongst mankind. I am convinced that we shall find neither peace nor goodwill among men through strife among men of different religions, through disputation among them. We shall find truth and peace and goodwill if we approach the humblest of mankind in a prayerful spirit. Anyway that is my humble appeal to Christians who may be present at this great meeting. It is a privilege that may not occur again to any of you in your lifetime.[113]

Hindu-Muslim Unity

During a year of Hindu-Muslim riots (in 1926) Gandhi stated the source of his belief in the possibility of Hindu-Muslim unity. It was theological: "Even if the whole of India ranged on one side were to declare that Hindu-Muslim unity is impossible, I will declare that it is perfectly possible. I will say that, if there is anything like God or Truth on earth, Hindu-Muslim unity is possible.[114]

Along with uplifting *khadi* and the *harijans*, Hindu–Muslim unity was a vital article of Gandhi's creed. Affirming his faith in these beliefs against all challenges was his way to be true to his Maker.[115] Thus when all of

---

*A reference to the young prince and to his mother, the regent.

Gandhi's efforts on behalf of Hindu-Muslim unity seemed to have failed, he could confidently entrust the issue to God, the source of all unity:

> And so I have now washed my hands. I am helpless. I have exhausted all my effort. But I am a believer in God, as I never for a moment lost faith in Him, as I content myself with the joy and sorrow that He wills for me. I may feel helpless, but I never lose hope. Something within me tells me that Hindu-Muslim unity must come and will come sooner than we might dare to hope, that God will one day force it on us, in spite of ourselves. That is why I said that it has passed into the hands of God.[116]

On the grounds of the unity of God, truth, life, and faith, Gandhi pointed out to the warring factions of both Hinduism and Islam that their animosities were more destructive than beneficial to either side.[117] He also pointed out the contradictions involved, such as the mockery of the concept of brotherhood if it excluded people belonging to other faiths.[118] The theological basis of Gandhi's values required that the Hindu-Muslim unity he sought be not merely a matter of expediency, but a permanent institution and a life-attitude. He wrote to Hakim Ajmal Khan:

> This unity, therefore, cannot be a mere policy to be discarded when it does not suit us. We can discard it only when we are tired of swaraj. Hindu-Muslim unity must be our creed to last for all time and under all circumstances. Nor must that unity be a menace to the minorities, the Parsis, the Christians, the Jews or the powerful Sikhs. If we seek to crush any of them, we shall some day want to fight each other.[119]

Gandhi saw God not as merely a witness to the question of Hindu-Muslim unity, but as a concerned participant in its problems.

THE EMERGING CONCEPTS OF GOD

Gandhi's belief in the power of *satyagraha* provided the foundation for his efforts both in noncooperation and in the Constructive Program. Through his experience of and reflections on *satyagraha* there emerge various concepts of God that are integral to his theology.

God as Master of Gandhi's Life

References to God so abound in Gandhi's mature writings that an irate English correspondent once wrote to him about the "God stunt" in *Young India*. Gandhi publicized this cynical comment.[120] The fact that he neither defended himself nor refuted his correspondent indicates that Gandhi's God-talk was part of his nature, not a show or playacting. In the phrase of Rabin-

dranath Tagore, Gandhi's words came "out from the depth of truth."[121] But
Gandhi did see God as the master of play, in whose hands he was the play-
thing. In a letter to Durga Desai in January 1931, reflecting on why he had not
joined the Round Table Conference, Gandhi wrote:

> My heart simply did not consent, however much I tried to persuade
> myself. The reins are held by that Master of the Play. Why, then, need
> we worry at all? On the contrary, we should daily leave the reins more
> and more in His hands and strengthen His hands.[122]

Likewise, on accepting the viceroy's invitation to participate in discussions
leading to the Gandhi-Irwin pact, he wrote to Prabhashankar Pattani in February 1931:

> I always pray to God that I, who am standing at Death's door, may not
> put my signature to anything which might prove a trap for the country.
> I am going to Delhi today with this prayer in my heart. I do not feel
> presumptuous like the dog in the story who was walking under the cart.
> I know the limits of my strength. I am but a particle of dust. Even such a
> particle has a place in God's creation, provided it submits to being trod-
> den on. Everything is done by that Supreme Potter. He may use me as
> He wills.[123]

Thus God ruled Gandhi's life and influenced his decisions, even those of a
political nature. Gandhi claimed to think of God every moment of the day.
During waking hours, he maintained, there was no time when he was not
aware of God dwelling within and observing everything. This awareness was
intellectual, and achieved through long practice. He did not claim that his
heart had such awareness, since he did not think himself free from all fear.
One who actually feels the presence of God in his or her heart would be
wholly free from blind attachment to the body. Yet so complete and firm was
his intellectual acceptance of the idea that he felt it slowly sinking into his
heart.[124] He spoke of God as the one true friend: "The number of one's co-
workers may be a million, but there can be only one friend and that is God. It
is my view, and my experience, that other friendships are an obstacle in the
way of friendship with God."[125] In his decisions to fast, Gandhi claimed to
have listened like a slave to the voice of that "most exacting Master," who
had never forsaken him even in his darkest hour.[126] God was not only friend
and master, but also father and mother all in one.[127]

God as Judge in His Moral Holiness

A young judge once wrote to Gandhi objecting to relief work in Gujarat as
contravening the ethical maxim, "Reap as you sow." His assumption was
that relief work prevented the victims of the natural disaster, famine, from

reaping what they had morally sown. Gandhi responded in *Navajivan*, writing that since God was Judge, it was not for human beings to usurp his place and withhold service to the victims of the disaster:

That a man reaps as he sows is an immutable principle which admits of no exception. The above extract [from the young judge's letter, summarized above] is an example of how the principle can be misinterpreted. Many persons think in this way, and the question deserves consideration because I know that the correspondent has not advanced his pleas merely for argument's sake. The maxim "Reap as you sow" is true for all times. Holy books in Sanskrit state the same thing, and so does the Bible. Nowhere does the maxim imply that we are to inflict on the doer what his deed deserves. The present correspondent, however, has put such a construction on the original sentence, and that has led to a terrible misunderstanding of its meaning. When we say "man reaps as he sows," we mean that God will bestow on him his due and not that any of us might sit in God's place and mete out justice to the doer according as he thinks of the latter's deed. If we had the right to judge a man's deed and reward or punish him as the case may demand, there would be nothing left for anyone to do for anyone else. In that case, the idea of service would perish. But the fact is that the world has not perished. Countless men have been rendering service to one another. From this we see that the meaning of the great maxim in question is not what the correspondent conceives it to be, but it is what I have suggested above.[128]

The correspondent was subordinating both God and human to an ethical law or maxim, a trend not uncommon in traditional orthodox Hinduism. Gandhi's interpretation, in placing both God and human above the maxim or law, was a reinterpretation and reform of Hinduism itself. This interpretation struck at the doctrinal roots of enslavement in Hindu society. Yet spatial imagery portraying God and human as being "above" law or maxim should not be interpreted to connote any separation of God and person from the moral law of the universe of humankind. Gandhi had occasion to clarify the issue of God in relation to the law years later on the question of sexual ethics: "And what is God but the law?" he asked, and went on to state that "to obey God is to perform the [l]aw."[129] God and the moral law of the universe of humankind were not two realities extrinsic to each other, but identical within the vision of the moral believer. Gandhi believed that "God is ethics and morality,"[130] both moral agent and the prime source of all norms of morality.

A reader of *Young India* had once objected to the introduction of the name of God into the Congress pledge of noncooperation. Gandhi's answer to him contained many different definitions of God, all of which were implicitly moral, and which, taken together, illustrate both the relativity and the consistency of faith.

We may all have different definitions of "God." If we could all give our own definitions of God there would be as many definitions as there are men and women. But behind all the variety of definitions there would be also a certain sameness which would be unmistakable. For the root is one. God is that undefinable something which we all feel but which we do not know. . . . To me God is truth and love; God is ethics and morality; God is fearlessness. God is the source of Light and Life and yet He is above and beyond all these. God is conscience. He is even the atheism of the atheist. For in His boundless love God permits the atheist to live. He is the searcher of hearts. He transcends speech and reason. He knows us and our hearts better than we do ourselves. He does not take us at our word for He knows that we often do not mean it, some knowingly and others unknowingly. He is a personal God to those who need His personal presence. He is embodied to those who need His touch. He is the purest essence. He simply Is to those who have faith. He is all things to all men. He is in us and yet above and beyond us. One may banish the word "God" from the Congress but one has no power to banish the Thing Itself. What is a solemn affirmation if it is not the same thing as in the name of God? And surely conscience is but a poor and laborious paraphrase of the simple combination of three letters called God. He cannot cease to be because hideous immoralities or inhuman brutalities are committed in His name. He is long suffering. He is patient but He is also terrible. He is the most exacting personage in the world and the world to come. He metes out the same measure to us that we mete out to our neighbors—men and brutes. With Him ignorance is no excuse. And withal He is ever forgiving for He always gives us the chance to repent. He is the greatest democrat the world knows, for He leaves us "unfettered" to make our own choice between evil and good. He is the greatest tyrant ever known, for He often dashes the cup from our lips and, under cover of free will, leaves us a margin so wholly inadequate as to provide only mirth for Himself at our expense. Therefore it is that Hinduism calls it all His sport—*lila*, or calls it an illusion—*maya*. We are *not*, He alone *Is*. And if we will be, we must eternally sing His praise and do His will. Let us dance to the tune of His *bansi*—lute, and all would be well.[131]

Elsewhere Gandhi described God as *atman* (soul) that has attained *moksha*,[132] as *chaitanya*, which is the principle of life and consciousness,[133] and as pure consciousness.[134]

God-Human Union

In his commentary on the *Gita* under the aspect of *anasaktiyoga* (unselfish action) there emerges a mystical description of God. Commenting on verse 36 of Discourse X, "Of deceivers I am the dice-play; of the splendid, the splendour; I am victory, I am resolution, I am the goodness of the good," Gandhi states that the matter in question is not the good or evil nature of things but "the directing and immanent power of God." He examines verses describing God as the Unmanifest: "Arjuna said: 1. Of the devotees who thus worship Thee, incessantly attached, and those who worship the Imperishable Unmanifest, which are the better yogis? The Lord said: 5. The greater is the travail of those whose mind is fixed on the Unmanifest; for it is hard for embodied mortals to gain the Unmanifest-Goal." Gandhi's comment is:

Mortal man can only imagine the Unmanifest, the Impersonal, and as his language fails him he often negatively describes it as "Neti," "Neti" [Not-That, Not-That]. And so even iconoclasts are at bottom no better than idol-worshippers. To worship a book, to go to church, or to pray with one's face in a particular direction—all these are forms of worshipping the Formless in an image or idol. And yet both the idol-breaker and the idol-worshipper cannot lose sight of the fact that there is something which is beyond all form, Unthinkable, Formless, Impersonal, Changeless. The highest goal of the devotee is to become one with the object of his devotion. The *bhakta* extinguishes himself and merges into, becomes, *Bhagavan*. This state can best be reached by devoting oneself to some form, and so it is said that the short cut to the Unmanifest is really the longest and the most difficult.

On the verses: "12. I will expound to thee that which is to be known and knowing which one enjoys immortality; it is the supreme Brahman which has no beginning, which is called neither Being nor non-Being," and "15. Without all beings, yet within; immovable yet moving; so subtle that it cannot be perceived; so far and yet so near It is" Gandhi comments:

The Supreme can be described neither as Being nor as non-Being. It is beyond definition or description, above all attributes. . . . He who knows It is within It, close to It, mobility and immobility, peace and restlessness, we owe to It, for it has motion and yet it is motionless.

On verse 22, "What is called in this body the Witness, the Assentor, the Sustainer, the Experiencer, the Great Lord and also the Supreme *Atman*, is the Supreme Being," and verse 23, "He who thus knows *purusha* and *prakriti* with its *gunas* is not born again, no matter how he live and move," Gandhi says:

. . . This *sloka* may not be taken to support any kind of libertinism. It shows the virtue of self-surrender and selfless devotion. All actions bind the self, but if all are dedicated to the Lord they do not bind, rather they release him. He who has thus extinguished the "self" or the thought of "I" and who acts as ever in the great Witness's eye, will never sin nor err. The self-sense is at the root of all error or sin. Where the "I" has been extinguished, there is no sin. This *sloka* shows how to steer clear of all sin.

On verses 27 and 28 in Discourse XIII Gandhi writes: "He who sees the same God everywhere merges in Him and sees naught else; he thus does not yield to passion, does not become his own foe and thus attains Freedom." And on verse 30: "To realize that everything rests in Brahman is to attain to the state of Brahman. The *jiva* becomes *Siva*."[135]

The unifying element in Gandhi's descriptions of God lies in the unity of his vision of faith. As he once wrote, politics itself is all-inclusive, so he did not divide political, social, religious, and economic activities into watertight compartments. Rather, he looked upon them all as an indivisible whole, each running into the rest and affected by the rest. Gandhi knew that political freedom properly so called would depend upon internal reforms and India's ability to solve its many domestic problems.[136] Not one of the many descriptions of God by Gandhi is absolute; each is perspectival and relative to the one speaking in faith. Any absolutist description would have been a contradiction of theory and praxis.

God as Truth

Gandhi described God as truth in the sense of being, that which is, whose essence it is to be (*sat*). Among all of Gandhi's names or images for God, this is perhaps the most central, providing a unity to Gandhi's thought and life. The primary meaning of *satya* (derived from *sat*) is "to be," "to exist." Changelessness is inherent in the Indian definition of being, and therefore truth and God also have the qualities of changelessness. This ontological meaning is never divorced from the moral meaning in Gandhi.

Not only is it the intrinsic characteristic of God to be, but that quality is exclusively his. "Only God is, nothing else is."[137] Everything else is fleeting. The ontic quality of God finds its religious expression in Gandhi in terms of God's immanence. And Gandhi's perception of God's presence in all of us binds him at once to all. God's presence, then, is a unitive presence. "God is present in all of us. For my part, every moment I experience the truth that though many we are all one."[138] And again, "He is not outside of us. He is in the hearts of us all."[139]

For Gandhi, truth was the only appropriate designation for God. The various names for God, such as Vishnu, Maheshvar, Brahma, Bhagavan, and Ishvar, either had no meaning or had a meaning that was imperfect. " 'Truth' is the only term which is perfect as a description of God." Truth has no body. Each person therefore imagines it in the form which appeals to him or her. The form that each worships is a creation of one's own living imagination. Each image will be true, so long as it meets the spiritual needs of that particular worshipper of God.[140]

In a speech at Lausanne, Switzerland, on December 8, 1931, Gandhi told the story of finding his name for God. In early youth he had learned the thousand names of God from Hindu scriptures. Later on he had found many names for God in Islam as well. To him the significance of these many names of God was that God has as many names as there are creatures: each creature is a name of God. For his own part, Gandhi had concluded that God is truth, and he had even gone a step further and defined truth as God.[141] In another version of the story, recounted in a letter to Pandit Narayan Khare, Gandhi wrote: "I do not remember whether or not I had before me the *mantra, Hiranmayena*, etc., when it occurred to me that Truth is God; when such things occur to me, they spring straight from the heart as if they were original intuitions. For me, these truths have the certainty of personal experience."[142] Even before he had concluded that truth was God, he had acted as if it were so, always having known God as truth, and never having doubted the existence of truth even when he had doubted the existence of God. He defined this truth as the pure consciousness that alone holds the universe together and that therefore was God.[143]

Although Gandhi found the nearest approach to truth to be through love, he did not define God first and foremost through love because of the many meanings of the term "love." Love in the sense of *ahimsa* and nonviolence had very few followers in the world, and human love, as passion, was degrading to Gandhi. Gandhi reconciled truth and love in the equation of end and means, terms that to him were mutually convertible.[144] Still other reasons for Gandhi's definition of God through truth were that truth was not impersonal; that it avoided idolatry; and that it was known relatively,[145] an absolute definition of truth being an impossibility[146] because of our condition of knowing, which is relative and relational. Gandhi saw it therefore as significant that Pilate's question to Jesus about the truth did not receive a reply. He seems to imply an unanswerability about the question, unless the answer were "Truth is God," which would indeed make perfect sense in the Gospel context.

The understanding and observance of relative truth in thought, word, and action was the way to know God and attain *moksha*, or spiritual liberation, while still encased in the body. God and spiritual liberation were integral to the Gandhian concept of *swaraj*. As he himself claimed, his goals and ideas were inseparably interwoven. His own self-concept in the practice of truth was that of an ascetic or trainee rather than one who claimed to have attained to its perfection. He did not profess to be a *jivan-mukta*, that is, one who had reached *moksha* in the body.[147] The moral and ascetical-mystical implications of the discipline of truth are as great as those emanating from the concept of God. Truth therefore was more than abstinence from telling lies. All moral observances could be summed up under the practice of truth. Intrinsic to that observance would be service to all[148] as well as *satyagraha*. From the idea of the presence of the God of truth in all, Gandhi infers that "the sin of one is the sin of all." He adds: "And hence it is not up to us to destroy the evil-doer.

We should, on the contrary, suffer for him."[149] Since truth cannot exist without love, it had to include nonviolence, *brahmacharya*, nonstealing, and other *yamas*.

If even one person followed truth to its perfect degree, *swaraj* was a certainty. If a large number strove to follow truth even in some measure, *swaraj* could be won. It could be won also by a few pursuing truth with the utmost consciousness and sincerity. But it was Gandhi's earnest desire that all would learn to follow truth rigorously as a matter of principle.[150]

God as Savior

The image of God as savior is neither dominant nor frequent in Gandhi's writings, certainly not as frequent as truth, except in his repeated reference to God as the help of the helpless. Notwithstanding this infrequency, the image of God as savior is important to the theme of liberation, and the central theological image of truth certainly subsumes it. Despite the emphasis in Gandhi's life and teachings on moral striving, Gandhi never loses his awareness of the primacy of God and his dependence on God.

Gandhi believed that in pure justice there could be no cruelty. When the question was raised as to whether the earthquake in Japan at the end of World War I was the result of divine wrath, Gandhi replied that God never acted out of pride and that to attribute cruelty to him was to measure him with a human yardstick. He did believe, however, that "If a nation is sunk in sin and God wants to save it, He might send an earthquake with that aim." This would be a saving act of God rather than a punitive act.[151]

When an anonymous writer charged Gandhi with a grievous error in having mercy-killed an ailing calf, Gandhi pointed out that if in the long run he discovered his act to be in error, it would prove to be a serious irreligious act in the name of religion, reprehensible in anyone, not the least so in himself. Without diminishing his responsibility for the act, however, Gandhi added: "I believe that if in spite of the best intentions one is led into committing mistakes, they do not really result in harm to the world or, for the matter of that, any individual. God always saves the world from the consequences of unintended errors of men who live in fear of Him."[152]

A more pointed reference to God as savior occurs in Gandhi's thoughts on the question of the untouchables' entry into temples. Gandhi assumed in his reasoning that temples were meant for sinners, as the place where they could wash away their sins. To those Hindus who argued that the *harijans* found themselves in their current plight because of their past sins, Gandhi asked that they concede the first right to the *harijans* to worship in the temples, adding: "God has been described by all scriptures of the world as a Protector and Saviour of the sinner."[153]

Implicit references to God as savior or to the saving presence and activity of God occur in sundry writings. While advising a patient to adhere to medical instructions, for example, Gandhi described God as the only true doctor or healer.[154] Elsewhere God is described as the model of free and selfless action, to be imitated by his devotees.[155] In a *Young India* article of November 1, 1928, Gandhi quoted approvingly extracts from an English correspondent who wrote that the English people's oppression of themselves and others was due to their not heeding the laws of God written in their hearts, the law of their freedom. Since God and his law are one for Gandhi, and Gandhi locates God's presence in the heart, the law of freedom is God's own liberating presence in the human being.[156] God's liberating and saving presence within a person extends to human activity as well, particularly to *yajna* (sacrificial action) which is dedicated to God in service rather than to the self. God works from within those acts to save the performer of such acts, who in turn knows God to be the real performer.[157] That God operates from within human actions and situations to save human beings is affirmed by Gandhi when he refers to the human need of God's grace, the futility of anything without it,[158] and the possibility of everything within that grace.[159]

Swaraj *as the Kingdom of God*

Gandhi's view of *swaraj* was dependent upon his faith, thereby bridging the gap between politics and religion. The state of enslavement was opposed to the laws of God, as inscribed in the laws of nature. It was a basic disorder in God's creation, accounting for other disorders and unrests in India.[160] Gandhi lived for India's freedom and would die for it, because it was part of truth. Only a free India could worship the true God.[161] Therefore, while service was the highest expression of religion, service of the motherland was the best religion.[162] Spiritual liberation was the realization that God alone Is. The realization itself, which comes through the heart, can be brought about only by service. Thus Gandhi's own self-realization in God was bound up necessarily with freedom for India.[163] He further expressed his own dependence on God for winning *swaraj* as follows:

> I have never dreamt that I could win swaraj merely through my effort or assisted only by Hindus. I stand in need of the assistance of Mussalmans, Parsis, Christians, Sikhs, Jews and all other Indians. I need the assistance even of Englishmen. But I know too that all this combined assistance is worthless if I have not the other assistance, that is, from God. All is vain without His help. And if He is with this struggle, no other help is necessary. . . . A satyagrahi has no power he can call his own. All the power he may seem to possess is from and of God.[164]

Gandhi often described *swaraj* in religious terms. It was interior freedom and conformity to the divine statute.[165] As was mentioned in chapter 2, Gandhi's idea of *swaraj* was not merely a transfer of power from British to Indian hands, but a power regulated or informed by the law of right reason, that is, of truth and justice, making for a sense of security for all. This could be described as *Ramarajya,* or the rule of *dharma,* that is, the rule of law.[166] *Ramarajya* was also a synonym for the "Kingdom of Righteousness."[167] Asked why he defined *swaraj* as *Ramraj,* Gandhi replied, "I defined swaraj as Ramraj as I often do because it is a graphic description for a moral government based upon truth and non-violence, in other words, universal religion."[168]

A GANDHIAN THEOLOGICAL ANTHROPOLOGY

Gandhi's political theology of *swaraj* implies a theological anthropology. The human being in theological perspective is an "ideal" type, a mental construct [169] from elements of experience and reality in a logically precise conception. The notion that is used in social sciences as an analytical tool becomes in practical knowledge and reason a standard of measurement, a norm. The theological human being in Gandhi's thought was the ideal type that Gandhi kept before him as a model on which to pattern his life. The ideal type of *homo theologicus* in Gandhi's writings is not an analytical, conceptual category, but a conceptual category of a practical order, affecting Gandhi's very mode of life. It would be an error to equate this ideal type with the factual, historical character of Gandhi. Gandhi believed that for himself, as well as for any persons the perfection of the ideal type could never be attained; but striving toward it was the noblest pursuit to which one could dedicate one's life.

For Gandhi, the human being is essentially "the person before God," and God is existentially "God in faith." God is the creator, Father of the universe; therefore, everything is a living proof of God. If anything exists, God exists. God is even the atheism of the atheist. As that which alone Is, God is absolute truth. As creature and child, the human being is also truth, although relative, a truth in need of "realization." Creation, or existence, is grace, bounty, divine play, *lila.* Everything, including the will to self-realization or truth-realization, is sustained by divine grace. However thin its margin, freedom is real. It defines humans in their existence—in conscious life and selfhood. It also elevates them above the rest of animal creation.

The realization of self, or truth, is a process of conflict, of struggle between good and evil, between God and the Devil. To the extent that the person loves and identifies with goodness, the person is free. In love and goodness there is no room for violence. Identification with, and love of, goodness is implicitly identification with, and love of, the ideal type of person, the human before God. To the extent that the ideal type becomes realized, one realizes truth and freedom, and to that extent becomes less violent. Such a person does not identify the "self" with the body, but treats the body as an instrument of the self or the truth. For the truth, therefore, the person is ready not only to labor and sacrifice but also to die; ready to shed the body rather than to kill in self-defense. This is the way to truth—to self-realization. Living in accordance with relative truth, the only truth to which the human being has access, is the way to bear witness to absolute truth.

In speaking of these things, Gandhi did so from his own experience and striving. The Mahatma as man before God, in worship and faith, can be seen in the words he spoke to the press while breaking his fast in 1939:

> I claim to know my millions. All the 24 hours of the day I am with them. They are my first care and last, because I recognize no God except the God that is to be found in the hearts of the dumb millions. They do not recognize His presence; I do. And I worship the God that is Truth or a Truth which is God through the service of these millions.[170]

"The person before God" is also before all creation as a "representative of God to serve all the lives and thus to express God's dignity and love."[171] This idea Gandhi derived from the peculiarly Hindu belief in the unity of all life, which allows the possibility of salvation not just for human beings, but for all of God's creatures. The human being is not the lord of creation but, rather, the servant of God's creation. The oneness of human life extends to *all forms* of life, which therefore cannot be exploited by human beings for their own purposes.

> Hinduism excludes all exploitation. There is no limit whatsoever to the measure of sacrifice that one may make in order to realize this oneness with all life, but certainly the immensity of the ideal sets a limit to your wants. That, you will see, is the antithesis of the position of the modern civilization which says: "Increase your wants." Those who hold that belief think that increase of wants means an increase of knowledge whereby you understand the Infinite better. On the contrary Hinduism rules out indulgence and multiplication of wants as these hamper one's growth to the ultimate identity with the Universal Self.[172]

God works through earthly and human agents.[173] The human being is God's steward and co-worker, by God's grace, and the conservator of creation. If the human mind is turned Godward, it ultimately merges in God.[174]

> Krishna of the *Gita* is perfection and right knowledge personified; but the picture is imaginary. That does not mean that Krishna, the adored of his people, never lived. But perfection is imagined. The idea of a perfect incarnation is an after-growth. In Hinduism, incarnation is ascribed to one who has performed some extraordinary service to mankind. All embodied life is in reality an incarnation of God, but it is not usual to consider every living being an incarnation. Future generations pay this homage to one who, in his own generation, has been extraordinarily religious in his conduct. I can see nothing wrong in this

procedure; it takes nothing from God's greatness, and there is no violence done to Truth. There is an Urdu saying which means: "Adam is not God but he is a spark of the Divine." And therefore he who is the most religiously behaved has most of the divine spark in him. It is in accordance with this train of thought, that Krishna enjoys, in Hinduism, the status of the most perfect incarnation. The belief in incarnation is a testimony of man's lofty spiritual ambition. Man is not at peace with himself till he has become like unto God. The endeavour to reach this state is the supreme, the only ambition worth having. And this is self-realization. This self-realization is the subject of the *Gita*, as it is of all scriptures. [175]

Elsewhere Gandhi added to this interpretation: "Perfect satyagraha means perfect *avatar*, incarnation, or descent of God." [176]

4

The Way of the Cross as the Way to Swaraj

The Gandhian era in Indian history coincided with a time of great conflict. The questions of the fate of the untouchables and the future of Hindu-Muslim unity were being played out against the background of India's struggle for liberation. In the process of leading India to *swaraj*, Gandhi evolved a unique system of conflict resolution.[1] This system, based on *satyagraha* with its components of *satya, ahimsa,* and *tapasya,* drew heavily upon the Christian model of contrition, repentance, conversion, and reform. While remaining a Hindu, Gandhi extracted much of value from Christian dogma and integrated it into his practices—leaving as his legacy to Christians a challenge to do the same.

In this chapter, following a brief survey of the conceptual framework on which Gandhi's action was based, we shall analyze three specific conflicts. One illustrates the Indo-British conflict, another the Hindu-Muslim conflict, and the third a conflict within Hinduism. We shall conclude with an explication of the Christological elements and features in Gandhi's theory and practice of conflict resolution.

THE GANDHIAN CONCEPTUAL FRAMEWORK FOR CONFLICT RESOLUTION

Satya: *Truth*

Satyagraha (holding onto truth, "truth-force") was Gandhi's way of managing and resolving conflict. But often truth is itself the source of the conflict. How could it also be the way to manage and resolve conflict? The absolute or total truth could not be the source of conflict, for if it were attained in human knowledge there would be no conflict at all. But relative truth is all that is given to human beings, and by its light human problems must be resolved. Gandhi wrote in his *Autobiography*: ". . . as long as I have not realized this Absolute Truth, so long must I hold by the relative truth as I have conceived it. That relative truth must meanwhile be my beacon, my shield and buckler."[2] Gandhi concerned himself more with the way and the means to the absolute truth than with the absolute truth itself. *Satyagraha*, as Gandhi's way and means to the absolute truth, was itself relative truth. *Satyagraha* was a practical confirmation of the relativity of the truth to which we attain. It is remarkable that Gandhi made the source of conflicts also the way to their solution when he applied the relativity of the knowledge of God as truth to social and politicoeconomic conflict solution. N. K. Bose applauds Gandhi for what he effected by making God and truth convertible:

> With this changed creed, he could easily accommodate as fellow-seekers those who looked on Humanity or any other object as their God, and for which they were prepared to sacrifice their all. By enthroning Truth on the highest pedestal, Gandhi thus truly became a catholic, and lost all trace of separateness from every other honest man who worshipped gods other than his own.[3]

If God was truth, "the nearest approach to truth was through love."[4] Human inability to know the absolute truth required an unceasing openness in the approach to those who differed. Since what appears to be truth to one may appear to be error to another, the "pursuit of truth did not admit of violence being inflicted on one's opponent but that he must be weaned from error by patience and sympathy."[5] Holding onto truth nonviolently is a constituent element of *satyagraha*. In other words, nonviolence is a constituent element of truth itself. Gandhi said of *satyagraha* as applying to conflict situations, "It excludes the use of violence because man is not capable of knowing the absolute truth and therefore not competent to punish."[6]

Answering the Hunter commission's inquiry about *satyagraha* and truth, Gandhi, whose final aim was to know and to see God face to face, maintained that it was for the individual to determine the truth in contexts where people's notion of truth differed. He was confident that this course would not lead to confusion in spite of the necessary difference in every honest striving after truth.[7] Gandhi's concept of truth, which is nonabsolute, avoids the practical difficulty of ethical relativism through the introduction of nonviolence as an operative principle of *satyagraha* in interpersonal relations and conflicts.[8]

In making nonviolence an operative principle of *satyagraha*, Gandhi adopted the social and moral criteria for judging the truth in a given situation. Truth is that which brings about agreement or community—that in which the many meet and in which differences are resolved.[9] Conversely, that which brings about community or agreement is truth. In an individual world of relative truth, society is the objective standard of truth or the standard of objective truth.[10] The truth that is not absolute relates to and partakes of human needs, and hence the individual's search for truth takes place in terms of the community of which he or she is a part. In Gandhi's words, "The quest for Truth cannot be prosecuted in a cave,"[11] that is, the relation of truth to community implies, for Gandhi, the absence of secrecy. Secrecy, implying privacy of knowledge and action, is an exclusion or minimization of the community of knowledge and action, and as such it is a violation of the integrity of truth. Only within a framework of the integrity of truth is individual integrity attainable. Hence there is no room for secrecy in *satyagraha*.[12] The sociological nature of Gandhi's theory and perception of truth and knowledge is obvious. Gandhi's truth is not static, but dynamic faith and action arrived at through *ahimsa*.

Ahimsa: *Nonviolence*

Ahimsa, in its Buddhist, Jain, and Hindu contexts, stands for noninjury to living beings, the attitude of the will not to injure, and in its broadest connotation all action that eschews injury to living beings. Gandhi refined its meaning by applying the term to human and social interactions especially, and by introducing the positive connotation of *ahimsa* as love:

> *Ahimsa* is not the crude thing it has been made to appear. Not to hurt any living thing is no doubt a part of *ahimsa*. But it is its least expression. The principle of *ahimsa* is hurt by every evil thought, by undue haste, by lying, by hatred, by wishing ill to anybody.[13]

> I accept the interpretation of Ahimsa namely that it is not merely a negative state of harmlessness but it is a positive state of love, of doing good even to the evil doer. But it does not mean helping the evil-doer to continue the wrong or tolerating it by passive acquiescence. On the contrary, love, the active state of Ahimsa, requires you to resist the wrong-doer by dissociating yourself from him even though it may offend him or injure him physically.[14]

Joan Bondurant, in *Conquest of Violence: The Gandhian Philosophy of Conflict*, has called attention to the "proximity of this concept to the Christian charity and to the Greek *agape*,"[15] noting that positive action, a Constructive Program, is required for every *satyagraha*. Thus the truth-love combination is the nucleus of the Gandhian solution to the problem of means. Gandhi wrote:

> . . . without *ahimsa* it is not possible to seek and find Truth. *Ahimsa* and Truth are so intertwined that it is practically impossible to disentangle and separate them. They are like the two sides of a coin, or rather of a smooth unstamped metallic disc. Who can say, which is the obverse, and which is the reverse? Nevertheless *ahimsa* is the means; Truth is the end. Means to be means must always be within our reach, and so *ahimsa*

is our supreme duty. If we take care of the means, we are bound to reach the end sooner or later. When once we have grasped this point, final victory is beyond question.[16]

Even while admitting the difficulty of its practice,[17] Gandhi made strict adherence to *ahimsa* the criterion and the test of one's truth and truthfulness. Nonviolence in this sense is at once a supreme moral value and the norm of truthful action and of social truths.[18] One's social action should not injure anyone, indeed, the ideal of *ahimsa* was that one may not harbor an uncharitable thought even against those who consider themselves as one's enemies. Would-be members of Gandhi's ashram had to accept and strive after this level of *ahimsa*.[19]

Tapasya: *Self-Suffering*

The deeper meaning of *ahimsa*, or nonviolence in action, is self-suffering, the acceptance of pain within oneself instead of its infliction on the opponent. Such submission to pain is of the very nature of the love that is *ahimsa*. "Love never claims, it ever gives. Love ever suffers, never resents, never revenges itself."[20] And again, "The test of love is *tapasya* and *tapasya* means self-suffering."[21] Thus Gandhi saw active nonviolence as conscious suffering.[22]

Satyagraha as "truth-force" is expressed in the individual as self-suffering. Self-suffering is not a "meek submission to the will of the evil-doer, but it means the pitting of one's whole soul against the will of the tyrant. Working under this law of our being, it is possible for a single individual to defy the whole might of an unjust empire."[23] The suffering is the penalty for refusal to submit to the will of the tyrant. In preferring suffering to submission to evil, one is at once suffering for truth and justice and identifying oneself with truth, thus affirming one's indivisibility from truth at the very point of self-sacrifice. The human and the divine dignity of the individual is thus established by voluntary self- suffering.

Whereas *tapasya* as penance was an ancient and rather self-centered practice in India, Gandhi turned it inside out by de-centering the self. In Gandhi's version the penitent concentrated on another's self, for whose moral persuasion and conversion the penance was undertaken. Just as nonsubmission to evil was a model for action, so *tapasya* was a model for suffering, or "passion."

Self-suffering is not an inability to use violence, but a viable choice in the face of violence. It is not the weapon of the weak, drawn from the armory of cowardice, to be deployed indiscriminately. "Suffering injury in one's own person is . . . of the essence of non-violence and is the chosen substitute for violence to others."[24]

Expediency is not ruled out in the choice of self-suffering, but if *satyagraha* is to be true to its name in conflict situations, self-suffering and voluntary submission to injury are not a last resort, but a policy choice made early in the course of the conflict. Initially *satyagraha* may involve the sacrifice of many lives, but in the long run the loss of life through self-suffering will be less than that through the alternative of violence. Life lost in self-suffering ennobles the voluntary victims while enriching the world by their example.[25]

Gandhi took care to distinguish self-suffering from passive resistance. The latter implied a physical incapacity to resort to violence combined with an inner compulsion or drive toward violence.[26] Passive resistance was therefore the "non-violence of the weak." Gandhi spoke of the ambiguities of passive resistance as follows:

> Passive resistance may be offered side by side with the use of arms. Satyagraha and brute force, being each a negation of the other, can never go together. In passive resistance there is always present an idea of harassing the other party and there is a simultaneous readiness to undergo any hardships entailed upon us by such activity; while in Satyagraha there is not the remotest idea of injuring the opponent. Satyagraha postulates the conquest of the adversary by suffering in one's own person.[27]

Gandhi's self-suffering nonviolence presupposed the courage to take up arms in the face of a threat or danger. Cowardice and nonviolence were poles apart. "I do believe," wrote Gandhi, "that where there is only a choice between cowardice and violence, I would advise violence."[28] Nonviolent conduct is never demoralizing, cowardice always is.[29] Further:"Non-violence cannot be taught to a person who fears to die and has no power of resistance. . . . He harbors violence and hatred in his heart and would kill his enemy if he could without hurting himself. He is a stranger to non-violence."[30] Courage, which was the prerequisite for self-suffering, was as much a matter of nurture and training as the arts of violence and warfare were. "The votary of non-violence has to cultivate the capacity for sacrifice of the highest type in order to be free from fear. . . . He who has not overcome all fear cannot practice *ahimsa* to perfection."[31]

Satyagraha *as Contritional-Conversional Model of Conflict Resolution*

The analysis of *satyagraha* into its component concepts of *satya*, *ahimsa*, and *tapasya* (truth, nonviolence, and self-suffering) illuminates the potential in *satyagraha* for several stages in the winning over of an opponent in any given conflict. The first stage is persuasion through reasoning, which would correspond to the level of *satya*. The second stage is emotional persuasion through suffering, in an attempt to capture the heart of the opponent. This would correspond to *tapasya*. Third, if persuasion through both reason and emotion fail, the *satyagrahi* may resort to nonviolent coercion through acts of noncooperation and civil disobedience.[32] This would correspond to the level of *ahimsa*. However, these three levels are not mutually exclusive in Gandhi's theory, so that any or all levels could be present simultaneously in a given conflict situation.

Irrespective of which levels of appeal are present in a conflict, Gandhi's model of conflict resolution can be identified as contritional, penitential, or conversional, and hence Christological. Insofar as contrition, penitence, and conversion are religio-spiritual experiences, Gandhi bridges the gap between religion and politics in his model for conflict resolution.

In this context, it is useful to recall the young Gandhi's own contrite confession to his father, and the latter's tears of trust, grief, and self-affliction washing the boy's conscience clean as the experiential base of Gandhi's approach to conflicts (see p. 9, above). To understand the Christological moorings of this approach, we must focus attention on the Catholic ritual of sacramental penance. The ritual of penitence involves a frank confession of moral failure to a priest, who represents Christ, after which the priest pronounces the words of absolution and pardon in Christ's name. Contrition of some sort is indeed presupposed, even if only at the level of a selfish guilt-feeling over the wrongdoing. Pardon and absolution are pronounced as derived from the power of the passion and death of Christ. The voluntary sufferings of the sinless Christ, by whose merits the sinner is forgiven, perfects the penitent's contrition, and the very reconciliation with Christ prompts the penitent sinner to reform his or her life. The initiative for this repentance rests not with the penitent, but with Christ and his sufferings.

Although Gandhi did not avow any Christian influence in his boyhood confession, implicit in the interpretation of it in his autobiography is the Catholic rite of penance. His father's tears mirror Christ's gracious initiative with regard to those who have strayed. In Gandhi's later years the roles of self-sufferer, reconciler, and reformer, as exemplified by Christ and by Gandhi's father, were appropriated by the Mahatma. Gandhi enlarged their scope in his application of the principle of vicarious suffering to situations of socio-political conflicts and their resolution. In doing so, Gandhi took over the role of the vicarious sufferer who, by that very suffering, is able to challenge the lives, attitudes, and actions of individuals and societies and to initiate repentance and reform through admission of the wrongness of the previously espoused lives, attitudes, and actions. Furthermore, Gandhi overcame the limitation of the age-old Indian doctrine of *karma*, with its moral world of exclusively individual retribution, by extending the individualist implications of *karma* to the level of society as a whole. He believed that all people were related and united both in sin and in salvation. Hence the sin of one person is the sin of all, and the liberation of one person is the redemption of humankind. Both sin and salvation are communal realities, communal experiences.

Inflictors of suffering are ignorant of their victims' kinship to them. If they realized this kinship, they could not continue to inflict the suffering. The victimized member of society has to bring his oppressors to that recognition through suffering. The use of suffering as a method is preferable to the use of violence in that it allows the preservation of the spiritual unity and kinship of all people.

The practice of exclusive possession and enjoyment of material goods hinders the realization of spiritual unity. It is an act of violence to, and theft from, the truth of spiritual, familial unity. The remedy for this malaise must consist of return, or homecoming (*moksha*) to the spiritual truth (self-realization) in community, through acts, first, of renunciation of what was stolen and, second, of restoration of the same to the community. This is the active hermeneutic role in social history of the observance of the five *yamas*, namely, *ahimsa, satya, asteya, brahmacharya*, and *asangraha* (nonviolence, truth, nonstealing, celibacy, and nonpossessiveness).

In the face of those who ignore the spiritual unity of humankind, anyone who witnesses to that unity by a life of renunciation, restoration, and voluntary suffering is a savior and truly a son of God. If one suffers and lays down one's life in witness to spiritual unity under God, that life is precious to humanity. It challenges, inspires, instructs, and enables others to attain their own redemption through a process of contrition, repentance, conversion, or reform.

Christ was to Gandhi an ideal *satyagrahi* whom he could imitate even in the realm of sociopolitical conflict and its resolution in truth. To illustrate this, let us analyze three conflict situations[33] and then explicate in Gandhi's own words the Christological principles that were operational therein.

ANALYSES OF CONFLICT SITUATIONS

The Salt Satyagraha (1930-31)

The Salt *Satyagraha* was a part of the civil disobedience movement from March 1930 to March 1931. Headquartered in Bombay, it was a national movement launching *satyagraha* in every province.

Its immediate objective was the rescinding of the Salt Laws, which made the salt market a government monopoly; the tax on salt was especially hard on the poor. Gandhi's ultimate objective in the Salt *Satyagraha* was the same as that of the civil disobedience movement in general, namely, *purna swaraj* (complete independence). Gandhi chose the Salt Laws for the purpose because "they not only appeared to be basically unjust in themselves, but because they symbolized an unpopular, unrepresentative, and alien government. British official sources described the object of the *satyagraha* as 'nothing less than to cause a complete paralysis of the administrative machinery.' "[34]

In an initial protest against the Salt Laws, Gandhi led members of his Ahmedabad ashram on a two-hundred-mile march on foot to Dandi, on the western coast of India. As the movement grew, participants included Indians throughout the country—Hindus and Muslims, men and women.

"Thousands of . . . [women]—many being of good family and high educational attainments—suddenly emerged from the seclusion of their homes and in some instances actually from *purdah*,* in order to join Congress demonstrations and assist in picketing."[35] Governmental sources noted with concern the active sympathy and financial support given by the Hindu mercantile and industrial community. The *satyagrahis* soon found themselves ranged against government officials supported by the police force (both British and Indian) and by units of the army.

The organization of the civil disobedience movement, which had been delegated by the congress to Gandhi, reflected the organizational structure of the congress. The congress president—then Jawaharlal Nehru—was given extensive powers to act on behalf of the executive committee in case it could not meet. He was empowered to nominate a successor in the event of his arrest. The successor had the power of nominating another in turn. Provincial leaders were given the necessary powers to foster the continuity of the movement. *Khadi* (hand-spun cloth) was made the uniform for congress and the movement. Since there was no remuneration for participants or their families, it was "constructive work" for members of the congress to be engaged in civil disobedience, to be in prison, or to be at the spinning wheel or "some constructive work advancing Swaraj."

Preparation for the civil disobedience movement included the training of unarmed volunteers to control large crowds; the choice of the Salt Laws for violation; the instructing of the people in the principles of *satyagraha*, the objectives of the Salt *Satyagraha*, and the necessity for engaging in constructive work; abstinence from intoxicants; the renouncing of untouchability; the pledge of *satyagraha* to be taken by all who joined the movement, even to the point of being jailed or suffering in other ways; seeking no monetary help for one's family from congress funds; obeying implicitly the orders of those in charge of the campaign.

The preliminary action for the Salt *Satyagraha* as the vehicle to launch the whole civil disobedience movement for *purna swaraj* included notice of the congress's intention to agitate for independence through civil disobedience; and Gandhi's letter to the viceroy, Lord Irwin, detailing to him the grievances of the people and describing the *satyagraha* plan to be implemented if there were no negotiated settlement of the grievances.[36]

The actual implementation of the Salt *Satyagraha* encompassed a series of actions:

1. On March 12 Gandhi and his *satyagrahis* commenced the march to Dandi, inviting people all along the way to participate in the action and in other nonviolent constructive programs.

2. The *satyagrahis* reached Dandi on April 5, and the next day, after prayer, they prepared sea salt on the beach, which was a technical breach of the Salt Laws.

*The veil worn by women to shield them from observation by strangers.

3. In a statement to the press, Gandhi announced that it was then open to anyone who would risk prosecution to manufacture salt wherever they wished.

4. To instruct the people in the meaning of the salt-tax violation and the methods of preparing salt, leaflets were issued throughout the country.

5. People responded with such enthusiasm to violations of the salt ban that, in Nehru's words, salt-making spread like a prairie fire and he felt ashamed "for having questioned the efficacy of this method when it was first proposed by Gandhiji."

6. All over India shops observed *hartal* to protest the arrests of the leaders.

7. Jawaharlal Nehru was arrested on April 14. His father succeeded him as president of the congress; and Gandhi, arrested on May 5, was replaced by Abbas Tyabji.

8. Village headmen and other subordinate officers resigned their posts in large numbers in sympathy with the *satyagrahis*.

9. In many places symbolic acts, such as throwing a copy of the Salt Acts into the sea at Bombay, were performed to demonstrate the death of the British law in the land.

10. In a few places, among them Bardoli, people refused to pay the salt tax.

11. Riots erupted in some places, although leaders worked to preserve the nonviolent nature of the movement. The movement was not suspended because of the violence, but Gandhi refused to recognize as *satyagrahis* those who did not fulfill their pledge.

12. After the march to Dandi, Gandhi wrote a second letter to the viceroy, stating that his next move would be to take possession of the government-operated Dharasana Salt Works. Such action could be prevented by removal of the salt tax—or by the arrest of every *satyagrahi* in India.

13. Throughout the nonviolent raid on Dharasana, the *satyagrahis* refrained from striking the police or even from deflecting their blows. Instead they rushed onto the salt pans, wave upon wave, and even pleaded with the police to join them. In some instances the police refused to continue the assault on the *satyagrahis*.[37]

14. When the onset of the monsoon season necessitated a halt of the raids on salt works, disobedience took the form of a boycott of foreign products, particularly of cloth and liquor. Shops selling imported goods were persistently picketed.

15. The special ordinances of the government suppressing publicity and assembly rights were consistently disobeyed by *satyagrahis*, many of whom were arrested.

16. After continuing manifestations of noncooperation and civil disobedience, and the government's declared intention to "fight it with all our strength," talks between Gandhi and the viceroy, Lord Irwin, ended in a settlement marked by modification of the salt regulations and release of all imprisoned *satyagrahis*.

The immediate objective of the Salt *Satyagraha* was realized to a large

extent by a new official interpretation of the Salt Laws, which allowed residents of villages adjoining salt-producing areas to make salt for domestic use
and local sale. In other provisions of the Gandhi-Irwin Pact, the government
agreed to grant amnesty to all convicted of nonviolent offenses of the civil
disobedience, to withdraw the restraining ordinances, and to restore confis-
cated, forfeited, or attached properties. In return civil disobedience, including publications in support of it and attempts to influence civil and military
servants or village officials against the government, was to be discontinued.
The constitutional provisions of the agreement included the assurance that in
future discussions on constitutional reform, representatives of the congress
would be invited to take part, and that the next Round Table Conference
would take up questions of federation, reservation of portfolios in the government, financial credit, and the position of the minorities.

The Poona "Fast Unto Death" (1932)

Gandhi's fast of September 1932 was the dramatic beginning of his *satyagraha* against untouchability, triggering a whole series of social reforms
throughout the country.

The immediate objective of the fast was to secure the reversal of the British
government's decision that the depressed classes would form a separate electorate.[38] The ultimate objective was nothing less than the total abolition of
untouchability. Gandhi and other reformers found themselves in opposition
not only to the British government but also to tradition-bound orthodox Hindus and interpreters of the *Shastras* (written tradition), as well as some representatives of the depressed classes themselves (notably R. D. Ambedkar) who
opposed other caste Hindus, thus helping to perpetuate the caste system.

Gandhi's preparation for the fast was more interior than exterior. He told
the people, "If the Hindu mass mind is not yet prepared to banish untouchability root and branch, it must sacrifice me without the slightest hesitation."[39]
To Sarojini Naidu, one of his associates, he wrote that the call to the fast had
been so sudden and peremptory that there was little time to prepare the people for it: "There was no call from within for years. But the [British] Cabinet's decision [to make the depressed classes a separate electorate] came like a
violent alarm waking me from my slumber and telling me this is the time."[40]
And thus seizing the psychological moment, Gandhi implored the blessing of
friends on his decision rather than seeking their opinion or counsel.

Gandhi's first announcement of his intention to sacrifice his life by a fast
unto death was made in the Round Table Conference where a separate electorate for the depressed classes had become a controversial subject, following
the official recognition, on August 17, of the depressed classes as a minority
community and a separate electorate. Gandhi wrote to the British prime
minister, Ramsay MacDonald, informing him that he would embark on "a
perpetual fast unto death from food of any kind" from noon of September

20. That fast, he added, would cease "if during its progress the British Government, of its own motion or under pressure of public opinion, revise their decision and withdraw their scheme of communal electorates for the 'depressed' classes."[41] Gandhi also made a statement to the press concerning his resolve to fast unto death in opposition to the separate communal electorates for the untouchables and, should it actually continue until death, as his ultimate protest against untouchability itself.

The conditions outlined by Gandhi in his letter to the prime minister were fulfilled by the sixth day of the fast, and so Gandhi broke the fast then. The constructive work of the anti-untouchability *satyagraha*, however, continued and occupied Gandhi's attention very nearly to the exclusion of all else. From the time of the fast the congress made removal of untouchability part of its official policy.

The results of the Poona fast may be summarized as follows:

1. The summoning of a conference by Pandit Madan Mohan Malaviya, which met first at Bombay and then at Poona, with Dr. Ambedkar being persuaded to join it.

2. The Poona Pact, according to which a common electorate for *all* Hindus was agreed upon, subject to two conditions: first, 148 seats in the provincial legislatures were to be reserved for the depressed classes (instead of the 71 previously theirs), and 18 percent of the seats in the central legislature allotted to the general electorate for British India were to be reserved for them; second, there was to be a primary for the voters of the depressed classes alone, in which four candidates would be selected for each reserved seat; the election by the general (Hindu) constituencies was restricted to these alone.

3. The ratification of the Poona Pact by the Hindu Mahasabha and acceptance of it by the British government, which amended the constitution to incorporate the provisions of the Poona Pact.

4. The launching of the anti-untouchability campaign by Gandhi immediately after the ending of his fast.

5. The passing of the Bombay Resolution* by Hindu leaders, under the chairmanship of Malaviya, on September 25, 1932, rejecting untouchability in principle and giving statutory status to the abolition of social disabilities imposed on the so-called untouchable classes, including the bar on their admission to temples.[42]

---

*The text reads: "The Conference resolves that, henceforth, amongst Hindus no one shall be regarded as an untouchable by reason of his birth and that those who have been so regarded hitherto will have the same right as other Hindus in regard to the use of the public wells, public schools, public roads and all other public institutions. This right shall have statutory recognition at the first opportunity and shall be one of the earliest Acts of Swaraj Parliament, if it shall not have received such recognition before that time.

"It is further agreed that it shall be the duty of all Hindu leaders to secure, by every legitimate and peaceful means, an early removal of all social disabilities now imposed by custom upon the so-called untouchable classes, including the bar in respect to admission to temples." (As quoted in Majumdar, *The History and Culture of the Indian People*, 11: 523.)

6. The throwing open of many public wells throughout India to the erstwhile untouchable classes, thanks to the appeal of Gandhi and the other Hindu leaders.

7. The founding of the *Harijan* Sevak Sangh, with G. D. Birla as president and Amritlal Thakkar of the Servants of India Society as secretary, to work actively for the abolition of untouchability.

8. The commencement of a twenty-one-day fast by Gandhi for purification of himself and his associates for their "greater vigilance and watchfulness in connection with the Harijan cause," which also led, incidentally, to Gandhi's unconditional release by the government from jail.

9. The launching of *Harijan*, a periodical in three languages, dedicated to social reform.*

10. Gandhi's call to the congress to suspend the mass civil disobedience movement, which effectively ended it. Thereafter it would be resumed only as individual civil disobedience.[43]

Gandhi was well aware that the Poona Pact was only a beginning: "The agony of the soul is not going to end until every trace of untouchability is gone. . . . I shall undergo as many fasts as are necessary in order to purify Hinduism of this unbearable taint."[44] Although the British government accepted only the fact of a common electorate for all Hindus, Gandhi assured the depressed classes that he was "wedded to the whole of that Agreement" and that they could hold his life "as hostage for its due fulfillment."[45] The twenty-one-day fast immediately following the "fast unto death" was undertaken as a sign of Gandhi's earnestness in this undertaking. Not only had the immediate objective of the "fast unto death" been accomplished, but the nation as a whole was made joltingly alive to the problem of untouchability and all the social evil implied in it.

The Last Fast: For Hindu-Muslim Unity (1948)

The fast in Delhi, commencing on January 13, 1948, was Gandhi's last great action, or "passion," before his death two weeks later from an assassin's bullet.[46]

Gandhi's immediate objective in the fast was the restoration of freedom of residence and of movement for Muslims in the Delhi area. His ultimate objective was a perfect communal harmony between Hindus and Muslims, specifically in Delhi but ultimately for Hindus and Muslims everywhere and for friendly relations between India and the new country of Pakistan.

Gandhi acted alone in deciding upon the fast. However, both government and religious leaders worked to bring about a program of action designed to fulfill the goals of Gandhi's fast. Active in this way were Jawaharlal Nehru, Abul Kalam Azad, Sardar Patel, Delhi's chief of police and his deputy,

---

*The three editions were *Harijan* (in English), *Harijan Sevak* (in Hindi), and *Harijanbandhu* (in Gujarati).

and representatives of the Hindu Mahasabha and the R.S.S. The home of Rajendra Prasad, president of the congress, was the venue of prolonged negotiations in Delhi. Opposition to this fast came primarily from a group of fanatical Hindu nationalists.

As primarily an individual act, Gandhi's last fast is difficult to analyze under the aspect of organization. Whatever organization might result had to come from the consciences of all to whom the fast was directed. The preparation for this fast was also of an interior and spiritual order. Gandhi consulted no one, and it came as a surprise to all. Although there was a lull in Hindu–Muslim tensions then, Gandhi still sensed a spirit of interreligious killing abroad in the land. He brooded over it for several days:

> It was only when in terms of human effort I had exhausted all resources . . . that I put my head on God's lap. . . . God sent me the fast. . . . Let our sole prayer be that God may vouchsafe me strength of spirit during the fast that the temptation to live may not lead me into the hasty or premature termination of the fast.[47]

The decision to fast in January 1948 left Gandhi with a feeling of happiness for the first time in months.[48] Gone was his sense of helplessness in the face of recent events. India had become independent, and the Muslim-majority areas of India had become self-governing as Pakistan (divided into East and West Pakistan and separated from each other by over one thousand miles). In Muslim Pakistan, however, there were many millions of Hindus and Sikhs. The frontier that divided India and Pakistan also separated factories from raw materials and crops from markets. The army was divided; the treasury was to be divided. The non-Muslims of Pakistan feared for their future and the Muslims still within India lived in anxiety. Fighting broke out between the dominant majorities and the frightened minorities in each country. Calcutta was torn by riots.

On August 31, 1947, an attempt was made on the life of Gandhi, who was staying in a Muslim home in Calcutta at the time. Although his presence had not forestalled religious hatred, Gandhi hoped that a fast by him at that time would have an effect.[49] If it touched the heart of Calcutta, it could touch the hearts of all warring factions in the Punjab. Peace returned to Calcutta by the third day of that fast. (Even five hundred of the policemen in the city had observed a twenty-four-hour fast in sympathy with Gandhi.)

On September 7, 1947, Gandhi left Calcutta for New Delhi en route to the Punjab. But Delhi was itself raging with riots as Hindu and Sikh refugees were pouring in, fleeing from strife in the Punjab. Dr. Zakir Hussain and his Jamia Millia Islamia were threatened by the engulfing sea of angry Hindus and Sikhs. Gandhi's visit to Delhi helped to restore calm. He visited several refugee camps without armed escort. Asked on one occasion, by an anti-Muslim partisan, whether or not Hinduism permitted the killing of an evil-doer, Gandhi answered that one evildoer may not punish another. He addressed prayer meetings every day, appealing for trust and humanity and the banishment of fear and hatred. Attending a Sikh celebration, Gandhi condemned their violence against the Muslims. As a Hindu, he was stern with Hindus.[50] Politicians no longer seemed to heed his advice in party and governmental affairs. They were more concerned with their own power or efforts to attain it while Gandhi was proposing programs to remove the political corruption that threatened to strangulate independence at its very birth.[51] By early January 1948 the killings in Delhi had ceased, but the fact that eminent Muslims like Dr. Zakir Hussain and Shaheed Suhrawardy of Bengal could not move about Delhi as freely as he himself did left Gandhi in an "agony." He felt helpless—and never in his life had he put up with helplessness.

And so the fast sent him "by God" in January 1948 brought Gandhi a measure of inner peace. This fast—for Hindu-Muslim unity— was total. He abstained even from drinking water. He knew that no fast weakened one within the first twenty-four hours, but doctors warned him that if he did survive a total fast, his health would be permanently impaired. To a man staking his very life, however, good health and ill health were not matters of concern. He walked to address the prayer meetings on the first and second days. Thereafter he could not walk, and spoke into the microphone from his bed. His voice was getting feebler day by day. On the third day he dictated a reminder to the India Union government to pay immediately to the government of Pakistan its share of the assets from the partition of India. Long queues of people filed past the emaciated Gandhi day after day, in veneration and prayer, with sobs and tears. Nehru too came—and wept. In his prayer messages, which were read out for him after the third day, Gandhi warned of the danger to all India if religious strife continued in Delhi. He asked the people to leave him in God's hands, and to turn the searchlight inward upon themselves. He requested that people not ask him to terminate his fast, unless in their journey of life they had "turned deliberately from Satan to God."[52]

Upon the pledges of all leaders in Delhi to maintain nonviolent peace in the city, Gandhi broke the fast on January 18, 1948, amid readings from the Scriptures of several faiths and the chanting of multireligious hymns. Gandhi interpreted the pledges given him as meaning that "come what may, there will be complete friendship between the Hindus, Moslems, Sikhs, Christians, and Jews, a friendship not to be broken."[53] Some dissidents quickly repudiated their pledges, however, and on the second day after the conclusion of the fast, Gandhi narrowly escaped death when a young man threw a bomb at him at the prayer meeting.

The immediate results of Gandhi's fast were:

1. The pledge taken by all representatives of non-Muslims to respect life, property, and faith of the Muslims, which included: permitting Muslims to hold their annual fair near Delhi in safety; ensuring freedom of movement for Muslims in Delhi; restoring to the Muslims the mosques taken over by Hindus and Sikhs; respecting the areas set apart for Muslims; doing all this by

the personal efforts of the signatories and without the aid of police or armed forces.

2. Hindu-Muslim fraternization, such as a procession of 150 Muslim residents of Subzimandi being given an ovation and the Muslims being feted by the Hindus of the locality.

3. The paying over of monetary assets owed to Pakistan by India.

4. The ending of communal tensions in many areas outside Delhi as well as in the city. Sir Muhammad Zafrulla Khan, the foreign minister of Pakistan, for instance, informed the United Nations Security Council that "a new and tremendous wave of feeling and desire for friendship between the two dominions is sweeping the subcontinent in response to the fast."[54]

Gandhi's fast was indirectly the cause of his assassination, the very success of the fast having roused the anger of some fanatics to conspire against him under the misguided motivation of defending Hinduism from its internal enemy—Gandhi! His death only sealed, in his blood, the cause for which he had fasted, to reconcile Hindus and Muslims. In his death he also reconciled the two great leaders Jawaharlal Nehru and Vallabhbhai Patel, who did not see eye to eye, likewise sealing their unity by his own blood. Pyarelal called Gandhi's death "the one perfect act of his life." Nehru, in his tribute, said that "the light that shone in this country was no ordinary light. The light that has illumined this country for these many years will illumine this country for many more years, and a thousand years later that light will still be seen in this country, and the world will see it and it will give solace to innumerable hearts."[55]

GANDHIAN CHRISTOLOGY

Christology can be seen from two points of view—as description or as prescription. For Gandhi, the descriptive aspect, which takes the form of worship and dogma, is subservient to the prescriptive aspect, which consists of imitation of Christ or moral identification with him as manifesting the underlying truth of the spiritual unity of all humankind. As we have noted, Gandhi saw Christ as an ideal *satyagrahi*.

Gandhi's Christology can be discovered in the context of the Christian concept of service to one's fellow humans, which was a guiding principle of his life. Gandhi's search through *satyagraha* was not for his own salvation, but for communal growth in truth, involving whole races and peoples converging in mutual recognition and love. As James Douglass points out:

When God is sought as truth, he draws the seekers into a growing community of love. The concrete way in which Gandhi suffered toward this community of seeking men is the point at which his experiments coincide most perfectly with the life and death of Christ.[56]

According to Douglass, the significance of Gandhi can be seen in the authentically Christian terms of a socially and politically active suffering love.[57] (Gandhi once wrote: "To me God is Truth and love. . . . He is long-suffering.")

A Christology inspired by the spirit or self-understanding of Jesus, as that self-understanding is appropriated in faith, must recognize in Gandhi's discipleship to—and imitation of—truth or self-sacrificing love, an eminent example of what Karl Rahner terms "anonymous Christianity."[58] Gandhi's own self-understanding, as dedicated to truth and self-sacrificing love, implicitly reproduces a central aspect of Jesus' own self-understanding. In other words, the Hindu Gandhi fulfilled in his life the injunction of St. Paul to the Christians of Philippi: "In your minds you must be the same as Christ Jesus" (Phil. 2:5). It is noteworthy in this connection that the popular association of Gandhi in India was not so much with the great names in the world's political history, but with the great names in the religious history of the world.[59] As influential as he was in shaping the political history of the country, Gandhi was looked upon primarily as a man of faith.

Servant of God

Gandhi saw himself primarily as a servant of God and thus a servant of humanity. The report of the Thirty-ninth Indian National Congress (1924) quotes him as tracing the value of his life to this calling: "My time is valuable, for I deem myself a servant of God."[60] As early as his South African days, on the occasion of the birth of the disobedience pledge, Gandhi had referred to himself as "an adviser and servant of the community."[61]

Likewise, on the occasion of his fast for the *harijan* cause in 1933, Gandhi answered the critical appeals of General Smuts, Rajagopalachari, Dr. Ansari, and his own son, Devadas, as follows:

> My claim to hear the voice of God is no new claim. Unfortunately there is no way that I know of proving the claim except through results. God will not be God if He allowed Himself to be object of proof by His creatures. But He does give His willing slave the power to pass through the fiercest of ordeals. I have been a willing slave to this most exacting Master for more than half a century. His voice has been increasingly audible as the years have rolled by.[62]

Gandhi saw the task of bringing about a change of heart in the millions of caste Hindus as God's own work, the achievement of the eradication of untouchability being beyond the limits of human power by itself: "Man cannot acquire such power even by self-purification or penance. By these means he merely becomes an instrument in the hands of God. He can do nothing more. I am experiencing this every day and every moment, and that makes me more and more humble."[63]

Gandhi sought to inculcate this same self-understanding in his fellow Indians, particularly in the members of his ashram. His idea of servanthood of God and humankind was not exclusive but was, at least potentially, universal. We see it illustrated in his talk at prayer to the members of his ashram: "We are going to become servants—servants of India, servants of the world, and through these means, servants of God. It is through this humble service that we shall catch a glimpse of God."[64] Gandhi spelled out the meaning of this servanthood of God in terms of the subordination and obedience of the human will to God's. Thus in a letter to a friend, Emma Harker, he wrote, "God does not do as we will, but on the contrary, He bends us to His will. Let us therefore bend ourselves voluntarily to the will of that Imperial Taskmaster."[65] Gandhi also stated that votaries of *ahimsa* do nothing of their own will; all their actions are prompted by God.[66]

As a union of wills, Gandhi's servanthood to God precluded any distance between God and himself. Servanthood implied reliance on the strength of the Master and avowal of one's own weakness and helplessness in fulfilling any task apart from one's God-given strength. Thus, even in the political context of being commissioned to attend the second Round Table Conference in London as the sole representative of the congress, Gandhi could state:

I must go to London with God as my only guide. He is a jealous Lord. He will allow no one to share His authority. One has therefore to appear before Him in all one's weakness, empty-handed and in a spirit of full surrender, and then He enables you to stand before a whole world and protects you from all harm.[67]

And further, God is "always at the service of his devotees; He is ever the Servant of His servants. He justifies the devotee's faith."[68]

Atonement

Satyagraha in the form of atonement is made possible by the presence of God in all. God is the power that unites and reconciles where there has been division and enmity. He uses those who are comparatively more pure to atone for those who are less pure. Thus in the context of the anti-untouchability campaign, Gandhi could state: "The vicarious penance of the comparatively pure is needed to bring about a change in the hearts of both *savarnas* and *Harijans*."[69] Gandhi's faith in God's saving presence in all people was at the source of his concept of *satyagraha*. With reference to this presence of God, Gandhi wrote:

From this it follows that the sin of one is the sin of all. And hence it is not up to us to destroy the evil-doer. We should, on the contrary, suffer for him. From this thought was born the idea of satyagraha and of civil disobedience of law. Criminal, violent or uncivil disobedience is sin and ought to be abjured. Non-violent disobedience can be a holy duty.[70]

There are, however, limits to atonement. "Atonement is possible only when some error is committed in ignorance." And hence "there can be no atonement for untruth spoken knowingly. Or the only possible atonement would be never to do so again."[71] Atonement is meant to effect true repentance, to reform one's life. Thus "there can be no absolution from the sin of telling a lie knowingly no matter how severe the *prayashchitta* [penance] one undergoes for it. *Prayashchitta* wins forgiveness only for one who has told a lie in ignorance."[72] Since the presence of God is the source of all atonement, atonement is possible only for those who are wedded to truth and are standing in God's presence. Being wedded to truth and standing in God's presence are incompatible with deliberate untruth or sin. *Satyagraha's* role is to remove ignorance and thus to remove the sin.

Gandhi's commitment to truth found expression as self-suffering, through which he hoped to influence wrongdoers to reexamine their actions, removing the veil of ignorance that caused them to sin. As one wedded to truth and standing in God's presence, Gandhi was sensitive to the presence of violence and animosity; such evidence of sin caused in him intolerable pain. Believing that "nothing is impossible for those who are prepared to suffer,"[73] Gandhi turned his suffering to the constructive task of atonement—as seen in his many *satyagraha* campaigns and especially in the three conflict situations analyzed above. Given the universality of God's presence in humankind, such atonement could not remain merely a religious experience but must lead to transformations in the social and political spheres as well.

Incarnation of God

What is the relation of the sufferer for truth—the servant of God who makes atonement for the sin of all—to God? Is that person the incarnation of God? Many Hindus did regard the Mahatma as an incarnation of Vishnu. Louis Fischer records an instance in which a man asked Gandhi, at a prayer speech some days before his assassination, to declare himself an incarnation of God; Gandhi, tired from a fast ended less than forty-eight hours earlier, replied to him with a smile, "Sit down and be quiet."[74]

Hindu belief held that a number of historical figures had been incarnations, or avatars, of God, as well as that God had descended in various animal forms. Since human beings are incarnate, it is natural for them to imagine God by giving God a form. But Gandhi pointed out that this is just a way to make it easier for a person to apprehend God.[75]

And when we speak of His *avatars* to protect *dharma* whenever *dharma* declines and *adharma* flourishes, it is true only in the manner and to the extent which I have just described; how else could we say that the birthless One took birth? There is no reason to believe that any historical figure was the incarnation of God or God as a historical figure was born in human or any other form. If a person is endowed with all the qualities of God, he may be called an incarnation of God. It was because of their divine qualities that all those great men of the past* were regarded by people as either plenary or partial incarnations. And yet, knowing this, different devotees have described the same God in the Rama of Valmiki or Tulsidas† and there is no harm in singing those *bhajans*. If we bear in mind what I said earlier, we would not be deluded. If someone wishes to confuse us confronting us with conundrums, we should tell him that we do not worship embodied Rama as conceived by anyone; we worship our own Rama who is flawless and formless. As we cannot reach Him direct, we sing *bhajans* that describe Him as personified, and then try to apprehend Him in His purity.[76]

For human beings, bondage to the body involves the self in *karma*, or action; without the body there would be no need for *karma*. God has no body; so he has no need to perform *karma*. But Shri Krishna in the *Gita* says that even though God has no body, he does not cease from *karma*. He should therefore be thought of as having a body. The entire visible creation is his body. Gandhi embraced the Vaishnavite idea of the cosmos as the body, image, or sphere of the self-manifestation of God. "In the Ashram we keep no idol or image because there is before us God's image in the form of the world and we should know God through it."[77]

Just as the body of God is not God, the body of a human being is not the self of the person. To pursue truth, and thus to reach God, we must cease mistaking the body for ourselves. The pursuit of truth and nonviolence postulates that we die. The body is the root of the ego; attachment to the body holds the self in bondage to the ego. Attachment to, or possessiveness of, the body is a source of violence. "One who desires to have a vision of God will have to transcend the body, to despise it, to court death."[78]

The distinction between body and self allows for an ethical, Christian understanding of God. According to Johann B. Metz, the implications of the body-self distinction are (*a*) the freedom of spirit over matter, (*b*) the contingency and non-necessity of creation as dependent on God's own free play of grace, and (*c*) the transference of the incarnation of God from the mythical metaphysical-physical level to the ethical-physical level of socially verifiable meaning. In other words, it involves a shift in the understanding of the incarnation of God from either a mythical world-view or a predominantly

---

*Gandhi is here referring to Rama and Krishna, believed to be incarnations, or *avatars*, of God in Vaishnavite Hinduism.

†Valmiki is believed to be the author of the epic *Ramayana*, the story of Rama in Sanskrit. Tulsidas is the author of the *Ramayana* in the Hindi language.

metaphysical theory to an understanding based upon the practical following of Christ.[79] Incarnation at this level is not a matter of one's own claim but of social acclaim in the sense of the faith of a community of believers.

In order to reach God, Gandhi believed, one must first accept one's helplessness, one's ultimate dependence on God. Out of this grows the refusal of self-defense. Once one has reached the level of realization of God, prayer and fasting, coming from the heart and accompanied by a consciousness of the presence of God, are a remedy for the sin of violence.[80] True realization of God cannot be expressed in words.

> It is one thing to believe in God and quite another to realize God emotionally and act accordingly. . . . One can realize God only by ridding oneself totally of attachment, aversion, etc., and in no other way. I hold that one who claims to have realized God has not truly done so. Realization can be experienced, but is beyond description.[81]

Gandhi's View of Christ

Gandhi's view of Christ does not reinforce Christian dogma, but goes beyond dogma to embrace Christian morality. From his youth, Gandhi had evaluated the *Vedas* and the *Upanishads* on the basis of their ethical or practical teachings. Miracles had no interest for him as apology or proof. Upon his first reading of the Bible he was repelled by the literal meaning of many biblical texts, refusing to take them as the Word of God. In evaluating all Scriptures, his criterion was morality—not sectarian, but universal morality. If religions gave conflicting counsel, Gandhi applied three criteria by which to discriminate among them: (1) the superiority of truth over everything that conflicted with it; (2) rejection of everything that conflicted with nonviolence; and (3) on things that could be reasoned out, rejection of everything that conflicted with reason.[82] Thus that which reconciled Gandhi to any teaching of Jesus was not his alleged miracles, but the conformity of his teaching with Gandhi's criteria of universal morality.

In this light, Jesus was to Gandhi a great world-teacher among others: "He was to the devotees of his generation no doubt the only begotten son of God."[83] For Gandhi, however, to believe that Jesus was the "only begotten son of God" was contrary to reason; the word "son" therefore can be used only in a figurative sense. Gandhi claimed that the adjective "begotten" had for him "a deeper and possibly a grander meaning than its literal meaning." It implied "spiritual birth. In his own times he [Jesus] was the nearest to God."[84] In this sense any person with the qualities of Jesus is a begotten son of God: "If a man is spiritually miles ahead of us we may say that he is in a special sense the son of God, though we are all children of God. We repudiate the relationship in our lives, whereas his life is a witness to that relationship."[85] Jesus affected Gandhi's life no less because he regarded him as one among the many begotten sons of God. For Gandhi, Jesus was "as divine as Krishna or Rama or Mahomed or Zoroaster."[86]

Gandhi believed that Jesus had attained the highest degree of perfection possible for a person, given the limitations of the flesh. He discounted miracles for much the same theological reasons as Rudolf Bultmann would at a later date, namely, the actual negation of the divine transcendence involved in the conception, despite every intent to affirm that transcendence. Gandhi wrote:

> I believe in the perfectibility of human nature. Jesus came as near to perfection as possible. To say that he was perfect is to deny God's superiority to man. And then in this matter I have a theory of my own. Being necessarily limited by the bonds of flesh, we can attain perfection only after dissolution of the body. Therefore God alone is absolutely perfect. When He descends to earth, He of His own accord limits Himself. Jesus died on the Cross because he was limited by the flesh. I do not need either the prophecies or the miracles to establish Jesus's greatness as a teacher. Nothing can be more miraculous than the three years of his ministry. . . . I do not deny that Jesus had certain psychic powers and he was undoubtedly filled with the love of humanity. . . . But he brought to life not people who were dead but who were believed to be dead. The laws of Nature are changeless, unchangeable, and there are no miracles in the sense of infringement or interruption of Nature's laws.* But we limited beings fancy all kinds of things and impute our limitations to God. We may copy God, but not He us.[87]

Gandhi is affirming the perfection of Jesus at the moment of his death rather than locating it at any one moment or even within the total duration of his life. Gandhi associates perfection with the resurrection and relates worship to the perfection seen by the eyes of believers. Thus, asked about the worship of "incarnations" who were historical figures, he said:

> Christians worship the Christ who was resurrected. In the same manner those who worship Rama and Krishna worship Rama and Krishna who are more living than you are, or certainly more living than I am. They live now and will live until eternity. . . . I worship the living Rama and Krishna, the incarnation of all that is True and Good and Perfect.[88]

Gandhi believed in the pluralism of religions as reflecting God's will to save all. He distrusted dogma,[89] and believed in the essential equality of reli-

---

*Gandhi is not saying that miracles infringe and interrupt nature's laws, or denying miracles, but that they work *with* the laws of nature and do not change them. He fights false apologetic use of miracles. Miracles can be understood as manifestations of the power of faith (cf. Gerd Theissen, *Urchristiliche Wundergeschichten* [Göttingen: Gütersloher Verlagshaus, 1974]).

gions.[90]* Equality of religions meant that each religion provided truth to its respective adherents in their beliefs, gave them a framework in which to relate to God, and provided them with moral standards. All religions are divine in their inspiration, though equally imperfect in that they are received and transmitted by human instruments. Different religions are therefore beautiful flowers from the same garden; or they are branches of the same majestic tree. Hence they are equally true.[91] They are also equal in their capacity to grow.[92]

This same argument of equality applies to the personages of the various religions. Thus the prophets within the Bible—Moses and Jesus, for example—are equal on the "historical plane."[93] He acknowledged the Christ of C. F. Andrews, who was not the Christ of "a narrow sect, but the Anointed of humanity, whom he sees in Ramakrishna, Chaitanya, and many other teachers of other faiths."[94]

Gandhi located himself and his nonviolence within the great tradition of nonviolence, which he traced from the Buddha through Christ even to Muhammad. He saw it as his duty to enrich this tradition. The burden of the tradition was not just an individual mission, but a collective tradition.[95] Refuting an article in *The Statesman*, which said that the example of Jesus proved the definitive failure of nonviolence in the worldly sense, Gandhi replied:

> Though I cannot claim to be a Christian in the sectarian sense, the example of Jesus' suffering is a factor in the composition of my undying faith in non-violence which rules all my actions, worldly and temporal. And I know that there are hundreds of Christians who believe likewise. Jesus lived and died in vain if he did not teach us to regulate the whole of life by the eternal Law of Love.[96]

It was Gandhi's conviction that the root of the evil of violence was the want of a living faith in a living God. He considered it a tragedy that peoples of the earth who claimed to believe in the message of Jesus, whom they described as the Prince of Peace, showed little of that belief in actual practice. It pained him to see Christian divines limiting the scope of Jesus' message to select individuals. He wished to "convince honest doubters that the love that Jesus taught and practiced was not a mere personal virtue, but that it was essentially a social and collective virtue."[97]

Gandhi's feeling was that most Christians tended to reject the moral substance of Christ's teaching for the metaphysical symbols embodied in dogmas or creedal formulas. If the morals of a person were a matter of no concern, the particular form of worship in a church, mosque, or temple was not only an empty formula but might even be a hindrance to individual or social growth. And insistence on a particular form or repetition of a credo

---

Sarvadharmasamanatva, meaning equality of all religions, was one of the vows observed in the daily life of Gandhi's ashram.

might be a potential cause of violent quarrels, which would have the effect of discrediting the basis of all religions, that is, belief in God.[98] Gandhi saw Jesus' atonement, which should have been an example for imitation, flouted by many Christians in their understanding of it as a substitution, and wasted on those who did not change their lives.[99] Rejecting such Christianity for the true message of Christ, he stated: "I rebel against orthodox Christianity, as I am convinced that it has distorted the message of Jesus. He was an Asiatic whose message was delivered through many media and when it had the backing of the Roman emperor, it became an imperialist faith as it remains to this day."[100] While Gandhi disputed the claim of Christianity to be the only true religion, he looked upon it as one of the true religions—a noble one, which along with others had contributed to raising the moral height of humankind, though it had yet to fulfill its potential in contributing to nonviolence.[101]

Gandhi and the Cross

As James Douglass has pointed out, "When the Gospel has become a fixture of culture, and thus been crowned with irrelevance, the discipline required to pass over to the standpoint of Jesus crucified must receive its inspiration from beyond that culture."[102] From that point of view, it might seem providential that Gandhi remained a Hindu despite the many and persistent attempts that had been made toward his conversion.

Douglass uses Gandhi and his interpretation of *satyagraha* for a rediscovery of the humanity of Christ and the cross as the necessary condition for a rediscovery of the divinization or lordship of Christ. The cross serves as the point of the passing from the "incarnational heresy" to the universal transcendence or inclusiveness of the incarnation as suffering love. But Douglass would seem to part company with Gandhi in stressing Christocentrism,[103] whereas Gandhi was always centered on God. For Gandhi the cross is the symbol of the theocentric rather than the Christocentric life. He dared not think of Christ's birth without his death on the cross, and could proclaim as his Christmas message: "Living Christ means a living Cross, without it life is a living death."[104]

The universality and transcendence that Gandhi recognized in Jesus was related to the universal appeal he recognized in the cross and in Jesus' Sermon on the Mount. The sermon, relating to nonretaliation and nonresistance to evil, echoed something he had learned and made a part of his being from childhood.[105] The universality he saw in the cross was a potential universality, depending on the meaning given to the cross. Self-suffering was applicable to any individual or any nation, although Christian usage, confining it to Jesus, had failed to recognize this.[106] For Gandhi the universality of Jesus' message was due to the power of his death, which had confirmed his [Jesus'] own word.[107] Orthopraxis was more important, powerful, and authoritative than orthodoxy. The crucifix was to Gandhi an eloquent sermon proclaiming "that nations, like individuals, could only be made through the agony of the

Cross and in no other way.''[108] On the basis of this unique interpretation and application of the Sermon on the Mount, Gandhi could claim to be a Christian,[109] unfettered by any sect or church or denomination.

Gandhi made his own meaning of the universality of the cross and of Christ when he declared, "God did not bear the Cross only 1900 years ago, but He bears it today, and He dies and is resurrected from day to day.''[110] The cross exists for all who are receptive to it. Where people are not receptive and suffering takes place in a moral vacuum, however, the suffering so suffered is itself the cross, and the dynamics of redemption can be understood in terms of *ahimsa*, or nonviolence. The dynamism of the cross is to bring the inflictor to recognize with the victim the unity of all in Christ. The dynamism of nonviolence is to move the inflictor to recognize with the victim their common humanity. To bring about this recognition of faith, suffering is necessary. The saving revelation of God takes place through the forgiving and redeeming love of the willing victim.

To affirm Gandhi's faith in Christ is not to claim Gandhi for Christianity, nor is it merely to see the full meaning of Christ through Gandhi.[111] Through his existential identification with the God of suffering and saving love, Gandhi passes into the redeeming reality of the incarnation,[112] opening and showing the way for us to do the same.

5

Gandhi's Vision
of a Liberated Society

GLOBAL VISION

Gandhi saw India's struggle for independence as a preparation for the country's world mission, its "religious [not political] supremacy of the world"—the supremacy of *ahimsa* (nonviolence). In fulfillment of that mission India should, when free, "offer herself a willing and pure sacrifice for the betterment of the world"[1]—a world in danger of perishing under the weight of the material comforts that were enslaving it. "India's destiny lies not along the bloody way of the West, of which she shows signs of tiredness, but along the bloodless way of peace that comes from a simple and godly life."[2]

Through the deliverance of India, Gandhi sought the deliverance of the so-called weaker races of the earth from the crushing heels of Western exploitation. The independence of India was not a matter merely of self-interest, but the way and the symbol for every nation to become independent and self-giving.[3] Thus Gandhi envisaged a time when England would rejoice in India's friendship, and India would not reject the proferred hand because it had once despoiled the country.[4]

Political self-government could be attained by "precisely the same means" as those required for individual self-government—namely, internal strength and ability to fight against the heaviest odds, and a continuous striving to sustain the goal once attained.[5] Nonviolence was an indicator of inward freedom to which outward freedom, or political independence, would be in exact proportion.[6] Gandhi desired that India should set an object lesson in nonviolence to a world weary of violence and hatred.[7]

Political power, therefore, was not an end in itself, but "one of the means of enabling people to better their condition in every department of life."[8] Truth was the end, and freedom, political power, and independence were

117

a part of truth. Only in truth and freedom could God be worshiped. Only a free people could worship the true God. By implication, the God of slaves could not be the true God, but only an idol of human creation.

The universality of *swaraj* and the character of political power as means necessarily enlarged Gandhi's objective. He wanted to free India from any yoke whatsoever, not merely the British yoke. Hence *swaraj* was a spiritual movement of self-purification,[9] for the realization of the greater mission of the brotherhood of all peoples:[10] "I want India to rise so the whole world may benefit. I do not want India to rise on the ruin of other nations."[11]

The mutual regard among individuals within a nation, which was the principle of national cohesion, would someday be extended to the whole universe, "even as we have extended the family law to form nations—a larger family."[12] Voluntary interdependence was to be the goal of world-states;[13] barriers were human creations, not from God.[14] Interdependence was a necessary condition for wholeness, for integrity:

> Man is a social being. Without inter-relation with society he cannot realize his oneness with the universe or suppress his egotism. His social interdependence enables him to test his faith and to prove himself on the touchstone of reality. If man were so placed or could so place himself as to be absolutely above all dependence on his fellow-beings he would become so proud and arrogant as to be a veritable burden and nuisance to the world. Dependence on society teaches him the lesson of humanity. . . . A man cannot become self-sufficient even in respect of all the various operations from the growing of cotton to the spinning of the yarn. He has at some stage or other to take the aid of the members of his family. And if one may take help from one's own family, why not from one's neighbors? Or otherwise what is the significance of the great saying "The world is my family"?[15]

Not only is freedom positively open-ended in the sense of self-realization, of self-perfection, but it becomes possible to realize self-perfection only at the culminating point of sacrifice. The perfection of freedom is the free self-sacrifice itself.[16] Sacrifice as a value has to be structured into the various levels of social groupings from the family to the world. In such a structure there will be little room for exploitation:

> We want freedom for our country but not at the expense or exploitation of others, not so as to degrade other countries. I do not want the freedom of India if it means the extinction of England or the disappearance of Englishmen. I want the freedom of my country so other countries may learn something from my free country, so the resources of my country might be utilized for the benefit of mankind. Just as the cult of patriotism teaches us today that the individual has to die for the family, the family has to die for the village, the village for the district, the

district for the province and the province for the country, even so a country has to be free in order that it may die if necessary for the benefit of the world. My love, therefore, of nationalism or my idea of nationalism is that my country may become free, that if need be the whole country may die so the human race may live. There is no room for race-hatred there. Let that be our nationalism.[17]

Gandhi saw narrowness, selfishness, and exclusivity as the evil in nationalism, but he did not see nationalism itself as evil. Nationalism, in its highest form, is a state of unity and unanimity, and as such is a prerequisite for internationalism.[18]

THEANDRIC UNIVERSALISM

Gandhi's vision of a liberated society was a unitive vision born of spiritual communion and identification with all people and all living things: "I believe," he said, "in the essential unity of man and . . . of all that lives. Therefore, I believe that if one man gains, . . . the whole world gains with him, and if one man falls, the whole world falls to that extent." This universal communion applied even to one's enemies: "I do not help opponents without at the same time helping myself and my co-workers."[19]

The depth dimension of the essential unity and the resultant spiritual communion was theological. God is "the purest essence" who simply *is* and "is all things to all men" and who alone *is* while "nothing else is." Gandhi perceived the *satvic* (substantive, ontic) reality of God as truth, being, essence, in terms of his immanence, which binds everyone and everything together: "God is present in all of us. For my part, every moment I experience the truth that, though many, we are all one."

The systematic character of Gandhi's vision of the essential unity of all life is seen in his translation of that vision into social, political, and economic terms. Nor could Gandhi—or any one else, for that matter—lead an integrally religious life unless he identified himself with the whole of humankind, which he could not do without participation in political and economic affairs.[20] As Raghavan Iyer has pointed out in his book on Gandhi's moral and political thought, Gandhi implicitly challenged the Augustinian distinction between the political and the religious.[21] Gandhi, like the Buddha, rejected the distinction between the natural and the supernatural, between the religious and the political. Neither *artha* (political economy) nor *moksha* (salvation-liberation) could be cut off from *dharma* (morality).[22] Hence Gandhi's political economy embraces the good of all.

I do not believe in the doctrine of the greatest good for the greatest number. It means in its nakedness that in order to achieve the supposed good of fifty-one percent the interest of forty-nine percent may be, or rather should be, sacrificed. It is a heartless doctrine and has done harm to humanity. The only real, dignified, human doctrine is the greatest good of all, and this can be achieved only by uttermost self-sacrifice.[23]

THE CRITICAL ALTERNATIVE

The liberated society that Gandhi envisaged was a critical alternative to those already in existence. Gandhi could not envisage a liberated society that was not intrinsically moral. No action could be moral that was not voluntary and deliberate. An action dictated by fear or coercion of any kind would be violent and thus cease to be moral.[24] True democracy must be marked by freedom from fear and coercion in all areas of social, political, and economic life. Gandhi's fight against popular fear, cowardice, and violence, on the one hand, and the organized violence of British power, on the other, was a moral warfare for the liberation of the people and the establishment of a liberated and moral society. It is obvious that the moral society envisaged by Gandhi and for which he worked was an ideal rather than already in existence. The existing reality was immoral. While the situation of the moral person in an immoral society was a source of pessimism for Augustine, Luther, Schopenhauer, and Reinhold Niebuhr, the presence and reality of the moral human was a source of optimism for Gandhi. His nondichotomized, more integrated and unitive vision of faith and works in the context of salvation and historical liberation come like a welcome breath of fresh air in a stuffy room.

Gandhi's overriding moral concern required that there be no sharp distinction between economics and ethics: "Economics that hurt the moral well-being of an individual or a nation are immoral and, therefore, sinful. Thus the economics that permit one country to prey upon another are immoral."[25] On the contrary, "True economics never militates against the highest ethical standard, just as all true ethics to be worth its name must at the same time be also good economics. . . . True economics . . . stands for social justice, it promotes the good of all equally including the weakest, and is indispensable for decent life."[26] There could be no *Ramarajya* in a state of iniquitious inequalities in which a few rolled in riches while the masses did not get enough to eat. The coming of *Ramarajya* had to be simultaneous with the abolition of such inequalities.[27]

A Liberated Economy

In his *Autobiography*[28] Gandhi summed up the message of Ruskin's *Unto This Last* in three concepts: community, equality, and dignity of labor. The core of Ruskin's work as summarized by Gandhi in *Sarvodaya* (The Welfare of All) is the question of whether or not economics is a science at all[29] and the consideration of the bearing of economics on socioeconomic thought and praxis. Ruskin was critical of the treatment of economics as the science of wealth,[30] because it omitted all religious, cultural, human, and moral considerations.[31]

The alternative proposed by Ruskin and endorsed by Gandhi was a definition of economics in "political," moral, and religious terms.[32] Such a definition would affect all socioeconomic thought and praxis. Political economy would be unitive in vision and practice. Under it, wealth would be moral, human, and "political" (communal) in the root meaning of the term. Human life and people in general, happy and healthy, would be the real wealth. [33] The worth of material possessions would come from their positive or negative moral value—on how they were gained and what they were used for.[34] Control over the lives of others through money-power was contrary to human freedom and dignity, and therefore immoral. It could have no place in political economy. An economy in which wealth and value are socially and morally construed[35] would be a stable economy,[36] one in which the supply and demand of labor and remuneration would be stable, with equal pay for equal work, the incompetent worker not being allowed to offer service at a reduced price, which could cause a deterioration in the quality of work and the product.[37] Those in the labor ranks and the professions would suffer rather than the quality of the work. Gandhi judged these ideas of Ruskin to be relevant and necessary to a free India; they were akin to his own values.

Economic equality was a master key to perfect *swaraj*. Hence Gandhian economics was egalitarian. Egalitarian economy did not mean equal income irrespective of work and talent. The equality Gandhi envisioned did not remove incentive or stifle talent.[38] Economic equality meant, rather, an equalization of social status in which working classes would be neither isolated nor separated. It meant: (1) the abolition of conflict between capital and labor; (2) equal right to the necessities of life;[39] the abolition of privilege and monopoly;[40] and (3) leveling down the rich minority and raising up the semistarved millions. The gulf between rich and poor was contradictory to a nonviolent system of government. However, a voluntary abdication of riches and of the power that riches give, and a sharing of them for the common good, was the right way to bring about the needed economic equality. The certain alternative to voluntary abdication was a bloody revolution.[41]

Gandhi always recognized a hierarchy in human needs: "A semi-starved nation can have neither religion nor art nor organization."[42] In that recognition was his knowledge that a complete, voluntary renunciation of one's possessions was not within the natural capacity of most people, and that what could realistically be expected of the wealthy class was that they should hold their riches and talents in trust and use them for the service of society.[43]

Gandhi's notion of *swaraj* did not imply the end of capital. He knew that accumulated capital constituted ruling power. He wanted to see right relations established between capital and labor, without the supremacy of the one over the other. He saw no natural antagonism between the two. "The rich and the poor will always be with us."[44] Nor did he think all capitalists and landlords were "exploiters by an inherent necessity." Rather, he traced all exploitation to the willing or forced cooperation of the exploited.[45] Since there was no irreconcilable antagonism between the interests of capital and labor, there was no need to destroy the capitalist. The destruction of the capitalist must finally mean the destruction of the worker. Besides, "no human being is so bad as to be beyond redemption, no human being is so perfect as to warrant his destroying him whom he wrongly considers to be wholly evil."[46] Further, as cooperators in their own exploitation, labor has only to say no to its cooperation in order to remedy the evil, leaving the burden of wooing labor on capital. Despite all its power, capital would be helpless if labor were to assert its dignity in a firm no without retaliation.[47]

Although Gandhi could not picture a time when no person would be richer than another, he did see a time when the better-off would spurn to enrich themselves at the expense of the poor, and the poor would cease to envy the rich. "Even in a most perfect world, we shall fail to avoid inequalities, but we can and must avoid strife and bitterness."[48] This, however, implied no slackening of his determination to fight poverty in India's villages.

Gandhi wanted the "economic constitution" of India—and indeed of the world—to ensure that no one would suffer from want of food and clothing, that everyone would have work enough to provide a basic, decent living. To realize this objective universally, the means of production of the elementary necessities of life must remain in the control of the people; they must not become either a vehicle for exploitation or a monopoly of any nation or group.[49]

Industrialism as Gandhi experienced it was exploitation of one nation by another. Therefore it was bound to prove a curse for humankind. Gandhi refused to think in terms of an industrialized India that could exploit other nations.[50] Industrialization, built on selfishness and want of consideration for the neighbor, was not the remedy for India's poverty. Gandhi wanted to concentrate industrialization on self-sustaining villages, engaging in manufacturing goods mainly for their own use. If this character of village industry was maintained, Gandhi would not object to the villagers using those modern machines and tools that they could make and afford to maintain. These should not become a means of exploitation of others.[51]

What Gandhi objected to was not machinery as such, but the "craze" for labor-saving machinery that simultaneously threw thousands out on the streets without jobs and food. Gandhi opposed the industrialization that was fueled by greed rather than *sarvodaya* (the welfare of all).

The supreme consideration in industrialization should be the human being. "As a moderately intelligent man"—in his own understatement—Gandhi knew the indispensability of industry in modern times. He was gravely concerned, however, about "producing too much too fast." Machines could come as and when they became necessary. Priority had to go to nonviolent self-dependence. A people who knew how to regulate themselves would know how to control the machine.[52] To be controllable, it had to be of an elementary type placeable in the houses of the millions and therefore labor-intensive. As such, it could not and did not have to be capital-intensive, complex, and mass-productive.[53] Contrary to Jawaharlal Nehru's position that industrialization, when socialized, would be free from the evils of capitalism, Gandhi held the evils to be structurally inherent in industrialism, which no amount of socialization could eradicate.[54]

The economics and civilization of a densely populated country like India are bound to differ from those of a sparsely populated country. Gandhi did not view India as overpopulated or the land as insufficient for its numbers. Rather, the people had to become industrious, making the land yield its plenty, producing what was needed and using what was produced—and thus making the way of life more rational.[55]

A Liberated Polity

Politics concerns nations and the welfare of people. Therefore no seeker after God as truth could cut herself or himself off from politics. Politics bereft of religion would be defiling: "Therefore in politics also we have to establish the Kingdom of Heaven."[56]

British political practices had long accustomed India to think that power flowed to the people through legislative assemblies. Gandhi regarded this belief as a grave error, and traced it to a superficial study of British history and the parliamentary system. In truth, power resides in the people, and it is temporarily entrusted to their elected representatives. "Parliaments have no power or even existence independently of the people. . . . Civil disobedience is the storehouse of power." It could be effectively offered to redress a local wrong. While the militia can coerce even powerful minorities, they cannot bend the resolute will of a people who are ready to suffer to the utmost.[57] Swaraj would give the masses the capacity to regulate authority so as to prevent its abuse.[58] That would be real freedom and democracy.

Gandhi spelled out the democratic spirit of brotherhood in politics as follows: politicians must share the sorrows of the masses; understand their difficulties and anticipate their wants; become pariahs (untouchables) with the pariahs; see how it feels to clean the toilets of the upper classes and have the remains of their food thrown at them; know what it feels like to live in boxes, miscalled houses, like the laborers of Bombay; identify with the villagers who toil under the hot sun beating on their bent backs; and think how they would like to drink from the pool in which the villagers bathe and wash their clothes and pots, and in which the cattle drink and roll. Then politicans would truly represent the masses, and the masses would respond to every call from such politicians.[59] A living connection with the masses can be established only by working for the masses, through the masses, and in their midst, "not as their patrons, but as their servants."[60]

Gandhi applied the democratic spirit of brotherhood to minority/majority issues thus: when a respectable minority objects to any rule of conduct, it would be dignified for the majority to yield. A majority would be acting in violence when it acts in total disregard of any strongly felt opinion of a minority. No organization can run smoothly when it is divided into camps, each growling at the other and each determined to have its own way by whatever means.[61]

While eschewing and proscribing torture for any crime, no matter how vile,[62] in deference to those who did not believe wholeheartedly in nonviolence Gandhi acknowledged the impossibility of compelling people and societies to nonviolent methods, and therefore, even while pronouncing war an unmitigated evil that had to be abolished, he went on to say that in free India there would be military training for those who wished to take it.[63] As freedom won through violence was no freedom, the truth of freedom imposed by violence would be no truth either. Truth was greater in communion and concession to unity than in splendidly isolated self-righteousness. Gandhi practiced what he taught.

To evolve along nonviolent lines, India would have to decentralize its polity, administration, economy, and system of justice. Centralization itself involved violence, and it could not be defended without force. Decentralized and rurally organized India would risk foreign invasion less than urbanized, centralized India.[64]

Decentralization meant organizing the country on the basis of its small natural units of society, namely, the villages. Gandhi saw the anonymity and crowding of the cities as fostering violence and untruth. True freedom and love were more consistent with the simple life and face-to-face relationships of the villages.

Political pacts or treaties were to be based on the less fragile personal friendships of peoples rather than the more fragile self-interest of nation-states. The people in government were not to be regarded as enemies, but as friends. Any contrary course would be inconsistent with *ahimsa*, the spirit of love. This ideal of Gandhi's is in sharp contrast to the party politics now prevailing in India.

Though he did not relish the idea of a national government, Gandhi realized that there would be a central government administration. He did not want a parliamentary government. Instead, in his plan, each of India's 700,000 villages would be organized according to the will of its citizens, all of whom would have voting rights. The villages, each of which would have one vote, would elect their district administrations. The latter would elect the provincial administration, and these in turn would elect a president who was to be the national chief executive. If it resembled the Soviet system, Gandhi did not mind.[65]

The village was to become a self-governing unit living its own life. Therefore it had to be self-sustaining and capable of managing its affairs—even to the extent of defending itself as needed. Dependence on willing help from neighbors or from the outside world was not excluded, so long as it came from the free and voluntary play of mutual forces. The innumerable villages of India were to be structured as an ever-widening circle: "Life will not be a pyramid with the apex sustained by the bottom. But it will be an oceanic circle whose center will be the individual always ready to perish for the village, the latter ready to perish for the circle of villages. . . . Therefore, the outermost circumference will not wield power to crush the inner circle but give strength to all within and derive its own from the center."[66]

In contrast to the reality of Indian villages,[67] Gandhi envisaged the ideal Indian village as having proper sanitation, light and airy structures with roomy courtyards for gardening and sheltering cattle, clean streets, an accessible and pure water supply, houses of worship, a public meeting place, a village common for grazing cattle, a cooperative dairy, and a school system. Local disputes would be settled by a *panchayat* (a council of five elected by the people for a year). The village should produce all its food and clothing.[68] Land was also to be reserved for playground and recreation for children and adults. If more land was available, it was to be devoted to cash crops other than tobacco, opium, and other narcotics. A village theater was also to be maintained for public entertainment. As far as possible every activity was to be conducted on a cooperative basis without distinction of person.[69] As for acquiring the land itself, Gandhi envisaged that landless peasants would on their own initiative take land from the legal owners. He did not anticipate any compensation for the landlords, because that would be a fiscal impossibility. His gratitude to his millionaire friends did not prevent him from speaking his mind on this matter.[70]

There was to be compulsory service in the village guard. The *panchayat* would function as legislature, judiciary, and executive combined. If every villager was ready to suffer death in defense of self and village, the village would be able to defy the might of the whole world. Gandhi thought of this as perfect democracy based on the freedom of the individual as the architect of one's own government.[71]

Gandhi was confident that, with the cooperation of the people, nearly all of this model-village program (with the exception of the cottages) could be worked out on a budget within the means of the villagers and without government assistance. Nevertheless, he recognized the major obstacle to implementation of the program: the indifference of the villagers toward bettering their lot.[72] What was needed was a "village-mindedness": "When we have become village-minded, we will not want imitations of the West or machine-made products, but we will develop a true national taste in keeping with the vision of a new India, in which pauperism, starvation and idleness will be unknown."[73]

Gandhi hoped that congressmen would interest themselves in villages to the point of settling there and giving "a new life and a new dress" to such "essential village industries" as hand grinding, hand pounding, soapmaking, papermaking, matchmaking, tanning, and oil pressing. Gandhi summed up the kind of person it took to realize this vision in his ideal of a "true Congressman":

A true Congressman is a true servant. He ever gives, ever wants service. He is easily satisfied so long as his own comfort is concerned. He is always content to take a back seat. He is never communal or provincial. His country is his paramount consideration. He is brave to a fault because he has shed all earthly ambition, fear of Death himself. And he is generous because he is brave, forgiving because he is humble and conscious of his own failings and limitations.[74]

Education and Social Reform

As education had conditioned the nation to slavery, it was also to aid in the formation and flowering of a free society. Gandhi's basic education scheme would link the children, from the cities and the villages, to all that was best and lasting in India, keeping them rooted to the soil, "with a glorious vision of the future in the realization of which he or she begins to take his or her share from the very commencement of his or her career in school."[75] Education should fit boys and girls for manual work in later life, and not merely introduce them to the classics. India's children should from their infancy be taught the dignity of labor.[76]

Adult education likewise would open the minds of its students to the greatness and vastness of their country, thereby removing the narrowness of their minds with its resultant fear and resentment of everything new or different. Gandhi's program of adult education was to be a "true political education of the adult by word of mouth. . . . Side by side with the education by mouth will be the literary education."[77]

While he valued and encouraged education in the sciences, Gandhi also regarded spinning and weaving as a necessary part of any national educational system, so as to develop the hands, brain, and soul of children.[78] Education should be practical, related to the life and development of the nation.[79] It should also foster unity, catholicity and toleration, and a worldwide outlook. If one sees the points of contact, namely the unity and oneness of spirit, "there will be no need to divide this universe of ours between heaven and hell, no need to divide fellow-beings into virtuous and vicious, the eternally saved and the eternally damned." Instead love would inform one's actions and pervade one's life.[80]

In a land of many religions and sects, religious education was bound to pose problems. But if India were to avoid spiritual bankruptcy, religious instruction of its youth was as necessary as secular instruction.[81] Religious education had to be solely the concern of religious associations, but the teaching of fundamental ethics was the duty and function of the state.[82] A curriculum of religious instruction should include a study of the tenets of faiths other than one's own. In such study, students needed to cultivate a spirit of reverence and tolerance, which would give them "a spiritual assurance and a better appreciation of their own religion."[83]

In a liberated India, not only were duties to hold primacy over rights, but in the same spirit of duties and rights, women were to be equal partners with men in the mission of service. Oppressive laws and custom, for which man was responsible and in the shaping of which woman had no voice, had to be abolished. Rules of social conduct would have to be framed by mutual cooperation and consultation, and never imposed from the outside. Men thus would no longer be lords and masters, but instead friends, comrades, and co-workers. "Wives should not be dolls and objects of indulgence, but should be treated as honored comrades in common service. To this end, those who have not received a liberal education should receive such instruction as is possible from their husbands."[84]

Caste as distinctions of social status and superiority/inferiority was a sin against God and humankind and had to go.[85] Nevertheless, while ridding India of the evils of the caste system, Gandhi wanted to preserve what was good in the system, namely *varnashrama dharma*, the fourfold division of labor: imparting knowledge, defending the defenseless, carrying on agriculture and commerce, and all other services of physical labor. Actually the fourfold division had become mere labels. Therefore Gandhi envisaged bringing everyone to a voluntary *shudra* status to revive *varnashrama* in its true image.[86]

Able-bodied members of the family who would not work should not be supported. As long as poverty and hunger remained national problems, families should not spend money on costly education. The expansion of the mind must come from experience rather than the schoolroom. The golden rule to apply to all such cases of possessions and facilities was "resolutely to refuse to have what millions cannot." This implied cultivation of the spirit of poverty, and a change of lifestyle in keeping with that spirit.[87]

Social freedom also meant dealing with social problems such as addiction to alcohol and narcotic drugs.[88] In an India pulsating with new life, there would be not a leper or a beggar uncared for.[89] Civilization would consist not in the multiplication, but in the deliberate and voluntary reduction, of wants for the promotion of happiness, contentment, and the capacity for service.[90] "In the ideal state, doctors, lawyers and the like will work solely for the benefit of society, not for self. Obedience to the law of bread labor will bring about a silent revolution in the structure of society. Man's triumph will consist in substituting the struggle for existence by the struggle for mutual service. The law of the brute will be replaced by the law of man."[91]

Gandhi knew that the ultimate destiny of India, like that of any society, was bound up with what its citizens sought. Of his part Gandhi wrote:

I shall strive for a constitution, which will release India from all thraldom and patronage, and give her, if need be, the right to sin. I shall work for an India, in which the poorest shall feel that it is their country in whose making they have an effective voice; an India in which there shall be no high class and low class of people; an India in which all communities shall live in perfect harmony. There can be no room in such an India for the curse of untouchability or the curse of intoxicating drinks and drugs. Women will enjoy the same rights as men. Since we shall be at peace with all the rest of the world, neither exploiting, nor being exploited, we shall have the smallest army imaginable. All interests not in conflict with the interests of the dumb millions will be scrupulously respected, whether foreign or indigenous. Personally, I hate the distinction between foreign and indigenous. This is the India of my dreams. . . . I shall be satisfied with nothing less.[92]

6

Gandhi's Challenge
to Christianity

CHRISTIANITY AND CHRISTOLOGY

The Christian significance of Gandhi and his challenge to Christianity in India have been widely recognized. At least by the Christian missionaries and Indian Christians who formed part of his intimate circle of friends,* Gandhi's importance to Christianity was appreciated while he was yet alive. From the time of his death acknowledgment of his significance has increased.

In his study of the Christian relevance of Gandhi, *The Acknowledged Christ of the Indian Renaissance*, M. M. Thomas suggests that one of the most important tasks of the church is to reconstruct the Gandhian insights about the ethics of Christ within the framework of its doctrine of redemption in Christ.[1] While admitting Gandhi's Christian significance, however, he differs with Gandhi, as many Christian theologians do, on the issue of Gandhi's emphasis on the moral life of the believer, based on the Sermon on the Mount, as opposed to the centrality of the person of Christ.[2]

Though he emphasized the Sermon on the Mount, Gandhi never elevated ethical teaching or doctrine above faith. Through one's faith, one could commit oneself to a value enshrined in a doctrine and allow the power of that value to guide and direct one's life. Thus a life committed to value is a life of faith. Praxis is the empirical measure and criterion of faith.

Even when Gandhi speaks of the Sermon on the Mount as the whole of Christianity, he does so from the perspective of one whose life is committed to the values enshrined in that sermon. Following the example set by Jesus, Gandhi sees the essence of Christianity as a life of faith committed to the values of God and fellow humans. Jesus was more than merely an ethical

---

*C. F. Andrews, Aryanayagam, Verrier Elwin, S. K. George, Rajkumari Amrit Kaur, Ralph Richard Keithahn, Bharatan Kumarappa, and J. C. Kumarappa.

teacher. The way of Jesus' values was his way to the Father, the way to establish the kingdom of God. The grace of God is the constant milieu of Gandhian ethical commitment.

Gandhi does not deny divine self-disclosure in the person and self-understanding of Jesus. What he denies is the uniqueness of that self-disclosure to Jesus. The Gandhian faith makes central the person and deeds of every believer, not merely the person of Jesus, nor merely his sermon in the abstract.

The faith with which Gandhi committed himself to the imitation of the Christ of the Sermon on the Mount transformed Gandhi into an *alter Christus*, another Christ, just as it is the faith of any Christian, and not merely the ritual of baptism, that makes him or her an *alter Christus*. Since Gandhi was not baptized he was not a "Christian." Despite this, or maybe because of it, his faith was purer and freer than that of many Christians. And the words of a believer whose faith and vision are pure provide a theological challenge for those who call themselves Christians.

As M. M. Thomas points out, through Gandhi's life and death the meaning of suffering love and its application to struggles for social and political justice have been made available to the whole world. A Martin Luther King cannot be understood apart from Gandhi. In his practice and propagation of *ahimsa* in terms of vicarious suffering, which imputes a collective meaning to the doctrine of *karma* in addition to its individualistic meaning, Gandhi provides a meeting point between Indian Christianity and neo-Hinduism. Thomas acknowledges A. G. Hogg's description of the incarnation of God in Gandhian terms as the *satyagraha* of God,[3] though he does not recognize the necessity, as others have, to invert the description so as to see in Gandhi's *satyagraha* the incarnate presence and action of God.

There is a greater depth to Gandhi's sense of vicariousness than many Christians have detected. For Gandhi, vicariousness was not substitution, but spiritual and moral identification with a whole group of people. Whereas substitution excludes those for whom it takes place, vicariousness connotes total inclusiveness, extended to the realm of faith.

That Jesus holds the central place in Christian belief is a fact that Gandhi knew and accepted as valid within the context of Christian history and the Christian community. He even accepted it as Christian testimony when it was proclaimed within the context of a Christian subjectivity. What he could not accept was the objectification of Christianity, which denied the analogous subjectivity of the non-Christian; this changed a positive, subjective testimony into an aggressive denial of salvation to those who did not assent to an objectified Christological dogma.

Gandhi was aware of the liturgical or confessional origins of creedal formulations. In the "mood of exaltation" of worship, arising from communion with the worshiped and other worshipers, every affirmation about the object of worship is equally a self-affirmation of the worshiper. It is a confession by which one's whole moral and spiritual life is regulated, and the community's life ordered. In genuine in-group cultic testimony and sharing of experience this inclusive self-affirmation is so transparent to the witness that one does not lose one's moorings in kerygma. In the objectification of belief as the absolute truth or dogma, however, making this dogma the criterion of the truth of out-group faith, the transparency of self-affirmation is lost. The testimony unwittingly becomes a conquering religio-political ideology, even if in the name of Jesus.

Gandhi challenges Christians to the Christology of Jesus as servant rather than the Christology of the church about Jesus as Lord. Gandhi does not challenge the lordship of Jesus, but the unspoken lordship of the church. He reminds us of the pedagogical function of cult, as well as the role of the cult-object as teacher. Gandhi calls us to learn the full meaning of vicarious existence from Jesus, and to apply it in our worship, belief, missionary action, and suffering.

GANDHI'S THEOLOGY OF RELIGIONS

Despite the inspiration he found in the life of Jesus, Gandhi had misgivings about the Christian church. He saw Christianity as a comparatively young religion that would, one hoped, in the future move away from exclusiveness and violence and make a greater contribution to the world. That India was dominated by the country whose ruler was the head of the Church of England and of the established Church in India did not help to raise his estimation of Christianity. He saw the church as sanctioning both materialist civilization and the exploitation of one race by another. Hence he judged Christianity's contribution to India as essentially negative in character, though useful in that it helped Hinduism to set its house in order.[4]

As a Hindu, Gandhi had a right and a duty to point out the defects in Hinduism in order to help purify it. But this right did not extend to non-Hindus, whose ignorance of its practices prevented them from making reasonable judgments. Likewise, Gandhi, as a Hindu, was wary of criticizing the internal practices of other faiths.[5]

The basis of Gandhi's theology of religions was a strong belief in the equality of religions. Each religion was true, and each deserved his reverence and respect. "Each religion has its own contribution to make to human evolution. I regard the great faiths of the world as so many branches of a tree, each distinct from the other though having the same source."[6] All religions are rooted in a belief in God, yet each religion manifests this belief in its own way, uniquely suited to its own people. Gandhi would not have wanted a merging of various faiths into one religion. But he clearly foresaw the time when people of different religions would have the same regard for other faiths as they had for their own. As children of one and the same God, all had to find unity in diversity.[7] The fact that all prayer was addressed to the same God taught humankind that all belonged to one family and should bear love to one another.[8]

Since youth, Gandhi had tried to understand and adopt in his life every-thing that he had found to be of value in all the world religions. Thus he considered himself to be a *sanatani*—a universalist Hindu.[9] He believed in all the great prophets and saints of every religion. "My Hinduism is not sectarian. It includes all that I know to be best in Islam, Christianity, Buddhism and Zoroastrianism."[10] Hinduism does not rest on the authority of one book or one prophet, nor does it possess a common creed acceptable to all. While this renders a common definition of Hinduism somewhat difficult, Gandhi considered it the strength of Hinduism, because the very lack of a common definition had made its gradual evolution possible and given it its inclusive and assimilative character.[11] Yet far from aiming at the fusion of religions, *sanatana* Hinduism valued the distinctness of each religion.

Since Hinduism is founded on truth and nonviolence, there is no room in it for conflict with other religions. "It must be the daily prayer of every adherent of the Hindu faith that every known religion of the world should serve the whole of humanity."[12]

Asked by a Swiss monk if he saw a way to end the climate of "warring creeds in the world," Gandhi replied that it depended upon Christians and their making up their minds to unite with people of other faiths. But given their actions so far toward "universal acceptance of Christianity as they believe it," he did not think they would do so. As illustration he cited his experience with an English friend who had been trying for thirty years to convince him that there was nothing but damnation in Hinduism and that he must accept Christianity to be saved.[13]

For Gandhi the line between learning from another religion and converting to another religion was clear. As a Hindu his answers to religious questions would be found within Hinduism, and for Christians answers would be found within Christianity. Otherwise there is risk of one group patronizing another.[14] The idea that all people might someday belong to one religion also contradicted Gandhi's spiritual beliefs. To assume that any one faith was the only way to reach God was to posit limits on God's limitless grace.[15]

GANDHI'S CONTRIBUTION TO CHRISTIANITY

Following are three positive Christian evaluations of Gandhi, for which some debt is due the work of M. M. Thomas. All three, however, go beyond Thomas in the extent to which they credit Gandhi with making a positive contribution to Christianity.

The American missionary E. Stanley Jones describes Gandhi as a "natural Christian rather than an orthodox one"[16] who taught him more of the spirit of Christ than perhaps any other person in the East or the West.[17] He observes that Gandhi turned India's face to Christ and the cross and was calling not only India, but the whole world, including the Christian world, to the cross:[18]

Never in human history has so much light been shed on the Cross, as has been through this one man, and that man not even called a Christian. Had not our Christianity been vitiated by our identification with un-Christian attitudes and policies in public and private life, we should have seen at once the kinship between Gandhi's method and the Cross. Non-Christians saw it instinctively.[19]

While disagreeing with Gandhi on the unnecessariness of verbal evangelism, E. Stanley Jones agreed with Gandhi's emphasis on the ethical life based on the Sermon on the Mount.

C. F. Andrews was an English missionary minister of religion in India who became an intimate friend of Gandhi as well as his critic and interpreter.[20] He accepted Gandhi's emphasis on morality as expressing, more than dogma did, the essence of Christianity. He shared not only Gandhi's sense of Christ as the experience of a spiritual consciousness, but also his suspicion of the intellectual definitions of this experience in metaphysical formulations, and his rebellion against the exclusivism of dogmas promulgated as the essence of Christian faith.[21] Andrews eventually resigned from the priesthood.

There were some points on which Andrews differed with Gandhi. He believed that Gandhi's doctrine of the equality of religions was true neither to history nor to personal experience. He was critical of Gandhi's equation of the self of the human with the spirit, and of the body and materiality with the principle of selfishness or sin. He also challenged Gandhi's programs of boycott and noncooperation as violations of charity. Though eventually he appears to have changed his opinion, for a while Andrews feared, as did Rabindranath Tagore, that Gandhi might be self-deceived, and that his martyrdom for the cause of truth might degenerate into fanaticism.

The agreements between Gandhi and Andrews, however, far surpassed their differences. Gandhi excused Andrews's criticism of his views on celibacy and bodily mortification as part of his Protestant legacy. "Protestantism did many good things; but one of its few evils was that it ridiculed celibacy."[22] Andrews recognized the presence of Christ in the burning passion of Gandhi's sacrifice for the weak and the oppressed, and he declared, "To be a Christian means not the expression of an outward creed but the living of an inward life."[23] According to Andrews, Jesus Christ, the Son of man, was the reference point of Gandhi's religious and ethical life. Upon witnessing Gandhi's fast against violence during the early stage of the non-cooperation campaign, Andrews wrote:

Instinctively my gaze turned back to the frail, wasted tortured spirit on the terrace by my side, bearing the sins and sorrows of his people. With a rush of emotion, there came to memory the passage from the Book of Lamentations—"Is it nothing to you, all ye that pass by? Behold and see, if there is any sorrow like unto my sorrow?" And in that hour of vision, I knew more deeply, in my own personal life, the meaning of the Cross.[24]

With Gandhi, Andrews saw the missionary task as sharing religious experience rather than dogma, as communication in life rather than words.

S. K. George was an Indian Christian theologian who, having heard and responded to the challenge of Gandhi in his life and his theology, was dismissed from his job as professor of theology at Bishop's College, Calcutta, and severed his affiliation with the church. Gandhi made Jesus real to S. K. George. *Satyagraha* was Christianity in action, as the following, or imitation, of Christ. And Gandhi was the greatest ally of essential Christianity in India and "the greatest worker for the Kingdom of God in the world of today." Not to recognize this in Gandhi was to demonstrate gross inability to discern the working of God's spirit.[25] For the central message in Christianity is Christ's message of the kingdom of God and of the cross as the way to its realization. Thus the cross of Jesus is the supreme instance of triumphant *satyagraha*.

The "fact of Gandhi" was the challenge of a spiritual reality not unlike "the fact of Christ." Gandhi translated the power of suffering love, supremely illustrated in the cross of Christ, into the reality of mass action. Decrying the tendency in others to regard the cross merely as a means to personal salvation, S. K. George described Gandhi as one "in whom the central principle of the Cross has again incarnated itself." Hence Gandhi was calling Christianity back to its own truth.[26]

ORTHOPRAXIS AS GANDHIAN CHRISTOLOGY

If the central issue in Gandhi's criticism of Christianity is Christology as dogma, the resolution of Gandhi's criticism is through orthopraxis, or right action.[27] In most of the missionary practice with which Gandhi was familiar, non-Christian religions were regarded in Christian dogma as existing either in ignorance or in error. What Gandhi was opposed to, then, was not dogma, but the dogmatism of the Christian missionary evangelism of his time.

Current missionary practice has been modified by Vatican Council II's more positive teaching on non-Christian religions. And it may not be unreasonable to think that Gandhi, whose life and thought were echoed in several Protestant missionary conventions, may have indirectly made some contribution to the council's document on non-Christian religions and its Decree on the Church's Missionary Activity.

Vatican II represents a great advance in the attitude of the Catholic church toward non-Christian religions. Of Hinduism in particular, it says: ". . . in Hinduism men explore the divine mystery and express it both in the limitless riches of myth and the accurately defined insights of philosophy. They seek release from the trials of the present life by ascetical practices, profound meditation and recourse to God in confidence and love."[28] Following references to Buddhism and other religions, the declaration documents the church's principle of nonrejection of anything that is true and holy in these religions, as well as sincere respect for their teachings, which, even when differing from the teachings of the church, "nevertheless often reflect a ray of that truth which enlightens all men." Vatican Council II exhorts Catholics, prudently and lovingly, through dialogue and collaboration with the followers of other religions, and in witness of Christian faith and life, to acknowledge, preserve, and promote the spiritual and moral values as well as the social and cultural values found in non-Christian religions.[29] The Council's Decree on the Church's Missionary Activity (no. 13) speaks of conversion not as a guarantee of salvation but as a turning away from sin to the mystery of the love of God, to be marked by a progressive change of outlook and morals—all terms that are Gandhian. While insisting on a person's right to follow his or her own faith, unimpeded by others, the decree furthermore forbids the use of force, enticements, or other unworthy techniques in bringing about conversions. Gandhi would have rejoiced at these doctrinal developments.

While it remains the task of the church in India to integrate the various parts of the teachings of Vatican Council II into church life, some progress has been made since Gandhi's time. The church is more open, for example, to positive influences from other religions. Indian Christian theologians such as Raymond Panikkar are addressing themselves to the task of integrating Hinduism's challenge into their theological world.[30] However, there has always been some tension between the concept of Christ as exclusive, as seen in such New Testament texts as Acts 4:12, Mark 16:15–16, and John 3:16, 18, and the image of Christ as a universal figure, as seen in those New Testament texts that portray Christ as reconciling slave and master, man and woman, Jew and Gentile. As Panikkar writes:

> The Book of the Acts and the Pauline Epistles testify to us of the deep crisis of universalism through which the Church passed in the second decade of her history. Can we truly say that even after twenty centuries the Church has entirely surmounted this initial crisis of catholicity?[31]

Unlike biblical Jewish history, which reacted by violently repudiating its own ancestral polytheistic prehistory, India's Hinduism has moved smoothly from its Vedic polytheism by way of Upanishadic impersonal absolutism and Mahayana Buddhism's personal absolutism to Vaishnavite and Saivite monotheism. And yet it is able to condone apparent practical polytheism. The logic of this would seem to be that one theism does not contradict another but, rather, includes the justification for another. No manifestation of the perfection of God can serve as a denial of any other such manifestation.

In order to incarnate Christ in India's culture, Indian Christians may have to interpret the exclusivist passages of the New Testament as merely representing the early Christian repudiation of the Jewish repudiation of Jesus as the Christ. Thus exclusivist Christocentrism could be seen as representing the polemical phase of the early church's Christology, necessary in providing it with a new institutional identity distinct from its parental Judaism.[32] The advantage of this interpretation is that it would explain, even if not justify, the former attitude of exclusiveness and set the stage for a Hindu-Christian dialogue.

The place of Jesus Christ in Hinduism is among the many leaders and teachers revered as revealers of God and even as incarnations of God, in his aspect as the Lover and Redeemer of humankind. In fact, Hinduism's henotheistic conception of a favorite God, Ishta Devata, would allow an exclusive worship of Jesus for those who find in such worship the way to their God-realization.[33]

Christianity in such a setting would have to be undogmatic and true to the spiritual insight of Jesus of Nazareth, discovering and establishing links with liberal elements in all other religions and finding its rightful place in the larger fellowship of faiths to come, of which Hinduism, with its genuine catholicity, is an advanced even if imperfect example.[34] Such a Christianity, by its emphasis on morality as the way to union with God, would have a special contribution to make to the evolution of Hinduism itself. Rather than replacing Hinduism, it would be doing Gandhi's work in enabling Hinduism to come to a new fruition.[35]

Recognizing that ". . . every one of us is a son of God and capable of doing what Jesus did, if we but endeavour to express the Divine in us,"[36] Gandhi drew from Christianity to transform Hinduism in at least three significant ways. First, he realized the Christic presence of God in the poor and the untouchables, initiating actions to break down the barriers that surrounded them and bring them back into the Hindu fold. Second, influenced by Christian thinking, he reinterpreted *karma* as a social and communal expression of sin and salvation rather than an isolated, individualized relationship with God. Third, he saw the necessity of the cross or suffering love (*ahimsa*) for the God-realization of all people. In each instance, Gandhi saw social and political liberation as the manifestation of these specifically Christian contributions to his transformation of Hinduism. Therein also he demonstrated the locus of his Christology in praxis or action.

Gandhian Christology is an expression of the experience of liberation based on the spirituality of a liberator who is placed beside Jesus Christ, becomes another Christ, and does not replace or displace him. In accepting the depths of human weakness, Gandhi made the power of God manifest, as Jesus had before him. In his search for truth he bridged the gap between Christian theology and Hindu spirituality.[37] Where Max Weber had only analyzed the relationship between the Protestant ethic and the spirit of capitalism, without making any judgment upon it, and Marx had taken a committed stand for the dispossessed proletariat, but introduced a contradiction between religious faith and the process of social liberation, Gandhi resolved the contradiction by making religious faith an ally and an instrument in the social and political liberation of human beings. Social and political liberation were correlatives to spiritual liberation.

In his unflinching dedication to truth as God, in his relentless attempt to realize that truth through action and prayer, in his openness to correction and criticism, in his alignment with the poor and the voiceless, and in his suffering and death for justice sealed in fellowship and reconciliation, Gandhi can be seen as a man whose prayer, with Francis of Assisi and Ignatius of Loyola,* to be placed with Christ the liberator was answered abundantly.

*The Prayer of St. Francis

Lord, make me an instrument of Thy peace;
Where there is hatred, let me sow love;
where there is injury, pardon;
where there is doubt, faith;
where there is despair, hope;
where there is darkness, light;
and where there is sadness, joy.

O Divine Master, grant that I may
not so much seek to be consoled, as to console;
to be understood, as to understand;
to be loved, as to love;
for it is in giving that we receive;
it is in pardoning that we are pardoned;
and it is in dying that we are born to eternal life.

See also *The Spiritual Exercises of St. Ignatius of Loyola*, meditations on "The Kingdom of Christ" and "The Two Standards."

Notes

The following abbreviations are used throughout the Notes. Citations to books for which no author is listed are to works by Gandhi. Full bibliographical details for sources cited are given in the Bibliography if they do not appear in the Notes.

Autobiography   Mohandas K. Gandhi, *An Autobiography: The Story of My Experiments with Truth*. Because of the numerous editions of this book, in many countries, citations to it are by part and chapter number (roman numerals, as in the original), and not by page number. Thus, e.g., *Autobiography*, I: IX, refers to part I, chapter IX.

CW   *The Collected Works of Mahatma Gandhi*. Citations are to volume and page numbers. Thus, e.g., *CW* 31: 122, refers to volume 31, page 122.

HCIP   R. C. Majumdar, ed., *History and Culture of the Indian People*. Citations are to volume and page numbers. Thus, e.g., *HCIP* 11: 91, refers to volume 11, page 91.

SSA   Mohandas K. Gandhi, *Satyagraha in South Africa*.

1 GANDHI'S *LOCUS THEOLOGICUS:* THE HISTORICAL SETTING

1. See Johann Metz, *Faith in History and Society: Toward a Practical Fundamental Theology*.
2. See Matthew L. Lamb, *History, Method and Theology*.
3. Gregory Baum, *Truth beyond Relativism: Karl Mannheim's Sociology of Knowledge*, p. 71.
4. Ibid., pp.17–18.
5. Sebastian Kappen, *Jesus and Freedom*, p. 6.
6. Ibid., p. 7.cf. Ainslie T. Embree, ed., *The Hindu Tradition*, p. 238.
7. Kappen, *Jesus and Freedom*, p. 8.
8. Ibid., p. 9.
9. M. K. Gandhi, *Hind Swaraj*, chap. 7.

10. M. K. Gandhi, *An Autobiography: The Story of My Experiments with Truth* (hereafter cited as *Autobiography*), part I, chap. I.

11. *Autobiography*, I: I.

12. Ibid.

13. Ibid., I:II.

14. Ibid.

15. Ibid., I: VI.

16. Ibid.

17. Ibid., I: VII.

18. Ibid., I: VIII.

19. Ibid.

20. Ibid., I: IX.

21. Ibid.

22. Ibid., I: XI–XII.

23. Ibid., I: XIV.

24. Ibid., I: XX.

25. Ibid.

26. Ibid., I: XXIV.

27. Ibid., I: XXV.

28. Ibid., II: V.

29. Ibid., II: VII–X.

30. Ibid., II: XIV.

31. Ibid., II: XII.

32. Ibid., II: XIII.

33. Ibid., II: XXI.

34. Ibid., II: XIX.

35. Ibid., II: XXV; III: III.

36. Ibid., III: IV.

37. Ibid., III: X; *CW* 3: 113–14.

38. *Autobiography*, III: X.

39. Ibid., II: XI.

40. *Harijan*, Mar. 6, 1937; M. K. Gandhi, *Christian Missions*, p. 170.

41. *Autobiography*, II: XV.

42. Ibid.

43. Ibid., II: XI, XXII.

44. Ibid., III: XVIII.

45. *Young India*, Aug. 6, 1925; *Christian Missions*, p. 51.

46. *Autobiography*, III: XIX.

47. Ibid., II: XV.

48. Ibid.

49. Ibid.

50. Ibid.

51. Ibid., III: XII.

52. Ibid., III: XVII–XXVIII.

53. Ibid., IV: I.
54. Ibid., IV: III.
55. Ibid., IV: IV–V; III: IV–V.
56. *CW* 4: 5.
57. *Autobiography*, IV: XIX–XXI.
58. *Indian Opinion*, Dec. 31, 1906.
59. *Autobiography*, III: VII.
60. Letter of May 27, 1906.
61. *Autobiography*, III: XXVI, narrates the principle of *satyagraha* and the origin of the term.
62. *CW* 6: v–vii.
63. *Autobiography*, IV: XXVI.
64. *CW* 7: 118.
65. *CW* 7: 409.
66. *CW* 7: 67.
67. *SSA*, chap. 16.
68. *CW* 8: 447.
69. *CW* 7: 445.
70. *CW* 7: 467.
71. *CW* 8: vii–ix.
72. *CW* 8: 463.
73. *CW* 8: 464.
74. *CW* 8: 529.
75. *CW* 10: vii.
76. *CW* 12: 186.
77. Golden Number (50th issue) of *Indian Opinion*, December 1914; *CW* 12: appendix 28.
78. *CW* 12: x.
79. Regamey, *Non-Violence and the Christian Conscience*, p. 503.
80. Ibid., p. ix.
81. *Autobiography*, V: XI, XIV.
82. Ibid., V: XX–XXI.
83. Ibid., V: XXIII–XXV.
84. Ibid., V: XXVI.
85. Ibid., V: XXVII.
86. Ibid., V: XXVIII.
87. Ibid., V: XXIV–XXX.
88. Ibid., V: XXXII.
89. Ibid.
90. Ibid.
91. Ibid., V: XXXIV.
92. *HCIP* 11: 306.
93. *HCIP* 11: 315.
94. *HCIP* 11: 327–28.

95. *HCIP* 11: 337.
96. *HCIP* 11: 333–34.
97. *HCIP* 11: 337–49.
98. *HCIP* 11: 349–51.
99. *CW* 23: 114.
100. *CW* 32: 114.
101. *CW* 23: 97.
102. *CW* 23: 115.
103. *CW* 23: 118.
104. *CW* 23: 117.
105. *CW* 23: 119.
106. *CW* 23: 414–18.
107. *CW* 23: 229–35.
108. *CW* 23: 440–43.
109. *CW* 25: 175.
110. *CW* 25: 200.
111. *CW* 25: 356.
112. *CW* 26: 512.
113. *CW* 36: 217.
114. *CW* 26: 244.
115. *CW* 29: v.
116. *CW* 30: 542.
117. *CW* 30: 562.
118. *CW* 31: 122.
119. *CW* 31: 460.
120. *CW* 32: vi.
121. *CW* 35: 81.
122. *CW* 35: 263.
123. *HCIP* 11: 454–57.
124. *CW* 36: 14.
125. *CW* 36: 90.
126. *CW* 36: 243.
127. *CW* 34: 451.
128. *CW* 34: 452.
129. *CW* 34: 500.
130. Letter to Motilal Nehru, *CW* 37: 194.
131. *CW* 37: 212, 249.
132: *CW* 38: 290.
133. *CW* 38: 268.
134. *CW* 38: 284–85.
135. *CW* 40: 78.
136. For full text, see *CW* 42: appendix 1.
137. *CW* 42: 81.
138. *CW* 42: 444.
139. *CW* 42: 423.

140. *CW* 42: 382.
141. *CW* 42: 477–78.
142. *CW* 42: 497.
143. *HCIP* 11: 477–82.
144. *HCIP* 11: 482–84.
145. *HCIP* 11: 493.
146. *HCIP* 11: 501–4.
147. *CW* 49: 191.
148. *CW* 59: 3–12.
149. *HCIP* 11: 522–25.
150. *CW* 61: 21, 88.
151. *CW* 61: 212.
152. *CW* 63: 347, 417.
153. *CW* 63: 234–35.
154. *Harijan*, Jan. 7, 1939.
155. *Young India*, Sept. 25, 1925.
156. *Speeches and Writings of M. K. Gandhi*, pp. 273–75.
157. *Harijan*, Dec. 15, 1933.
158. Ibid., Dec. 12, 1936.
159. *CW* 64: 242.
160. *CW* 64: 195.
161. *CW* 64: 71.
162. *CW* 64: 71, 218.
163. *CW* 65: 37.
164. *CW* 65: 422.
165. *CW* 65: 99–100.
166. *CW* 65: 117–18.
167. *CW* 65: 407.
168. *CW* 65: 432.
169. *CW* 66: 16.
170. *CW* 66: 62.
171. *CW* 66: 155–56.
172. *CW* 66: 300–302.
173. *CW* 66: 350.
174. *CW* 66: 410.
175. *CW* 66: 371–72, 430–31.
176. *CW* 66: vii.
177. *CW* 66: 275.
178. *CW* 66: vii.
179. *CW* 66: 404–5.
180. *CW* 66: 137.
181. *CW* 66: 137–41.
182. *CW* 66: 97, 126, 279.
183. *CW* 66: 390.
184. *CW* 66: 102.

185. *CW* 66: 324.
186. *CW* 70: 162.
187. *CW* 70: 204.
188. *CW* 70: 175, 311.
189. *CW* 70: 257–58.
190. *CW* 70: 175, 311.
191. *CW* 70: 416–18.
192. *CW* 70: 411.
193. *CW* 70: 431.
194. *CW* 70: 259.
195. *CW* 70: 316.
196. *CW* 70: 337.
197. *CW* 70: 328.
198. *CW* 70: 205–6.
199. *HCIP* 11: 632–33.
200. *HCIP* 11: 635–38.
201. *HCIP* 11: 644–45.
202. *HCIP* 11: 650. For details the reader is referred to *HCIP*, 11: 28.
203. *HCIP* 11: 696–97.
204. *HCIP* 11: 712–13.
205. *HCIP* 11: 713–14.
206. *HCIP* 11: 716–20.
207. *HCIP* 11: 721.
208. *HCIP* 11: 722–26.
209. *HCIP* 11: 726.
210. *HCIP* 11: 727.
211. *HCIP* 11: 728.
212. Ibid.
213. *HCIP* 11: 733–39.
214. *HCIP* 11: 739.
215. *HCIP* 11: 740.
216. *HCIP* 11: 752.
217. Majumdar, *Advanced History*, p. 994.
218. Ibid.
219. Ibid.
220. Ibid.
221. Ibid.
222. Ibid., p. 995.
223. Ibid.
224. Ibid.
225. Ibid., pp. 995–96.
226. Louis Fischer, *The Life of Mahatma Gandhi*, pp. 467–75.
227. Ibid., pp. 475–502.
228. Ibid., pp. 502–5.

2   LIBERATION AS *SWARAJ*

1. There is as yet little secondary literature on these Gandhian concepts. James Brown McGinnis III, "Freedom and Its Realization in Gandhi's Philosophy and Practice of Non-Violence" is unpublished (Ph.D. dissertation, Saint Louis University, 1974). Published material includes J. Bandyopadyaya, *Social and Political Thought of Gandhi* (Bombay: Allied Publishers, 1969), pp. 63–84; and Margaret Chatterjee, "Gandhi's Concept of Freedom," in *The Philosophy of Mahatma Gandhi* (New Delhi: Gandhi Bhavan, University of Delhi, 1969), pp. 23–30.

2. *CW* 35: 456.

3. *CW* 14: 50.

4. *CW* 8: 373–75.

5. See M. K. Gandhi, "A Brief Biographical Sketch of the Hon. Dadabhai Naoroji," *Indian Opinion* 8, no. 36 (Sept.3, 1910); *CW* 10: 313.

6. *CW* 38: 296.

7. *Hind Swaraj*, pp. 1–13; *CW* 10: 8–14.

8. Ibid., pp. 14–18.

9. Gandhi originally wrote *Hind Swaraj* in Gujarati during his return voyage from England to South Africa on the *Kildman Castle* late in 1908. The first twelve chapters were published in *Indian Opinion*—a weekly that Gandhi was editing and publishing in South Africa—on Dec. 11, 1909, and the last eight chapters were published in the issue of Dec. 18, 1909. *Hind Swaraj* was printed as a separate book in January 1910 and proscribed by the government of Bombay in March 1910. The same month Gandhi hastened to publish an English translation. The first Indian edition in English was brought out by Ganesh and Co., Madras, in 1919. By 1924 they had issued six editions of the book; the same year saw an American edition of the work, edited by H. T. Mazumdar, under the title, *Sermon on the Sea*. The second Gujarati edition was issued in 1914, in South Africa, with a new preface by Gandhi. The Navajivan Publishing House published, in September 1923, a facsimile edition of the Gujarati original in Gandhi's own hand. The *Collected Works* series has adopted the Revised New Edition of 1939, indicating in footnotes any significant variations from the Gujarati original of 1909 (see *CW* 10: 6).

10. *Hind Swaraj*, p.65.

11. Ibid., pp. 19–21.

12. Ibid., pp. 22–23.

13. Ibid., pp. 28–32.

14. Ibid., pp. 32–35.

15. Ibid., pp. 35–36.

16. Ibid., pp. 36–38.

17. Ibid., pp. 39–40.

18. Ibid., pp. 40–42.

19. Ibid., pp. 40–47.

20. Ibid., pp. 53–57.

21. Ibid., pp. 57–60.

22. Ibid., pp. 60–64.

23. *CW* 14: 48–66.

24. See *CW* 14: 378–79, 426–28, 429, 434, 440–42, for the basis of Gandhi's *swaraj* program at this time.

25. *Young India*, Dec. 15, 1921; *CW* 22: 18.

26. From Gujarati, *Navajivan*, Jan. 8, 1922; *CW* 22: 150.

27. *CW* 22: 106.

28. From Gujarati, *Navajivan*, Mar. 12, 1922; *CW* 23: 72.

29. *Young India*, July 17, 1924; *CW* 24: 396.

30. *CW* 23: 37–39.

31. *Young India*, May 8, 1924; *CW* 24: 11.

32. *Young India*, Jan. 29, 1925; *CW* 26: 50.

33. *CW* 65: 102.

34. *Young India*, Mar. 3, 1927; *CW* 33: 138–40. *Young India*, Mar. 17, 1927; *CW* 33: 133.

35. Letter of Mar. 19, 1924, to C. Vijayaraghavachariar, a lawyer and congressman who had presided over the Nagpur session of the Indian National Congress in 1920.

36. *Young India*, Jan. 27, 1924; *CW* 25: 361.

37. *Young India*, Jan. 13, 1927; *CW* 32: 552–53.

38. *The Hindu*, Apr. 19, 1929, and May 3, 1929; *CW* 40: 259, 316. *Young India*, Dec. 15, 1921; *CW* 22: 15. *Young India*, Mar. 9, 1922; *CW* 23: 53.

39. *The Statesman*, May 2, 1925; *CW* 27: 1.

40. *Hindi Navajivan*, May 4, 1924; *CW* 23: 538.

41. *Young India*, Jan. 29, 1925; *CW* 26: 49f.

42. *Young India*, May 8, 1924; *CW* 24: 14.

43. Ibid.

44. *Young India*, June 12, 1924; *CW* 24: 227.

45. *Young India*, Jan. 22, 1925; *CW* 25: 514.

46. Desai, *Mahadevbhaini Diary*, 7: 93–95; *CW* 26: 6–7.

47. *Young India*, Dec. 26, 1924; *CW* 25: 479.

48. Desai, *Mahadevbhaini Diary*, 7: 347–49; *CW* 26: 508.

49. Ibid., 7: 160; *CW* 26: 148.

50. Ibid., 7: 138–39; *CW* 26: 128.

51. Gandhi's letter to *The Statesman*, July 31, 1925; *CW* 27: 463.

52. Letter to Madanmohan Sharma, May 7, 1926; *CW* 30: 417.

53. Speech at pubic meeting in Wardha, Dec. 20, 1926; *CW* 32: 441.

54. Speech at public meeting in Comilla, Jan. 5, 1927; *Amrita Bazar Patrika*, Jan. 7, 1927; *Young India*, Jan. 13, 1927; *CW* 32: 511, 571–72.

55. Speech at Madhubani, Jan. 20, 1927; *The Searchlight*, Jan. 26, 1927; *CW* 32: 590.

56. *Young India*, Nov. 10, 1927; *CW* 35: 225.

57. *Young India*, Dec. 1, 1927; *CW* 35: 353.

58. Letter to Dr. M. A. Ansari, Dec. 25, 1927; *CW* 35: 420.

59. *Young India*, Jan. 5, 1928; *CW* 35: 436.

60. Letter to Prabhashankar Pattani, Nov. 8, 1927; *CW* 35: 223.

61. Letter to P. T. Pillay, Tirunelvely district, May 4, 1928; *CW* 36: 293–94.

62. *Young India*, Jan. 9, 1930; *CW* 42: 374–75.

63. Ibid.; *CW* 42: 377.

64. *Hindi Navajivan*, Apr. 10, 1930; *CW* 43: 227–28.

65. *Young India*, June 18, 1931; *CW* 47: 4.

66. Ibid.; *CW* 47: 2–3.

67. *Harijanbandhu*, Nov. 22, 1936; *Harijan*, Nov. 14, 1936; *CW* 63: 417.

68. *Harijanbandhu*, Nov. 8, 1936; *Harijan*, Nov. 7, 1936; *CW* 63: 406.

69. *Young India*, Nov. 3, 1927; *CW* 35: 212.

70. *CW* 49: 324.

71. *Harijan*, Sept. 17, 1938; *CW* 67: 353.

72. *Harijan*, Mar. 25, 1939; *CW* 69: 53.

73. *CW* 68: 243–44.

74. *Harijanbandhu*, Jan. 3, 1937; *Harijan*, Jan. 3, 1937; *CW* 64: 191–92.

75. Unpublished letter to S. Natesan, May 23, 1940.

76. Unpublished letter to "Bhakti" (Madame Edmond Privat), dated New Delhi, Nov. 29, 1947.

77. Ibid.

3   GANDHI'S THEOLOGY OF *SWARAJ*

1. From Gujarati, *Indian Opinion*, Jan. 12, 1907; *CW* 6: 265.

2. *Indian Opinion*, Dec. 9, 1908; *CW* 9: 107–8.

3. Ibid.

4. From Gujarati, *Indian Opinion*, Jan. 23, 1909; *CW* 9: 160.

5. From Gujarati, *Indian Opinion*, Aug. 7, 1909; *CW* 9: 277.

6. *Indian Opinion*, Feb. 5, 1910; *CW* 10: 149.

7. *Indian Opinion*, Mar. 26, 1910; *CW* 10: 197.

8. From Gujarati, *Indian Opinion*, May 29, 1909; *CW* 9: 219.

9. From Gujarati, *Indian Opinion*, June 3, 1911; *CW* 11: 98.

10. Letter to Janakadhari Prasad, May 28, 1928; *CW* 36: 338.

11. Letter to Esther Menon, May 29, 1932; *CW* 49: 490.

12. To Mohammad Shafee, Mar. 26, 1926; *CW* 30: 180.

13. *CW* 30: 216.

14. Letter to his wife, Kasturbai, May 7, 1933; *CW* 55: 140.

15. *Harijan*, May 6, 1933; *CW* 55: 121.

16. Letter to Narandas Gandhi, May 3, 1933; *CW* 55: 140.

17. *Harijan*, Mar. 18, 1939; *CW* 69: 51.

18. Letter to Verrier Elwin, Aug. 21, 1937; *CW* 66: 63.

19. Speech at Islamia College, Peshawar, May 4, 1938; *CW* 67: 63.

20. Interview to L. W. Jardne, July 9, 1939; *CW* 69: 412.

21. *CW* 69: 226.

22. Interview to Chinese delegates, Jan. 1, 1939; *Harijan*, Jan. 28, 1939; *CW* 68: 271.

23. Letter to Gangabehn Vaidya, May 19, 1930; *CW* 32: 155–56.

24. *CW* 32: 490.

25. *CW* 61: 111–15.

26. *CW* 32: 200.

27. *CW* 68: 207.

28. Letter of Nov. 26, 1936; *CW* 64: 79.

29. *CW* 68:43.

30. *CW* 68: 117.

31. *CW* 70: 196–97.

32. *CW* 36: 296.

33. *Harijan*, June 18, 1938; *CW* 66: 175.

34. *Navajivan*, May 5, 1928; *CW* 36: 296.

35. *Harijan*, June 8, 1935; *CW* 61: 138.

36. *CW* 56: 171–72.

37. *Harijan*, Aug. 29, 1936; *CW* 63: 240.

38. *CW* 65: 134.

39. *SSA*, chap. 23; *CW* 29: 149.

40. *Young India*, Feb. 18, 1926; *CW* 30: 25.

41. *SSA*, chap. 12; *CW* 29: 86–91.

42. *Young India*, Oct. 11, 1928; *CW* 37: 350. *Young India*, June 14, 1928; *CW* 36: 399.

43. *CW* 48: 411–12; see also Joseph Thekkinedath: *Love of Neighbour in Mahatma Gandhi*.

44. Letters on the *Gita*; *CW* 49: 111.

45. Ibid.

46. *Navajivan*, Apr. 6, 1930; *CW* 43: 145.

47. *CW* 37: 113.

48. *Young India*, May 8, 1930; *CW* 43: 215.

49. *CW* 48: 412. *Prajabandhu*, Apr. 6, 1930; *CW* 43: 167.

50. On the First Cause argument, see *CW* 36: 209. for *Gita* comment, see *CW* 41: 125–27.

51. *CW* 41: 115.

52. *CW* 30: 437.

53. *Young India*, Dec. 8, 1927; *CW* 35: 311.

54. *CW* 30: 493.

55. *CW* 30: 571–72.

56. *Harijan*, Jan. 29, 1938; *CW* 66: 343.

57. Letter to Sreedharan Nair, Oct. 3, 1938; *CW* 66: 390.

58. Letter to Mirabehn, May 18, 1936; *CW* 62: 415.

59. *CW* 56: 156.

60. *CW* 49: 428.

61. *CW* 33: 278.

62. *CW* 48: 180.
63. *CW* 36: 276.
64. *Harijan*, Apr. 18, 1936; *CW* 62: 332-34.
65. Ibid.
66. *Hindi Navajivan*, Sept. 9, 1921; *CW* 31: 20.
67. *Young India*, Sept. 2, 1921; *CW* 31: 70.
68. Letter to Fulchand Shah, Jan. 22, 1925; *CW* 26: 32.
69. From Gujarati, *Navajivan*, May 2, 1926; *CW* 30: 399.
70. *Young India*, May 27, 1926; *CW* 30: 486-88.
71. Letter to A. C. C. Harvey, Jan. 11, 1927; *CW* 32: 547-48.
72. *CW* 65: 134.
73. *The Leader*, July 27, 1934; *CW* 58: 250.
74. *The Leader*, July 30, 1934; *CW* 58: 250.
75. Speech at Seva Sangh meeting, Apr. 20, 1937; *CW* 65: 126.
76. Speech in Madras, *The Hindu*, Mar. 24, 1925; *CW* 26: 393.
77. *The Hindu*, Sept. 24, 1927; *CW* 35: 21.
78. From Hindi, *Harijan Sevak*, Feb. 25, 1939; *CW* 68: 447.
79. *CW* 32: 439.
80. Letter of Jan. 18, 1931; *CW* 45: 99.
81. Speech at Seva Sangh meeting; *CW* 65: 133.
82. Letter of Dec. 9, 1938; *CW* 68: 197.
83. Letter to Durga Das, in Das, *India from Curzon to Nehru and After*.
84. *CW* 21: 372.
85. *Harijan*, Dec. 22, 1933; *CW* 56: 332-33.
86. Desai, *Epic of Travancore*, pp. 169-71; *CW* 64: 254.
87. *CW* 56: 485-86.
88. *CW* 56: 409.
89. *Harijanbandhu*, July 15, 1934; *CW* 58: 114-15.
90. *The Hindu*, Jan. 15, 1934; *CW* 56: 486.
91. *The Hindu*, Dec. 18, 1933; *CW* 56: 246.
92. Letter to L. Asar, Jan. 23, 1932; *CW* 49: 25.
93. *CW* 56: 485.
94. *CW* 56: 408.
95. *Harijan*, Nov. 24, 1933; *CW* 56: 271.
96. *The Hindu*, Oct. 6, 1927; *CW* 35: 82.
97. *Harijan Sevak*, Dec. 8, 1933; *CW* 56: 248.
98. *CW* 64: 254.
99. *CW* 58: 68-69; *CW* 70: 184.
100. *CW* 56: 247-48.
101. *CW* 35: 20-21.
102. *Navajivan*, Jan. 29, 1922; *CW* 35: 37, 486.
103. *Harijanbandhu*, Dec. 3, 1933; *CW* 56: 255.
104. *Harijan*, June 20, 1936; *CW* 66: 35-36.
105. Ibid.
106. *CW* 66: 39.
107. *CW* 66: 42.

108. *Harijan*, Nov. 24, 1933; *CW* 56: 271.

109. *Harijan*, Sept. 23, 1939; *CW* 70: 184.

110. *Harijan*, June 20, 1936; *CW* 66: 37.

111. *CW* 64: 257, 271, 281, 298-99.

112. *CW* 64: 243.

113. *CW* 64: 291.

114. Wardha speech, *Young India*, Dec. 30, 1926; *CW* 32: 441.

115. *CW* 32: 442.

116. Sewan speech, *Young India*, Jan. 27, 1927; *CW* 32: 571-72.

117. *CW* 32: 572.

118. *CW* 64: 208.

119. *CW* 23: 88.

120. *Young India*, Oct. 11, 1928; *CW* 37: 347.

121. Rabindranath Tagore, *Gitanjali*, (Macmillan, India, 1979), XXXV.

122. Letter of Jan. 4, 1931; *CW* 65: 59.

123. Letter of Feb. 16, 1931; *CW* 65: 180-81.

124. *CW* 69: 91.

125. *CW* 69: 248.

126. *Harijan*, May 6, 1933; *CW* 55: 121.

127. *The Hindu*, June 17, 1933; also *The Hindustan Times*, June 17, 1933; *CW* 55: 201.

128. From Gujarati, *Navajivan*, Jan. 5, 1930; *CW* 42: 366.

129. *Harijan*, Apr. 24, 1937; *CW* 65: 111.

130. *CW* 26: 224.

131. *Young India*, Mar. 5, 1925; *CW* 26: 224-25.

132. *CW* 11: 126.

133. *CW* 11: 189.

134. *CW* 11: 92.

135. *CW* 41: 125-28.

136. *CW* 30: 492.

137. Letter to Amrit Kaur; *CW* 64: 432.

138. From Gujarati, *Navajivan*, Mar. 16, 1930; *CW* 44: 82.

139. *CW* 45: 22.

140. Letter to Prabhudas Gandhi, May 20, 1932; *CW* 49: 461.

141. *CW* 48: 404.

142. Letter of Feb. 8, 1932; *CW* 49: 78.

143. Letter to boys and girls, Mar. 21, 1932; *CW* 49: 223.

144. *CW* 48: 404-5.

145. *CW* 61: 81.

146. *CW* 65: 398.

147. From Gujarati, *Navajivan*, Nov. 20, 1921; *CW* 21: 472-73.

148. *CW* 36: 276, 398-99.

149. From Gujarati, *Navajivan*, Mar. 16, 1930; *CW* 43: 82.

150. From Gujarati, *Navajivan*, Nov. 20, 1921; *CW* 21: 474-75.

151. *CW* 32: 164-65.

152. *Young India*, Jan. 3, 1929; *CW* 38: 139–40.

153. Speech at Mandla, Dec. 6, 1933; *CW* 56: 304.

154. *CW* 62: 119.

155. *CW* 44: 107–8.

156. *CW* 38: 1, 17–18.

157. *CW* 56: 6.

158. *CW* 38: 72.

159. *CW* 49: 328.

160. *Young India*, Jan. 8, 1925; *CW* 25: 552.

161. *Young India*, Apr. 3, 1924; *CW* 23: 340.

162. *CW* 14: 50.

163. *CW* 60: 159.

164. From Gujarati, *Navajivan*, Mar. 30, 1930; *CW* 43: 125–26.

165. *CW* 38: 1, 17–18.

166. *CW* 42: 22.

167. *CW* 46: 167.

168. *CW* 33: 9.

169. See Gerth and Wright, *From Max Weber*, p. 59.

170. *Harijan*, Mar. 11, 1939; *CW* 69: 33.

171. *Young India*, Mar. 24, 1927; *CW* 33: 186.

172. *Harijan*, Dec. 26, 1936; *CW* 64: 141.

173. *Harijan*, May 6, 1933; *CW* 55: 75.

174. *CW* 61: 92.

175. "Anasaktiyoga," *CW* 41: 94.

176. *CW* 60: 388.

4   THE WAY OF THE CROSS AS THE WAY TO *SWARAJ*

1. For analyses of the Gandhian philosophy of conflict and conflict resolution, see Joan Bondurant, *Conquest of Violence: The Gandhian Philosophy of Conflict*, and Arne Naess, *Gandhi and Group Conflict*.

2. *Autobiography*, Introduction.

3. N. K. Bose, *Studies in Gandhism*, p. 269.

4. D. G. Tendulkar, *Mahatma*, 3: 176.

5. Bondurant, *Conquest of Violence*, pp. 16–17.

6. *Speeches and Writings of Mahatma Gandhi*, p. 494.

7. *Young India, 1919–1922* (Madras: S. Ganesan, 1922), pp. 33–36; Tendulkar, *Mahatma*, 1: 342.

8. Bondurant, *Conquest of Violence*, pp. 20–21.

9. *Harijan*, July 18, 1948.

10. Bondurant, *Conquest of Violence*, p. 21.

11. *Ashram Observances in Action*, from the Gujarati; originally published in English as *History of the Satyagraha Ashram*. *Harijan*, July 18, 1948; *CW* 5: 194.

12. *Young India*, Dec. 25, 1925; Bondurant, *Conquest of Violence*, p. 22.

13. *From Yerawda Mandir: Ashram Observances*, p. 7.

14. *Young India*, Jan. 19, 1921, as quoted by Jag Parvesh Chander, *Teachings of Mahatma Gandhi* (Lahore: Indian Printing Works, 1945), p. 412.

15. Bondurant, *Conquest of Violence*, p. 24.

16. *From Yerawda Mandir: Ashram Observances*, p. 8.

17. Ibid.

18. Bondurant, *Conquest of Violence*, p. 25.

19. From an address to the YMCA, Madras, Feb. 16, 1916; quoted in Bondurant, *Conquest of Violence*, p. 26.

20. *Young India*, July 9, 1925; *CW* 27: 349.

21. *Young India*, June 12, 1922, as quoted in Chander, *Teachings of Mahatma Gandhi,* p. 352.

22. *Young India*, Aug. 11, 1920; *CW* 18: 133.

23. Ibid.

24. *Non-Violence in Peace and War*, p. 49.

25. Ibid.

26. *SSA*, p. 175.

27. Ibid., p. 179.

28. *Young India*, Aug. 11, 1920.

29. *Young India*, Oct. 31, 1929.

30. *Harijan*, July 20, 1935.

31. *Harijan*, Sept. 1, 1940.

32. Bondurant, *Conquest of Violence*, p. viii.

33. I am indebted to Joan Bondurant, *Conquest of Violence*, for the pattern of analysis I use in discussing the three following conflict situations.

34. Quoted by Bondurant, *Conquest of Violence*, p. 89.

35. Ibid., p. 90.

36. Letter to Lord Irwin, Mar. 2, 1930.

37. See Bondurant, *Conquest of Violence*, p. 96, for an incident recorded by American journalist Negley Farson.

38. *CW* 51: v.

39. *CW* 51: 71.

40. Ibid.

41. *CW* 50: 383–84.

42. See *HCIP* 11: 523.

43. *HCIP* 11: 521–24.

44. *CW* 51: 140–41.

45. *CW* 51: 145.

46. Gene Sharp, *Gandhi Wields the Weapon of Moral Power*, pp. 227–89, presents a detailed account of this fast.

47. Louis Fischer, *Life of Mahatma Gandhi*, p. 494.

48. Ibid., p. 495.

49. For a brief but sensitively analytical account of this fast, see Amiya Chakravarty, *A Saint at Work: A View of Gandhi's Work and Message*, pp. 23ff; also quoted by Sharp, pp. 258–60.

50. Fischer, *Life of Mahatma Gandhi*, pp. 475-90.

51. Ibid., p. 490.

52. Ibid., pp. 490-502.

53. Ibid., p. 502.

54. Ibid.

55. Interview given by Pyarelal to Jesudasan, on Jan. 8, 1979. Nehru's tribute is from the Indian government's *Homage to Mahatma Gandhi*, pp. 9-10.

56. James Douglass, *The Non-Violent Cross: A Theology of Revolution and Peace*, pp. 45-46.

57. *Young India*, Mar. 5, 1925; *CW* 26: 224-25. James Douglass, *The Non-Violent Cross*, pp. 66-69, quotes in full Webb Miller's account of the Dharasana incident of the Salt *Satyagraha* to substantiate the aspect of *satyagraha* as a politically active and revolutionary suffering love.

58. Karl Rahner, *Foundations of Christian Faith* (New York: Seabury Press, 1978), pp. 203-27; 293-321; *Theological Investigations*, vol. 6 (London: Darton, Longman and Todd, 1974), pp. 390ff.; Gerald A. McCool, ed., *A Rahner Reader* (New York: Seabury Press, 1975), pp. 211-24.

59. Louis Fischer, *Life of Mahatma Gandhi*, p. 473, documents Lord Mountbatten's testimony to this before the Royal Empire Society on Oct. 6, 1948.

60. *CW* 25: 465.

61. *CW* 29: 88.

62. *CW* 55: 121.

63. *CW* 58: 164.

64. *Navajivan*, Apr. 8, 1928; *CW* 36: 182.

65. *CW* 47: 344.

66. *CW* 60: 387.

67. *Young India*, Sept. 3, 1931; *CW* 67: 368-69.

68. *CW* 30: 112.

69. *Harijan*, Nov. 24, 1933; *CW* 56: 271.

70. *Navajivan*, Mar. 16, 1930; *CW* 43: 82.

71. Letter to Narayan Khare, Feb. 10, 1932; *CW* 49: 81.

72. Letter to Shrada Shah, Mar. 5, 1932; *CW* 49: 178.

73. From *SSA*, second part of Gandhi's preface, which was published in *Navajivan*, July 5, 1925. It also appeared in the original Gujarati edition of *SSA*. It was omitted in the English translation issued in 1928. See also *CW* 29: 6.

74. Fischer, *Life of Mahatma Gandhi*, p. 503.

75. *CW* 36: 164.

76. *CW* 36: 165.

77. Letter to Shrada Shah, Mar. 5, 1932; *CW* 49: 178.

78. *CW* 36: 165.

79. Johann Baptist Metz, *Faith in History and Society*, pp. 60-87, 200-205.

80. *Young India*, Aug. 13, 1931; *CW* 47: 286.

81. Letter to Hanumanprasad Poddar, Apr. 8, 1932; *CW* 49: 284–85.

82. *CW* 64: 398.

83. *CW* 62: 334.

84. *CW* 62: 334.

85. *CW* 64: 398.

86. *CW* 64: 397.

87. *Harijan*, Apr. 17, 1937; *CW* 65: 82.

88. *Harijan*, July 4, 1936; *CW* 63: 45.

89. See, for instance, Gandhi's letter to Donald Miller, July 11, 1936; *CW* 63: 137.

90. For Gandhi's exposition of the concept of the equality of all religions, see *From Yerawda Mandir*, chaps. 10–11.

91. *CW* 64: 326.

92. *CW* 64: 420.

93. *CW* 64: 420.

94. Letter to Kirby Page, La Habra, Calif., Oct. 17, 1937; *CW* 66: 250.

95. *CW* 68: 271.

96. *Harijan*, Jan. 7, 1939; *CW* 68: 278.

97. *Harijan*, Mar. 4, 1939; *CW* 68: 306–7.

98. *Harijan*, Jan. 30, 1937; *CW* 64: 327.

99. *CW* 62: 334.

100. *Harijan*, May 30, 1936; *CW* 62: 388.

101. *CW* 64: 398.

102. James Douglass, *The Non-Violent Cross*, p. 66.

103. Ibid., p. 64.

104. R. K. Prabhu, *What Jesus Means to Me*, p. 16.

105. Ibid., p. 13.

106. Anand T. Hingorani, *The Message of Jesus Christ*, pp. 22–23.

107. *CW* 66: 432.

108. Hingorani, *The Message of Jesus Christ*, p. 68.

109. Ibid., p. 44.

110. Ibid., pp. 37–38.

111. James Douglass, *The Non-Violent Cross*, p. 75.

112. Ibid., p. 76.

5   GANDHI'S VISION OF A LIBERATED SOCIETY

1. *Young India*, Sept. 17, 1925.

2. *Young India*, Oct. 7, 1926.

3. *Young India*, Jan. 12, 1928.

4. *Young India*, Jan. 29, 1925.

5. Mahadev Desai, *With Gandhi in Ceylon*, p. 93.

6. *Young India*, Nov. 1, 1928.

7. Mahadev Desai, *Gandhiji in Indian Villages*, p. 166.

8. *Young India*, July 2, 1931.

9. *Young India*, June 12, 1924.

10. *Young India*, Apr. 14, 1929.

11. *Young India*, Mar. 12, 1925.

12. *Young India*, Mar. 2, 1922.

13. *Young India*, July 17, 1924.

14. *Young India*, Dec. 31, 1931.

15. *Young India*, Mar. 21, 1929.

16. *Young India*, June 3, 1926.

17. M. Desai, *Gandhiji in Indian Villages*, p. 170.

18. *Young India*, June 18, 1925.

19. *Young India*, Dec. 4, 1924.

20. *Autobiography*, "Farewell."

21. Iyer, *The Moral and Political Thought of Mahatma Gandhi*, p. 46. For brief comparisons and contrasts of Gandhi's thought with other world thinkers, cf. ibid., pp. 38–61.

22. Ibid., pp. 49–50.

23. Letter to an Indian friend, July 4, 1932; in Desai, *Mahaderbhaini Diary*, p. 149.

24. *Ethical Religion*, p. 43.

25. *Young India*, Oct. 13, 1921.

26. *Harijan*, Oct. 9, 1937.

27. *Harijan*, June 1, 1947.

28. *Autobiography*, IV: XVIII.

29. Ruskin,*Unto This Last*, Essay I, p. 4.

30. Ibid., Essay II, p. 15.

31. Ibid., p. 16.

32. Ibid., Essay III, p. 30.

33. Ibid., Essay IV, p. 32.

34. Ibid., Essay III, p. 29.

35. Ibid., Essay II, p. 17.

36. Ibid., Essay III, p. 28.

37. Ibid., pp. 29–30.

38. *Young India*, Nov. 26, 1931.

39. *Young India*, Mar. 26, 1931.

40. *Harijan*, Nov. 2, 1934.

41. *Constructive Programme*, p. 26.

42. *Young India*, Feb. 17, 1927.

43. Speech to village volunteer workers, Apr. 11, 1945; in Pyarelal, *Mahatma Gandhi: The Last Phase*, 1: 66.

44. *Young India*, Jan. 8, 1925.

45. *Amrita Bazar Patrika*, Aug. 3, 1934.

46. *Young India*, Mar. 26, 1931.

47. Quoted in Louis Fischer, ed., *The Essential Gandhi*, p. 286.

48. *Young India*, Oct. 7, 1926.

49. *Young India*, Nov. 15, 1928.

50. *Young India*, Nov. 12, 1931.

51. *Harijan*, Aug. 29, 1936.

52. *Community Services News*, Sept.–Oct. 1946.
53. *Harijan*, Nov. 2, 1934.
54. *Harijan*, Sept. 29, 1940.
55. *Harijan*, Nov. 5, 1935.
56. *Young India*, June 18, 1925.
57. Fischer, *The Essential Gandhi*, p. 296.
58. *Young India*, Jan. 29, 1925.
59. *Young India*, Sept. 11, 1924.
60. *Young India*, Feb. 3, 1927.
61. *Young India*, June 9, 1927.
62. *Young India*, Feb. 26, 1925.
63. *Young India*, Sept. 13, 1928.
64. *Harijan*, Dec. 30, 1939.
65. Louis Fischer, *A Week with Gandhi*, pp. 55–56.
66. *Harijan*, July 28, 1946.
67. *Constructive Programme*, p. 15.
68. *Harijan*, Jan. 9, 1937.
69. *Harijan*, July 26, 1942.
70. Fischer, *A Week with Gandhi*, pp. 55–56.
71. *Harijan*, July 26, 1942.
72. *Harijan*, Jan. 9, 1937.
73. *Constructive Programme*, pp. 14–15.
74. *Young India*, Nov. 19, 1925.
75. *Constructive Programme*, pp. 15–16.
76. *Young India*, Sept. 1, 1921.
77. *Constructive Programme*, pp. 16–17.
78. *Young India*, Mar. 12, 1925.
79. *Young India*, June 24, 1928.
80. *Young India*, Feb. 9, 1928.
81. *Young India*, Aug. 25, 1927.
82. *Harijan*, Mar. 23, 1947.
83. *Young India*, Dec. 6, 1928.
84. *Constructive Programme*, pp. 17–18.
85. *Young India*, June 4, 1931.
86. *Harijan*, Mar. 25, 1933.
87. *Young India*, June 24, 1926.
88. *Constructive Programme*, pp. 10–11.
89. Ibid., p. 25.
90. *From Yerawda Mandir*, chap. VI.
91. *Harijan*, June 29, 1935.
92. *Young India*, Sept. 10, 1931.

6   GANDHI'S CHALLENGE TO CHRISTIANITY

1. M. M. Thomas, *The Acknowledged Christ of the Indian Renaissance*, pp. 234–36.

2. Ibid., pp. 193-238.

3. P. D. Devanandan, "Gandhi's Critique of Christianity," in *Preparation for Dialogue* (Bangalore, 1964), pp. 97-119.

4. *Young India*, Mar. 21, 1929.

5. *Harijan*, Mar. 13, 1937.

6. *Harijan*, Jan. 22, 1939.

7. *Harijan*, Feb. 2, 1934.

8. *Harijan*, May 26, 1946.

9. *Harijan*, Feb. 16, 1934.

10. *Harijan*, Apr. 30, 1938.

11. *Young India*, Jan. 29, 1925.

12. *Harijan*, Mar. 25, 1939.

13. *Harijan*, May 30, 1936.

14. *Harijan*, Mar. 6, 1937.

15. *Harijan*, July 18, 1936.

16. Ibid.

17. E. Stanley Jones, *Mahatma Gandhi: An Interpretation* (London, 1948), pp. 11ff.

18. Ibid., pp. 194-205.

19. Ibid., p. 137.

20. C. F. Andrews's works on Gandhi include *Mahatma Gandhi: His Own Story* and *Mahatma Gandhi's Ideas*.

21. M. M. Thomas, *The Acknowledged Christ*, pp. 218-19.

22. C. F. Andrews, *Mahatma Gandhi's Ideas*, pp. 337ff.

23. B. Chaturvedi and M. Sykes, *Charles Freer Andrews: A Narrative*, p. 102.

24. C. F. Andrews, *Mahatma Gandhi's Ideas*, p. 314.

25. S. K. George, *Gandhi's Challenge to Christianity*, p. xv.

26. Ibid., pp. 23, 29.

27. On dogma as relating to experience, cf. Matthew Lamb, "Dogma, Experience and Political Theology," Concilium 113, *Revelation and Experience,* ed. E. Schillebeeckx and Bas von Iersel (New York: Seabury Press, 1978), pp. 79-90.

28. "Declaration on the Relationship of the Church to Non-Christian Religions," no. 2 (Flannery edition).

29. Ibid.

30. See Raymond Panikkar, *The Unknown Christ of Hinduism* (London: Darton, Longman and Todd, 1964; revised and enlarged edition, London: Darton, Longman and Todd, and Maryknoll, N.Y.: Orbis Books, 1981); *The Trinity and World Religions*; and *The Trinity and the Religious Experience of Man.* To these may be added his articles "The Rules of the Game in the Religious Encounter," *Journal of Religious Studies* (Spring 1971), pp. 12-16; "Hinduism and Christianity" (extracts), *Mitte Me*, no. 5 (1963); "The Integration of Indian Philosophical and Religious Thought," *Clergy Monthly* (May 1958), pp. 64-68; "A Dialectical Excursus on the Unity or Plurality of Religions," *Monchanin—Information* 2, no. 10 (December

1969), pp. 2–10; "The Theandric Vocation" and "Indology as a Cross-Cultural Catalyst," *Numen* (1971), pp. 173–79. "Faith—A Constitutive Dimension of Man," *Journal of Ecumenical Studies* 8, no. 2 (1971); "The Meaning of Christ's Name in the Universal Economy of Salvation," *Documenta Missionalia* 5 (1972).

31. Panikkar, *The Trinity and the Religious Experience of Man*, p. 25.
32. Ibid., pp. 25–28.
33. S. K. George, *Gandhi's Challenge*, pp. 38–40.
34. Ibid., pp. xviiff.
35. M. M. Thomas, *The Acknowledged Christ*, pp. 217–18.
36. *Harijan*, Aug. 4, 1940.
37. Regamey, *Non-Violence and the Christian Conscience*, p. 19.

Glossary

adharma	failure in duty; lawlessness; immorality; unrighteousness
advaita	nondualism of God and the world, of God and human being
adyatmic	mystagogic; of mystical spirituality
ahimsa	noninjury; nonviolence; nonviolent love; suffering love
anasakti	spiritual detachment; nonattachment; spiritual freedom
anasaktiyoga	unselfish action
anekandavada	Jain epistemology bearing on the many-sidedness of truth and the consequent value of affirmations
aparigraha	nonpossession; nonpossessiveness
artha	substance; material goods; wealth; possessions; political economy
asangraha	nonpossessiveness
ashram	a Hindu monastery or hermitage; a place of contemplation and no physical labor
asteya	nonstealing
asuri	pertaining to the *asuras* or demons, hence demonic; purely mental; heartless; without feeling or compassion
atman	soul; the spirit of God in human beings
avarnas	those without color (*varna*), hence the casteless
avatar	descent (of God) on someone, hence incarnation of God
bansi	lute
Bhagavad Gita	see *Gita*
Bhagavan	personal God; a god-person; person of God; holy person; religious or sacred personality
Bhagavat	a Hindu classic
bhajans	hymns; popular religious chants
bhakta	devotee
bhakti	devotion to God as a way to salvation
bhogabhumi	land of enjoyments
Brahma	creator god; the first person in the Hindu triad; personal absolute
brahmacharya	literally, cult of Brahma; sacred studenthood; celibacy
Brahman	the impersonal Absolute

159

Brahmin	a person of the priestly caste, highest of the old fourfold Hindu social order
chaitanya	the principle of life and consciousness
charkha	spinning wheel
Daridranarayan	God of the poor
dharma	duty; law; righteousness; morality
duragraha	holding onto untruth, evil, violence; brute-force
dwaita	dualism of God and the world
Gita	a section of the *Mahabharta*; also known as *Bhagavad Gita*
guna(s)	a quality, intrinsic attribute, or modification of nature (*prakriti*)
harijans	literally, people of Hari; thus people of God; children of God
hartal	a strike
himsa	violence
Hind	a variant of the name "India"
Ishvar(a)	God as related or person
jiva	individual life; soul
jivan-mukta	one who attains liberation or salvation while yet alive on earth
karma	the force generated by a person's actions, the ethical consequences of which determine one's destiny in one's next existence
karmabhumi	land of duty
kesari	lion
khaddar	hand-spun cloth
khadi	hand-spinning, hand-spun cloth
khilafat	variant of "caliphate"
kidmatgar	servant of God
langoti	the minimal clothing of the poorest of the poor, just enough to cover nudity
lila	play; prank; flirtation; divine play; the game of God
Mahabharata	one of the two great Indian epic poems; the *Gita* forms a part of it
mantra	an incantation; a spell (of magic or prayer); a blessing or curse
Manusmriti	the code of Manu (Manu, the first man, is the Hindu Moses, i.e., law giver)
maya	appearance; nonreality; magical power of God; illusion; creation
moksha	heaven; home; salvation; liberation; freedom from bondage
nishkama karma	selfless, unattached action

panchama	the fifth class; those outside the four-fold order of society; the outcasts; the casteless; the untouchables
panchayat	council of five elected executives (in village government)
prakriti	nature; the material and potential principle in humankind and nature; the female active principle; principle of egotism
prayashchitta	penance for sin; expiation
Purana	The Story of Origin; myth; sacred history
purna swaraj	complete independence
purusha	person; the spiritual principle of personhood in humankind and nature; the male nonactive principle; witness
Raj	rule, ruler
Rama	one of the nine past *avatars*, or incarnations, of Vishnu
Ramanama	the name of Rama
Ramarajya	the reign or kingdom of Rama; the kingdom of God
Ramayana	one of the two great epics of India; it narrates the story of Rama
sadagraha	a variant of *satyagraha*; the first coinage for the concept, and later changed to *satyagraha*
sadhana	practice; asceticism; striving; achievement
sanatana(-ni)	universal, universalist
sarvodaya	the welfare of all
sat	truth, being
satvic	of the order of being; true; substantive; lightsome
satya	truthfulness
satyagraha	holding onto truth; suffering for justice; by extension, suffering for any cause or demand; soul-force; truth-force
satyagrahi	one who practices *satyagraha*
savarnas	the colored, i.e., the people of caste
sepoy	Indian soldier
Shastras	written traditions
Shuddhi	purification; ceremony of purification
shudra	the menial servant, the last and least of the Hindu social order
Siva	the high God in the Sivite religion; destroyer; third person in the Hindu triad
sloka	one sequence of verses; a set of verses; a logion; the basic unit in Sanskrit poetry
swadeshi	of the soil; indigenous; name of a movement to promote Indian products and national pride and dignity
swaraj	self-determination; self-government; autonomy
takli	spindle
tapasya	penance; mortification; expiation; self-suffering

varnashrama	literally, the order of colors; refers to the social order on the basis of division of labor
Vishnu	the high god in Vaishnavism; preserver; the second person in the Hindu triad
Vishwanath	Lord of the universe
yajna	sacrifice; selfless action
yamas	vows; discipline; knots; observances (the five *yamas* are *ahimsa*, *asangraha*, *asteya*, *brahmacharya*, and *satya*)

Bibliography

PRIMARY SOURCES

Books by Mohandas K. Gandhi

Ashram Observances in Action. Ahmedabad: Navajivan Publishing House, 1965.

An Autobiography: The Story of My Experiments with Truth. Ahmedabad: Navajivan Publishing House, 1945.

Christian Missions. Ahmedabad: Navajivan Publishing House, 1941.

The Collected Works of Mahatma Gandhi. Vols. 1–85 to date. New Delhi: Publications Division of the Ministry of Information and Broadcasting, Government of India, 1958–.

Constructive Programme. Ahmedabad: Navajivan Publishing House, 1968.

Ethical Religion. Madras: Ganesan, 1922.

From Yerawda Mandir: Ashram Observances. 3rd ed. Translated from Gujarati by V. G. Desai. Ahmedabad: Navajivan Publishing House, 1957.

Gandhi's Correspondence with the Government, 1942–1944. Ahmedabad: Navajivan Publishing House, 1957.

Hind Swaraj. 6th ed. Madras: G. A. Natesan & Co., 1932.

India of My Dreams. Ahmedabad: Navajivan Publishing House, 1947.

In Search of the Supreme. 3 vols. Ahmedabad: Navajivan Publishing House, 1962.

Non-Violence in Peace and War. 2nd ed. Ahmedabad: Navajivan Publishing House, 1944.

Speeches and Writings of Mahatma Gandhi. 4th ed. Madras: G. A. Natesan & Co., n.d.

Satyagraha in South Africa. Translated from Gujarati by V.G. Desai. Madras: Ganesan, 1928.

Sarvodaya (The Welfare of All). Ahmedabad: Navajivan Publishing House, 1968. Gandhi's paraphrase in Gujarati of John Ruskin's *Unto This Last*.

Compilations from Gandhi's Writings (listed in full under "Secondary Sources")

Fischer, Louis. *The Essential Gandhi*.

Hingorani, Anand T. *The Message of Jesus Christ*.

Prabhu, R. K. *What Jesus Means to Me*.

Prabhu, R. K., and U. R. Rao. *The Mind of Mahatma Gandhi*.

Periodicals Edited (and Largely Written) by Mohandas K. Gandhi.

Harijan (English edition)
Harijanbandhu (Gujarati edition)
Harijan Sevak (Hindi edition)
Indian Opinion (South Africa)
Navajivan
Young India

SECONDARY SOURCES

Books

Agarwala, N. N. *India's Savior Crucified: A Challenge for Us to Think and Act*. Agra: Agarwal, 1948.

Anderson, Sir Norman. *The World's Religions*. Grand Rapids, Michigan: B. Eerdmans Publishing Co., 1976.

Andrews, C. F. *Mahatma Gandhi's Ideas*. London: George Allen & Unwin, 1949.

———, ed. *Mahatma Gandhi: His Own Story*. London: George Allen Unwin, 1930.

Arokiasamy, S. *Dharma: Hindu and Christian According to Roberto de Nobili*. Rome: Pontifical Gregorian University (Doctoral dissertation, 1977).

Baum, Gregory. *Truth beyond Relativism: Karl Mannheim's Sociology of Knowledge*. Milwaukee: Marquette University Press, 1977.

Bondurant, Joan. *Conquest of Violence: The Gandhian Philosophy of Conflict*. Rev. ed. Berkeley and Los Angeles: University of California Press, 1965.

Bose, N. K. *Studies in Gandhism*. 2nd ed. Calcutta: India Associated Publishing Co., 1947.

Chakravarty, Amiya. *A Saint at Work: A View of Gandhi's Work and Message*. Philadelphia: The Young Friends Movement of the Philadelphia Yearly Meetings, 1950.

Chaturvedi, B., and M. Sykes. *Charles Freer Andrews: A Narrative*. London: George Allen & Unwin, 1949.

Das, Durga. *India from Curzon to Nehru and After*. New York: John Day Company, 1970.

Datta, Dhirendra Mahon. *The Philosophy of Mahatma Gandhi*. Madison: University of Wisconsin Press, 1953.

Desai, Mahadev. *Epic of Travancore*. Ahmedabad: Navajivan Publishing House, 1937.

————. *Gandhiji in Indian Villages*. Madras: Ganesan, 1927.

————. *Mahadevbhaini Diary*. 7 vols. Ahmedabad: Navajivan Publishing House, 1948–.

————. *With Gandhi in Ceylon*. Madras: Ganesan, 1928.

Devanandan, P. D. *Preparation for Dialogue*. Bangalore: Christian Institute for the Study of Religion and Society, 1964.

Douglass, James W. *The Non-Violent Cross: A Theology of Revolution and Peace*. New York: Macmillan Company, 1970.

Dulles, Avery. *The Survival of Dogma*. Garden City, N.Y.: Doubleday, 1970.

Embree, Ainslie T. *The Hindu Tradition*. New York: Random House, Vintage Books, 1972.

Erikson, Erik H. *Gandhi's Truth: On the Origins of Militant Non-Violence*. London: Faber and Faber, 1970; New York: W. Norton, 1969.

Fischer, Louis. *The Essential Gandhi: An Anthology*. New York: Random House, 1962.

————. *The Life of Mahatma Gandhi*. New York: Harper & Brothers, 1950.

————. *A Week with Gandhi*. New York: Duell, Sloan and Pearce, 1942.

Flannery, Austin, ed. *Vatican Council II: The Conciliar and Post-Conciliar Documents*. Boston: Daughters of St. Paul, 1975.

George, S. K. *Gandhi's Challenge to Christianity*. Ahmedabad: Navajivan Publishing House, 1960.

Gerth, H. H. and C. Wright Mills. *From Max Weber*. New York: Oxford University Press, 1973.

Hingorani, Anand T., comp. *The Message of Jesus Christ*. Bombay: Bharatiya Vidhya Bhavan, 1963.

Horsburgh, H. J. N. *Nonviolence and Aggression: A Study of Gandhi's Moral Equivalent of War*. New York: Oxford University Press, 1968.

Huttencach, Robert A. *Gandhi in South Africa*. Ithaca, N.Y.: Cornell University Press, 1971.

Ignatius of Loyola. *The Spiritual Exercises of St. Ignatius of Loyola*.

India, Government of. Ministry of Information and Broadcasting, ed. *Homage to Mahatma Gandhi*. New Delhi, 1949.

Iyer, Raghavan. *The Moral and Political Thought of Mahatma Gandhi*. New York: Oxford University Press, 1978.

Jones, E. Stanley. *Mahatma Gandhi: An Interpretation*. London: Hodder & Stoughton, 1948; New York: Albingdon-Cokesbury Press, 1948.

Kappen, Sebastian. *Jesus and Freedom*. Maryknoll, N.Y.: Orbis Books, 1977.

Karunakaren, K. P. *New Perspectives on Gandhi*. Simla: Indian Institute of Advanced Study, 1969.

Lamb, Matthew L. *History, Method and Theology*. Missoula, Mont.: Scholars Press, 1978.

Majumdar, R. C. *An Advanced History of India*. London: Macmillan and Co., 1950.

————, ed. *The History and Culture of the Indian People*. Vol. II. Bombay: Bharatiya Vidhya Bhavan, 1969.

McGinnis, James Brown III. "Freedom and Its Realization in Gandhi's Philosophy and Practice of Non-Violence." Ph. D. dissertation, St. Louis University, 1974.

Metz, Johann Baptist. *Faith in History and Society*. New York: Seabury Press, 1979.

Naess, Arne. *Gandhi and Group Conflict*. Oslo–Bergen–Troms: Universitetsforlaget, 1974.

Nanda, Bal Ram. *Mahatma Gandhi: A Biography*. Boston: Beacon Press, 1958.

Nehru, Jawaharlal. *Mahatma Gandhi*. Bombay: Asia Publishing House, 1966.

Niebuhr, Reinhold. *Moral Man and Immoral Society*. New York: Charles Scribner's Sons, 1966.

Panikkar, Raymond, *The Intra-Religious Dialogue*. New York: Paulist Press, 1978.

————. *The Trinity and World Religions*. Madras: Christian Literature Society, 1970.

Power, Paul F. *Gandhi on World Affairs*. Washington, D.C.: Public Affairs Press, 1960.

Prabhu, R. K., comp. *What Jesus Means to Me*. Ahmedabad: Navajivan Publishing House, 1959.

Prabhu, R. K., and U. R. Rao, comp. *The Mind of Mahatma Gandhi*. Bombay: Oxford University Press, 1945.

Pyarelal. *Mahatma Gandhi: The Last Phase*. 2 vols. Ahmedabad: Navajivan Publishing House, 1956, 1966.

Radhakrishnan, S., ed. *Mahatma Gandhi: Essays and Reflections on His Life and Work*. Allahabad: Kitabistan, 1944.

————, ed. *Mahatma Gandhi: 100 Years*. New Delhi: Gandhi Peace Foundation, 1968.

Ramachandran, G., and T. K. Mahadevan, eds. *Gandhi, His Relevance for Our Times*. Bombay: Bharatiya Vidhya Bhavan, 1967.

————, eds. *Quest for Gandhi*. New Dehli: Gandhi Peace Foundation, 1970.

Regamey, P. *Non-Violence and the Christian Conscience*. New York: Herder and Herder, 1966.

Reynolds, Reginald. *A Quest for Gandhi*. Garden City, N.Y.: Doubleday, 1952.

Ruskin, John. *Unto This Last*.

Samartha, S.J. *The Hindu Response to the Unbound Christ*. Madras: Chrisitan Literature Society, 1974.

Sharp, Gene. *Gandhi Wields the Weapon of Moral Power*. Ahmedabad: Navajivan Publishing Hosue, 1960.

————. *The Politics of Non-Violent Action*. Boston: Porter Sargent Publishers, 1973.

Shean, Vincent. *Mahatma Gandhi: A Great Life in Brief*. New York: Alfred A. Knopf, 1955.

Shiridharani, Krishnalal Jethalal. *War without Violence: A Study of Gandhi's Method and Its Accomplishments*. New York: Harcourt Brace and Company, 1939.

Tendulkar, D. G. *Mahatma*. 8 vols. Bombay: Jhaveri and Tendulkar, 1952.

Thekkinedath, Joseph. *Love of Neighbor in Mahatma Gandhi*. Alwaye: Pontifical Institute of Theology and Philosophy, 1973.

Thomas, M. M. *The Acknowledged Christ of the Indian Renaissance*. London: SCM Press, 1969.

United Nations Educational Scientific and Cultural Organization (UNESCO), ed. *All Men Are Brothers: Life and Thought of Mahatma Gandhi as Told in His Own Words*. Calcutta: Orient Longmans, 1959.

Vidyarthi, L. P., et al. *Gandhi and Social Sciences*. New Delhi: Bookhive, 1970.

Periodicals

Amrita Bazar Patrika (Calcutta)
The Bombay Chronicle
Clergy Monthly (India)
Community Services News
Concilium
Cosmopolitan
Gandhi Marg
The Hindu
The Hindustan Times
In Christo (India)
India
Indian Church History Review
The Journal of Religious Studies
The Leader (India)
Mitte Me
The Modern Review (Calcutta)
Monchanin Information
Morning Post
The Mountain Path (India)
Numen
Prajabandhu (India)
Rand Daily Mail (Johannesburg)
The Searchlight
The Statesman (Calcutta)
Times (London)
The Tribune

Bibliographies

Datta, Bimal Kumar. *Gandhiana: A Bibliography of Gandhi Literature Published in English Language Journals of Bengal*. Santiniketan: Central Library, 1970.

Deshpande, P. G. *Gandhiana: A Bibliography of Gandhian Literature*. Ahmedabad: Navajivan Publishing House, 1948.

Satyaprakash. *Gandhiana, 1962–1976*. Gurgaon: Indian Documentation Service, 1977.

Sharma, Jagadish Sharan. *Mahatma Gandhi: A Descriptive Bibliography*. Delhi: S. Chand, 1955.

Index

Action: associated with *yajna,* 69; threat of direct, 43, 45; moral, 120; nonviolent. *See also* nonviolence

Adyatmic, 32

Ahimsa, 9–10; in Buddhist, Jain, and Hindu contexts, 95; component part of *satyagraha,* 93, 97; and dynamics, of redemption, 116; and fear, 97; and five *yamas,* 72; has few followers, 87; proximity of, to Christian charity and Greek *agape,* 95; self-suffering as deeper meaning of, 96; supremacy of, for India's world mission, 117; in terms of human and social interactions, 95; testing ground for, 22; and truth, as means to end, 95; as vicarious suffering, 130

Ahmedabad, 21, 22; G's shift from, 62; session of Congress at (1921) 29; violence and labor unrest in (1938), 39

Ali, Mohammed and Shaukat, 32

All-India Congress Committee, 27, 42

All-India political party advocated by G, 40

All-India Spinners' Association, 31

All-Parties Conference, 33, 43; unsuccessful at Simla, 44

Allahabad, riots in, 39

Ambedkar, B. R., 35, 37, 102, 103

Amritsar: congress constitution drafted in, 27; session of congress in, 26; violence in, 23–26. *See also* Punjab

Anasakti, 35, 84

Anasuyabehn, 23

Andrews, C. F., 114, 129 fn., 133, 134

Anekandavada, 10

Anisakti (detachment), 35

Ansari, Dr., 108

Anthropology, theological, 90–99

Aparigraha, 72

Appar (a Tamil poet), 67

Arbitration: in Ahmedabad, 22; in South Africa, 12. *See* Congress, seven demands of

Army: in free India, 55–56; reorganized (1858), 3

Arnold, Edwin, 11

Arrests, 23, 24; new wave of, 36; rumor of, 23, wholesale, 33, 41

Artha, 119

Aryanayagam, 129 fn.

Ashram: and *ahimsa,* 96; equality of all religions vowed in, 114 fn.; established, 21; a lamp of sacrifice, 34; a member of, written to, 62; members of, in Salt March, 99; members of, as servants of God and humankind, 109; no idol or image in, 111; and *satyagraha,* 33; women of, written to, 76

Asiatic Ordinance, 17

Asiatic Registration Act, 19

Asteya, 72

Asuri, 70

Ataturk, Kemal, 31

Atheism: books inclining to, 9; new form of, 2; Sahara of, 11

Atlantic Charter, terms of not applicable to India, 41

Atlee, Clement, 44

Atman, 77, 85

Atonement: to effect social and political spheres, 110; Jesus', 74, 114; limits to, 109–110

Augustinian distinction challenged, 119

Avarnas, 78

Avatar, 10; perfect, 92

Azad, Abul Kalam, 104

Badshaki mosque, 24

Bahadur Company, 50–51. *See also* East India Company

Baker, A. W., 14

Banerji, Surendranath, 5

Bansi, 84

Bardoli, district of, 29; *satyagraha* successful in, 33

Bengal: divided into East and West (1905), 7; division of, seen by Indians as sinister British design, 49 fn., 50; Hindu minorities in, 43; and violence in (1947–48), 45

Bengal, East and West, 7; non-Muslim populations in, 44; partition of, 45, 50; prohibitive orders in, 28, 43, 44, 45

Benn, Wedgewood, 61

Besant, Mrs. Annie, 10; and *swaraj,* 48

Bhagavad Gita, 9, 11

Bhagavan, 86

Bhagavat, 9

Bhajans, 111

169